# The Independent Video Producer

# The Independent
# Video Producer

## Establishing a Profitable Video Business

## Bob Jacobs

**Focal
Press**

Boston   Oxford   Auckland   Johannesburg   Melbourne   New Delhi

## Library of Congress Cataloging-in-Publication Data

Jacobs, Robert M.
   The independent video producer : establishing a profitable video
business / Bob Jacobs.
     p.   cm.
   Includes bibliographical references.
   ISBN 0-240-80339-6 (alk. paper)
   1. Video recordings—Production and direction.  I. Title.
PN1992.94.J23     1999
791.45'0232—DC21

                                        98-53156
                                        CIP

## British Library Cataloguing-in-Publication Data

A catalogue record for this book is available from the British Library.
The publisher offers special discounts on bulk orders of this book.

For information, please contact:
   Manager of Special Sales
   Butterworth–Heinemann
   225 Wildwood Avenue
   Woburn, MA 01801-2041
   Tel: 781-904-2500
   Fax: 781-904-2620

For information on all Focal Press publications available, contact our World Wide Web home page at: http://www.focalpress.com

10 9 8 7 6 5 4 3 2 1

Printed in the United States of America

*This book is dedicated with love to my partner, my best friend, and my wife —all the same wonderful person—Martina Ann "Max" Jacobs.*

# Contents

## 4    Promoting and Marketing Your Company    110

# Acknowledgments

The author wishes to thank the following individuals and organizations for their valuable help and support during the research and writing of this book: Martina "Max" Jacobs; Ray Bradbury; Ralph Kendall Berge; Keith Salmon; Monique Eissing; Denise Van Ryzin; Lisa Romanowski; Henry Winkler; Tami Lane; Video Trend Associates; Ronald J. Bullock; Fay McCarthy; Theo Mayer and Peter Inova of Metavision; RAB; TvB; WEEK-TV; Sam Drummy (and his four Emmys!); Robert D. Coglianese, CPA; Berenice St. Bernard; Penney Ann Bassette; Gustav L. Abrador; my research assistants at Bradley University—M. Brandon Johnson, Melanie D. Laird, Susan C. Monce, Maureen L. Smith; the producers interviewed in Hollywood and elsewhere who granted me generous amounts of their time; Terri Jadick at Focal Press for her patient encouragement . . .

. . . and to the wonderful memory of Saul Bass and our beloved Verna Fields for their inspiration, not just to me, but to all creative people everywhere. They have left a void that can't be filled.

# Introduction

When in 1986 I wrote the book *How to Be an Independent Video Producer*, the Internet was not in common use, 3/4-inch U-Matic was the most common professional tape format, renting movies on videocassettes was still unique because so few homes had VCRs, COBOL was the computer language being taught to a few nerds in colleges, 256K memory was a big deal on the Macintosh home computers that were sprouting up as novelties, Saddam Hussein was not a household name, and movies and television shows had only one producer.

Much has changed since then.

That my computer now has 196MB of memory instead of 256K is really less important to the purpose of this book than the number of producers we see in the credits for today's movies and TV shows. When the hit comedy movie *Airplane* came out in 1980, the credits read: Producer—Jon Davison. In 1993, the smash hit *Jurassic Park*, directed by Stephen Spielberg, had two producers, Kathleen Kennedy and Gerald R. Molen, along with two associate producers, Lata Ryan and Colin Wilson. In that year, the Turner Pictures docudrama *Gettysburg* had three producer credits: Nick Lombardo, Robert Katz,

and Moctesuma Esparza. And in 1998, a modest feature film offering by Dreamworks SKG called *The Peacemaker* had *five* "producers" (Walter Parks, Branko Lastig, Pat Kehoe, Leslie Cockburn, and Andrew Cockburn) and three coexecutive "producers" (John Wells, Michael Grillo, and Lancie MacDonald). *Airplane* was an enormous financial and critical hit that still endures. *The Peacemaker* went quickly to video release and obscurity.

Today, the trend is to give a producer credit to anyone who contributes an idea, a dollar, or an introduction to somebody who might help finance a production or to some actor who is regarded as a box-office draw. Movies or videos can be made by committee, of course. But aside from adding to the confusion of what a producer actually does, this deadly practice makes for bad pictures and inflated egos. Many awful examples come to mind. The fact is that normally there is one producer—one person at the top of the food chain who is ultimately responsible for the success or failure of the product. This book is for that person.

Producing is much more an art than a science. The producer works best as a creative member of a dynamic team, whether in entertainment, industry, or education. Just because, in terms of responsibility, producers are at the top of that pyramid of creative energy known as a production team does not mean that they can do the job alone. The best producers know that they are leaders, not dictators; cocreators, not egomaniacs. In the end, however, they are the final word in making decisions, the place where the buck stops.

Ask ten nonproducers just what a producer does, and you'll probably get ten different answers. The typical director will tell you that the producer is the "business guy" who is largely concerned with budgets and schedules. The typical writer will say that the producer is the person who keeps insisting on changes in the script when the writer knows that it was fine the first time around. The typical editor will state that the producer is the one who has the final say in the "cut." All of them will be partially right, of course, but none will have told the whole story. That's because most people don't know the whole story.

A quick definition of the producer's role might run like this: The producer is an organizer, a manager, and a manipulator. The producer takes charge of a project, assembles all the necessary pieces or elements (including people and things), and sees the project through to completion. What this definition lacks constitutes the substance of this book.

Defining the producer's job seems simple enough if we use the one-liners above. But consider how absurd the following role definitions appear in abbreviation:

Video editor—pushes buttons to put together separate images
Director—moves actors around on the set
Cameraperson—points the camera and focuses it

These are all correct to a limited degree, but they are also misleading because they are so incomplete. We all know that these definitions are simplistic because of the enormous amount of information that has been written and spoken about these artistic sides of the craft of film and video production.

Because we live in an era of the director-auteur, the director takes ultimate credit for a production, and few laypeople question the validity of a single person laying claim to the entire work. Consider the following credits: *Titanic*—A James Cameron Film; *Schindler's List*—A Film by Stephen Spielberg. That's what leads the head credits in most movies. However, as the end credits roll and we see hundreds of names, it becomes clear that without this large number of artists and technicians, the director would have no movie at all on which to lay claim.

A video production, just like a film project, requires a team working in harmony and with a single purpose. All a writer needs to write a novel is a pencil and some paper. All a fine artist needs to create a sculpture or a painting are materials and tools. The art of movie and video production is one of the few in the long history of creativity in which no single person, regardless of talent or intelligence, can go it alone. Whether the piece is a 30-second television commercial or a 12-hour network miniseries, putting it all together takes a group of multifaceted individuals. Out of this group, the producer is the coordinator, the orchestrator, the single visionary, and the captain of the creative ship.

As the person at the top, you will have to be all things to all people. You will have to assess and respond to the various needs of everyone involved. Everyone will expect you to be a pillar of strength, always consistent, always available, always ready to give them what they need. In the words of Rudyard Kipling, "If you can keep your head when all about you are losing theirs and blaming it on you," then you are a producer and are managing as the principles of producing dictate that you must.

Because producers have the ultimate responsibility for the outcome of any project, they must know the basics of each of the technical and artistic functions involved in order to understand what can and cannot be achieved. Producers with no comprehension of elementary camera and lighting operations, for instance, will not be able to plan and budget properly for a project that needs a large number of camera setups.

Producers are also members of the top management. As such, they must have a firm grasp of pure business details like proposals, budgets, profit-and-loss sheets, tax consequences, accounting, state and federal regulations, and more. This is especially true of independent producers who must take care of these details themselves. This book assumes that you know how to make a video, so it does not cover basic production techniques like lighting and camera and editing. Rather, it covers the business side of independent production.

Everyone who works for, or who one day hopes to work for, producers must understand what producers are and what they are likely to expect from their casts and crews. Another purpose of this book is to provide a guide through the maze of misunderstanding between producers and their staffs.

You will be assisted part of the way by advice and counsel from some of the most outstanding producers in the television world. These include Saul Turtletaub, Stephen J. Cannell, Henry Winkler, and Ralph Kendall Berge. You'll also find quotes from some lesser-known professionals who run small, profitable video production companies. These interviews, coupled with the other information presented in this book, serve to make *The Independent Video Producer* a useful primer on establishing an independent production company. It can serve as a blueprint and guide.

As the United States continues to become an information systems society, the opportunities for independent video producers are virtually limitless. In the following pages, you'll find out why and how, with much determination, lots of energy, and a good bit of luck, you can take advantage of these opportunities. The evolving convergence of broadcast, cable, and the Internet opens doors of opportunity never before possible for information-age entrepreneurs. It is an exciting and heady time when new machineries of joy roll out a fantastic potential future for all of us.

This is a practical guide to help you prepare for that future. For professionals in the field, it will serve as a valuable refresher. For beginners in the business, or those still in college or university who are getting ready to venture out on their own, I hope to inform you about the nitty-gritty, true-life details that make up the business of producing and to arm you with enough information to make your entry into independent production a smooth one. I hope that your stay in this exhilarating realm of professional storytelling will be long, fulfilling, and profitable.

Chapter 1 covers the business end of producing, and Chapter 2 offers suggestions on managing people and productions. You'll learn how to set up an independent shop in Chapter 3, and you'll get some practical tips on promotion and marketing in Chapter 4. The next chapter discusses how to find and develop markets, and the final chapter gives procedural and practical business hints. The appendixes are filled with information on other publications and working documents. Especially intriguing is an in-depth interview with one of Hollywood's major line producers.

A new world awaits. The door opens here.

# 1

# The Business End of Producing

The independent producer, unlike someone who works in the womb of a large corporation, has one overriding preoccupation: to sell the product before producing it. Whether we call it "raising funds," "underwriting," "capitalizing," or any other euphemism, getting the money is what it's all about. Getting money involves the producer in the fine art of sales. All successful independent producers are salespeople in part. To be successful as an independent, you will find it extremely helpful if you have taken at least a couple of college courses in basic business principles, especially marketing, accounting, management, and sales. We talk about creativity all the time in our business. Generally, we're referring to the "art" in our project; to the creation of a script, of meaningful visual images, of complementary, perfectly recorded, and perfectly mixed sound; and to the final product that captures the imagination and wins the hearts of our viewers. But the business end of what we do—the down-and-dirty job of getting the project funded with other people's money (OPM)—requires some of the greatest creativity of all. And this aspect of creativity is the very foundation of the independent producer.

Whether you're selling a dramatic series to NBC, a movie about the first men to reach the North Pole to Turner Network Television, a local television concept to your network affiliate, or a sales promotion tape to a widget manufacturer in your town, the process is essentially the same. First, you must sell the client on yourself. In doing so, you help the client decide to let you produce a program. Selling yourself is a matter of projecting confidence, care about the client, and a professional attitude. One way to do this is to come to the project prepared and organized. To help you get started, here's a six-step process that others have used. The outline itself is very simple:

4. Assess the need
5. Write the proposal
6. Prepare a detailed budget breakdown
7. Demonstrate your cost-effectiveness
8. Make an effective presentation
9. Close the deal

Executing this simple procedure takes skill, talent, intelligence, perseverance, and hard work. We'll cover these steps one at a time, drawing on examples from the files of established, successful producers. No one

1

can guarantee that every idea you come up with will sell. However, you can improve your chances by getting organized at the outset and by following these guidelines.

## Assessing the Need

Many people have the false notion that after only one success, one hit show, a producer is given carte blanche from then on. They think that once your name is on a network show and you're rich and famous, all the doors in town are open. But as the line from *Porgy and Bess* goes, "It ain't necessarily so!"

Saul Turtletaub, who with partners Bernie Ornstein and Bud Yorkin produced the successful show *Sanford and Son*, sheds light on the truth of the matter: "The only thing a success does for a producer is to make the network executives willing to have a look at the next and the next idea. But if the new idea isn't a good one, if it doesn't fill a need of that executive, it doesn't matter what your name is or how many previous successes you've had. Every time I go in, I have to be as well prepared as if it were my first shot out of the box."[1]

Henry Winkler, whose company Fair Dinkum Productions produces feature films and syndicated television series like *Sightings*, brings to his successful business a philosophy that he adopted when he got the role of Fonzi on *Happy Days* Winkler says, "Never put a period at the end of a negative thought. If you do, the thought becomes a sentence, then a paragraph, and finally the obituary for your project." He also says, "Just because I'm the producer, I don't know everything. I surround myself with people who do know everything—about their own parts—and together we can't help succeeding." This is the most important advice you will ever get. Remember that a painter can paint with only a canvas, a brush, and some colors, but video is an art that can only be done by a team. No producer can go it alone. People are your most important asset. This understanding begins with your attitude toward the client, who is a person of vital importance to your new world.

The first thing you should try to establish at the outset of a project is a need. The word *need*, as it applies to network executives, is fairly straightforward. A television show *needs* to have the most viewers possible in order to increase the network's Nielsen ratings. Unfortunately for all of us, no one has yet discovered the magic formula that will always work to attract the diverse and fickle American TV audience for an entertainment program. The person who finds that magic formula will be rich indeed! Still, producers try to come up with ideas that will tap into the collective consciousness of the mass audience. They try to assess what viewers want, instead of what they need. Frequently in the movie-of-the-week business, the tap is as shallow as the lurid headlines in the pulp press. The movie-of-the-week is more likely to be the "disease-of-the-week" or the "trendy-cause-of-the-week" rather than something of substance or artistic merit. It's a matter of settling for the cheap and easy, frequently the lurid, instead of reaching deeper to deliver something of substance. Ted Turner has tried to buck that tide by producing historical dramas like *Gettysburg* and *Crazy Horse* on his cable movie channel, Turner Network Television. We'll explore one of these programs in depth later with former Turner Network Television producer Ralph Kendall Berge.

Assessing needs is much easier when you are trying to sell a commercial, a training tape, or an educational video. In these cases, the need is relatively simple to illuminate. When you tackle anything other than a network TV show, your work begins with some basic research about your prospective client. When you discover what that client needs, you have won half the sales battle.

Let's say that you're a producer in a medium-sized market (any community or group of communities in America with a population base between 200,000 to 350,0000). In that kind of market, there are a number of large chain operations, such as fast-food restaurants, national hotels and motels, and home improvement stores. You will also find a great many locally owned and operated businesses, and there is likely to be some small to moderate manufacturing. Most parts of the country have branches of major firms like Brunswick or Georgia-Pacific, along with smaller but no less viable local or regional companies. All of these are potential clients if you know what they need and how to give it to them.

## Determining Whom to Contact

The first thing to do at each business is find out the name of the person in charge of the area to which you would like to make a sale. In larger corporations, your contact will have a title like vice president of marketing, manager of training, or director of corporate communications. With smaller firms, you will more likely deal with an owner or a partner. With whomever you talk, keep this rule in mind: Never deal with anyone who can't say yes. There is nothing more frustrating than making a wonderful pitch, only to have the recipient say, "Gee, that was great. I'll have to tell my boss about it when he comes back from Bermuda." Many people within a company do not have the power to hire you, and there is no point in wasting your time or theirs on a pitch. This sounds cold, even rude, but it is a fundamental principle for any independent producer.

So how do you find out the name of that magic "yes" person? If it's a large corporation, send for a copy of the company's annual report to stockholders. This is usually a slick and glossy publication in which you'll find a list of all the corporate officers by title, along with the location of the company office at which they work. Remember that if you want to sell a training video to a branch, for example, you frequently have to make your presentation to the decision makers at corporate headquar-

ters. Although affiliates and subsidiaries of major corporations exercise a degree of local control and autonomy, the budgets for media, advertising, and training generally come from headquarters. There are exceptions to this rule, of course. One of these is the giant heavy-machinery manufacturer Caterpillar, Inc. CAT® divides its operation up into profit centers. Each of these is responsible for its own audiovisual budget and is free to decide whether to use the corporation's in-house production unit in Peoria, Illinois, or to choose outside suppliers. In Chapter 5, we will examine one of these profit centers and an independent producer who was chosen instead of the corporate unit. In the case of a smaller outfit, you can do a couple of simple things. First, visit the Chamber of Commerce or the Organization of Manufacturers and Commerce in the community where the firm is located. Most chambers publish annual lists of their local member businesses, with the names, telephone numbers, and addresses of the executives in each company. If the chamber doesn't provide this service, a friendly call to the receptionist at the target company will usually get you the information you want. Determining whom to contact is the first step on the road to your first project. The second step is even more fundamental.[2]

## Researching the Client

Now that you know the name of the firm and the person to contact, what are you going to say? How do you open the door to opportunity without sounding like one of those telemarketers you want to drown when they phone you at home? Think about this phase very carefully.

The typical slogan tossed off by a fledgling producer goes something like this: "I have a video production house, and I can meet all of your needs." This slogan appears in a dozen permutations somewhere in the literature of hundreds of production companies. And frankly, it stinks. First, it's too general; second, it's too sweeping; third, it's not true. You can't meet "all" of anybody's needs. No single entity can do that, even if it knows what all of those needs are. Your company slogan should be something like "We're at your service," and you should mean it. If you're like most people in this country today, you wonder what happened to the old-fashioned idea of service—of the customer always being right. If you make it your business to restore your clients' faith in that concept, you've won more than half your battle.

If you start your pitch by asking businesspeople to tell you what they need, you're likely to be shown the door. Executives today are overwhelmed with problems, and they don't want another one from you. Instead of asking questions, go in to your first call armed with a proposal for at least one specific project. Obviously, this means that you will have to do some research into the nature of the business. You will need to know some of the jargon spoken, be familiar with the competition, be knowledgeable about the company's position in its field, and know about its past experiences, if any, with video. This is simply doing your homework. An independent producer, therefore, must enjoy being a continuing student in a wide variety of fields.

Let's say that you've chosen to propose a training video for a business with a high employee turnover rate, such as a hotel or motel. You believe you can demonstrate to the management that significant cost savings can be realized by training the housekeeping staff with a video aid. Here's how to organize that presentation.

First, prepare charts and graphs or, even better, an electronic presentation. Base your argument on the standard pay scale for supervisors who must train new personnel in such tasks as making beds, cleaning rooms, taking inventory, stocking, and so forth. You can assume that each hotel or motel also spends some time stressing grooming, uniforms, and so on. Explain how your visual aid will save the hotel time or money. Saving money is a key need of all businesses.

You can make your case for a visual training aid on the grounds that these have been demonstrated to cut the time it takes to learn. Give examples; point out that the U.S. government implemented training films during World War II and drafted such luminaries as John Ford and Frank Capra to make them. Bolster your case by citing studies proving the effect of such things as television violence on the behavior of children. These are available through an Internet search. Call on your client's own reactions to motion pictures and television. Ask if the person has ever cried or laughed or been frightened while watching a movie or a program. Then point out that the emotion he or she remembers was evoked by the producer of that project. Even people who can't or don't like to read often respond to a movie or a video that entertains while it teaches. We'll explore this area in depth later with a case study about a project done for Caterpillar (see Figure 1–5).

Speak with authority about your subject matter. To present a good proposal about the case in point here, you must know a lot about the hotel/motel business. Short of taking a crash course in hotel/motel management, what can you do to educate yourself? You can contact a few of the many sources available that can help with your research. Most industries have associations. In many cases, you won't have access to the trade secrets of those associations unless you're a member. It doesn't hurt to try, though.[2] A quick search of the Internet on almost any subject will lead you to treasure troves of information, free for the taking. The Internet is a big ally in the battle of wits for production business. In general, you can get close to your topic simply by typing in the name of your target company followed by .com or .org. For example, http://www.caterpillar.com will take you to the home page of "Big Yellow," and http://www.johndeere.com will take you to "Big Green." If you're trying to pitch to a tractor company, that's about all you'll have to do to tap the source. Web links will take you into a whole world of mechanical wonders.

Two other major sources of information for producers are the Radio Advertising Bureau (RAB) and the Television Advertising Bureau (TvB). Both organizations provide research services to their members. The fees for membership depend on the market size of your area, but the access to information is worth the price. Research from these organizations is encapsulated and directed specifically at your target, and you'll save hours surfing the Net.

Figures 1–1 and 1–2 are reprints of the RAB and TvB "Instant Background" profiles for hotels and motels. Look them over carefully; with this type of information, you will be well prepared to make your initial call to any hotel or motel manager. When you know about and can discuss times of peak business, sources of revenue, how the bills are paid, and consumer attitudes by demographic breakdown, you will sound authoritative in the hotel/motel business. Without being overbearing or trying to tell clients that you know more than they do, you can gain their confidence as a colleague or, at worst, as a businessperson who cares enough to do the research.

Both the RAB and the TvB have profile information on every major kind of business in the United States, from shoe stores to heavy manufacturing concerns. These are invaluable resources for the independent producer. Membership in one or both bureaus also brings monthly tips on sales techniques and access to commercial spots that you can adapt to your needs.

## Staying Informed about Related Fields

As you can see, the good producer must be a veritable storehouse of information. He or she must read virtually everything available to keep up-to-date on technological and business trends, politics, social movements and trends, and so forth. Most producers subscribe to a large number of magazines, newspapers, and trade publications, the bulk of which are tax-deductible as professional expenses. Many trade journals are free to qualified people in the industry.

Author Ray Bradbury, who produced a very successful television series called *Ray Bradbury Theater*, advises young writers to be virtual sponges, "soaking up every poem, every short story, every novel, every magazine, every song, and every movie ever done. Make the library your second home," he says. "Take a year and read everything you can. Form a club and rent every movie on the shelf at the video store. Watch one every night. Read, read, read. When you're done, you'll have every great thought, every great scene, every great tune stuffed into your brain, and it will come flooding out just when you need it to save your life!" (personal communication). Bradbury's advice to young writers applies equally to producers. We must be true Renaissance people—all of us—in order to make the best judgment calls, to understand human motivation, to exercise artistic and practical leadership of those around us, and to recognize the immense canon of work atop of which we now stand. It is our duty to turn out the best-informed, most meaningful communication product that our talent, our art, and our intelligence can build. That is the Ethic, with a capital *E*, that must underpin our every undertaking. We are entrusted with other people's hopes, dreams, and honor, along with their money, when we perform. And that carries with it the responsibility to be at our peak. Most of us are not in this business for the money. We are in it for the love of doing it well. And it is simply amazing how often the information sponged up by savvy producers triggers good, sellable ideas or, even better, comes to their aid in a presentation or discussion with a client.

Many people these days claim that they don't have time to read. That's a load of old nonsense! Take an hour a day. Close your office door, and skim articles. Put a stack of literature next to your bed, and read every night before you go to sleep. Read over breakfast and lunch and in snatches as you go through your day. Put a reading rack in your bathroom. Turn on the reading lamp next to your recliner instead of the television set at night. After all, there

**RAB INSTANT BACKGROUND:**

# Hotels & Motels

Size of the Business. The U.S. Department of Commerce gives total receipts of the lodging industry:

| | | | |
|---|---|---|---|
| 1981 | $26.637 billion | 1979 | $22.226 billion |
| 1980 | 23.638 billion | 1978 | 19.443 billion |

There are about 2,525,000 rooms available today, of which the top 25 chains represent 45% (Travel Market Yearbook).

When Business Occurs. Percent of receipts by months (U.S. Dep't. of Commerce, 3-year average):

| | | | | | |
|---|---|---|---|---|---|
| January | 7.1% | May | 8.6% | September | 8.5% |
| February | 7.3 | June | 8.9 | October | 8.8 |
| March | 8.5 | July | 9.5 | November | 7.5 |
| April | 8.2 | August | 9.8 | December | 7.2 |

Occupancy Rates. For several years 67-70% of all rooms have been in use on the average day. By location, type, and size (Laventhol & Horwath):

| Location | | Region | | Size (No. of Rooms) | |
|---|---|---|---|---|---|
| Airport | 70.1% | Northeast | 71.6% | Under 150 | 68.3% |
| Suburban | 68.0 | N. Central | 61.2 | 150-299 | 66.6 |
| Highway | 67.2 | South | 66.8 | 300-600 | 66.5 |
| Downtown | 65.9 | West | 71.3 | Over 600 | 67.2 |

By Type and Incidence of Double Occupancy (Pannell, Kerr, Forster):

| Type | Occupancy | Double Occupancy As Percent Of Total Occupancy |
|---|---|---|
| All places | 67.6% | 48.4% |
| Transient Hotels | 66.9 | 40.0 |
| Resort Hotels | 68.4 | 87.5 |
| Motels with Restaurants | 68.1 | 43.2 |
| Motels without Restaurants | 70.2 | 45.3 |

Sources of Revenue. The Panell, Kerr, Forster study shows:

| | All Lodgings | Transient Hotels | Resort Hotels | Motels With Restaurant | No Restaurant |
|---|---|---|---|---|---|
| Rooms | 60.2% | 60.4% | 53.1% | 64.0% | 93.1% |
| Food | 23.8 | 24.3 | 26.6 | 21.6 | ---- |
| Beverages | 9.0 | 9.1 | 9.0 | 9.9 | ---- |
| All other | 7.0 | 6.2 | 11.3 | 4.5 | 6.9 |

Price Ranges. 12% of guests stay in deluxe/first class accomodations, 75% average/middle price, 13% economy or budget. This is the same for both business and pleasure travelers (Travel Market Yearbook).

**Figure 1-1** Radio Advertising Bureau profile for hotels and motels. (Reproduced with permission of the Radio Advertising Bureau.)

Handling of Reservations. 10% of a travel agent's business comes from lodging reservations, and 69% of agents have automated systems. 59% of reservations placed by agents are guaranteed (of them, 57% covered by client credit cards, 29% prepaid vouchers, 14% the agent's own credit) (Travel Weekly Harris Poll). Incidence of reservations to total hotel guests, and who places them (Laventhol & Horwath):

|  | Downtown | Airport | Suburban | Highway | Resort |
|---|---|---|---|---|---|
| Percent with Reservations | 81.9% | 66.6% | 62.1% | 67.0% | 88.4% |
| How Placed: Direct | 38.0 | 35.2 | 41.5 | 46.4 | 42.0 |
| Reservation Systems | 39.4 | 46.3 | 49.2 | 36.9 | 17.7 |
| Travel Agents | 16.0 | 12.2 | 8.1 | 10.8 | 24.4 |
| Other | 6.6 | 6.3 | 1.2 | 5.9 | 15.9 |

A Time survey of hotel guests found 61% of nonbusiness travelers made reservations more than one month in advance, but only 8% of business travelers did.

Decision-Making. 71% of travel agent vacation customers are given advice on choosing hotels; same for 41% of business customers (Travel Weekly). The Time survey found the guest chose which hotel to stay in 77% of the time, someone else in the company 31%, travel agent 4%, airline 2% (more than one influence could be listed, also more than one hotel could have been used on the same trip). The most important factors influencing choice were prior experience 25%, location 24%, recommendation from business associates 24%, image 8%, cost 7%, travel agent 3% (others unimportant). Percent of guests considering these facilities "very important":

| | | | |
|---|---|---|---|
| Beds | 84% | Restaurants | 66% |
| Friendly staff | 77 | Towels | 65 |
| Bathroom | 72 | Housekeeping services | 64 |
| Reservation service | 70 | Value for price | 59 |
| Safety, security | 69 | Wake-up call | 57 |

Meetings & Conventions. 92% of attendees stay at hotels/motels (Travel Market Yearbook). Percent of planners using (at various times):

|  | Associations | | Corporations |
|---|---|---|---|
|  | Major Conventions | Seminars | Company Meetings |
| Downtown Hotels/Motels | 61% | 56% | 54% |
| Resort Hotels/Motels | 36 | 38 | 61 |
| Suburban Hotels/Motels | 16 | 52 | 55 |
| Airport Hotels/Motels | 9 | 46 | 37 |

Profile of Guests. Half are repeat trade; 90% U.S. residents/10% foreign (Laventhol & Horwath).
Distribution of lodging expenditures (U.S. Travel Data Center):

| Purpose | | Age of Travel Party Head | | HH Income | |
|---|---|---|---|---|---|
| Business/convention | 29.0% | 18-24 | 11.1% | $35,000+ | 14.3% |
| Visit friends, | 10.4 | 25-34 | 19.1 | $25-34,999 | 17.7 |
| relatives | | 35-44 | 21.3 | $20-24,999 | 14.0 |
| Personal business | 8.8 | 45-54 | 18.5 | $15-19,999 | 17.2 |
| Outdoor recreation | 21.7 | 55-64 | 12.7 | $10-14,999 | 16.6 |
| Other tourism | 17.7 | 65+ | 17.3 | Under $10,000 | 20.2 |
| Other reasons | 12.4 | | | | |

| | | | | | |
|---|---|---|---|---|---|
| Vacation | 52.9% | Number on Trip: | 1 48.4% | 3 | 6.3% |
| Not a vacation | 47.1 | | 2 31.7 | 4+ | 13.6 |

**Figure 1-1 (cont.)** Radio Advertising Bureau profile for hotels and motels. (Reproduced with permission of the Radio Advertising Bureau.)

# CASE HISTORY

CATEGORY:      Hotels & Resorts
MARKET:        Baton Rouge
ADVERTISER:    Sheraton Hotel

The Sheraton Hotel in suburban Baton Rouge used television to expand the image of the hotel. Originally perceived as "just a hotel" by the local residents, the Sheraton has become a major meeting center for business and social activities.

The successful re-positioning of the hotel was accomplished by using two types of commercials. One promotes the various facilities of the hotel (dining room, meeting rooms) and special weekend packages. The other commercial is used to promote live entertainment in the lounge and is changed when a new act is appearing.

The Sheraton advertises on the local news and buys various specials, allocating 70% of its total advertising budget to television.

According to Jayne Rule, the hotel manager, "television has increased our sales and fulfilled our marketing objectives."

Source:    WBRZ-TV, Baton Rouge

B21

Television Bureau of Advertising, Inc., 1345 Avenue of the Americas, New York, NY 10105

**Figure 1-2** Television Advertising Bureau profile for a specific hotel. (Reproduced with permission of the Television Advertising Bureau.)

are 24 hours in each day, and you can certainly find an hour or two each day to do your homework. The fact is that most of us who practice this business find lots more time than that to read, and we actually enjoy it!

Here is a minimum list of suggested periodicals (quite aside from video trade journals) that will fill your gray matter with great, usable information: *Scientific American* (it is *not* as hard as it looks!), *Discover, Psychology Today, Time, Newsweek, U.S. News and World Report*, the *Wall Street Journal* (the best source of information about the business of business), the *New York Times*, the *Washington Post, Changing Times, Consumer Reports*, the *Hollywood Reporter, Variety, Inc.*, and *Rolling Stone*. Throw in the daily copy of your local newspaper, too.

Freelance producer-director Joel Schumacher, who is most famous for the *Batman* movie series, once stated some very practical observations about producing and the responsibilities that accompany it: "My dream was that I would go on and make productions and have this wonderful life. And it is a wonderful life. And I wouldn't trade it for anything in the world. But it isn't what I thought it was going to be. It's a people business. It's an ego business. You have to keep on going back in there when you maybe don't want to. And you have to keep on working on days when you don't feel like it, and you have to work with people that . . . sometimes you don't like. They're not kind and they're not supportive, and you still have to get the best out of them for the project, whether you want to be there or not. That's what it means to be the guy at the top. And that takes integrity."[3]

The producer must be able to keep three things in mind at all times: the project, the project, and the project! A producer uses what wags in the business refer to as "OPM" (other people's money). And when you're responsible for what happens with thousands and sometimes millions of dollars worth of OPM, you had better have plenty of integrity. There's an old saying that goes, "It's lonely at the top." Being in

business for yourself will show you how true that expression is. There is no one to give you the pats on the back that you may need. Instead, you are expected to give them to everyone around you. As the boss, you are expected to be a fountainhead of strength, justice, and support. At best, you will be second-guessed by everyone involved in the production; at worst, employees may ridicule you behind your back. It's natural for the troops to complain about the chow and to talk about how they could do the job so much better than the boss if given half a chance. That's human nature.

You will seldom, if ever, be fully understood, sympathized with, or complimented by those who work for you. This is a natural condition in most employer-employee relationships. If you are superb at your job and manage to find exceptional people, you may establish the close familylike relationship that some producers enjoy. You must be prepared, however, to work within the more traditional framework. You must be able to draw on your own wellsprings of satisfaction, thrive and grow under constant pressure from all sides, make decisions quickly, work with and inspire other people by your own example, and derive your primary pleasure from doing these things.

When it comes to trends, a producer should be at the leading edge in order to anticipate needs, forecast future developments, and speak knowledgeably with both clients and colleagues. Adding many of the aforementioned titles (you can choose one or two of the newsmagazines) to your reading list will help keep you on that edge. Add other titles as your own needs dictate. For example, if you want to break into the lucrative horse show trade, subscribe to such magazines as *Western Horseman* and *Horse and Rider*. If you want to clinch a deal with a boat manufacturer, you will find *Yachting, Sea and Pacific Motorboat*, and *Lakeland Boating* useful in preparing your presentation.

To find specific material, no matter how esoteric, go to your local library. The *Reader's Guide to Periodical Literature* lists

## Account Consultancy Questionnaire

**To the Client:** This consultancy form is a confidential document used by us to evaluate your media needs. The information that you give us will not be shared with anyone else. Your account executive will leave one copy of this form with you at the conclusion of the interview. There is no obligation to you for this consultancy. It is provided free of charge. You may use any of the results from it for any purpose you choose. We will use the results to formulate a proposal in writing to provide media services to you.

## Company Background

1. Name of Firm: _____

2. Type of business: _____

3. Number of years in business: _____

4. Company Officers:

| Name | Title | Duties | Phone |
| --- | --- | --- | --- |
| | | | |
| | | | |
| | | | |

5. Address: _____

6. Annual Gross Income: (optional) $ _____

7. Number of employees: _____

8. Who are your primary competitors in this area? _____

_____

9. What percentage of your business do you estimate the competition is taking away? _____

_____

## Assessing Your Needs

1. What are your company's strengths? _____

_____

2. What are your company's weaknesses? _____

_____

3. What would you personally like to change? _____

_____

4. What additional share of the market would you realistically like to obtain this year? _____

5. In what areas would you most like to reduce operating costs? _____

6. What are your operating costs in the following areas?

    [a] Training . . . . . . . . . . . . . . . . . $ _____

    [b] Advertising . . . . . . . . . . . . . . $ _____

    [c] Marketing . . . . . . . . . . . . . . . $ _____

    [d] Sales Promotion . . . . . . . . . $ _____

    [e] Safety . . . . . . . . . . . . . . . . . $ _____

**Figure 1–3** Questionnaire for evaluating media needs.

7. When does most of your business occur? _____

8. How many locations do you have? _____

9. Where are they? _____
_____

10. Do you have demographic figures on your target market?

    [a] Yes       [b] No

11. Would you like us to provide them at no cost to you?

    [a] Yes       [b] No

12. What is the media mix for your advertising?

    [a]_____% radio    [b]_____% TV    [c]_____% newspaper

    [d]_____% magazine    [e]_____% other _____

13. Do you employ an advertising agency?

    [a] Yes    [b] No

14. If so, name, address and contact: _____
_____

15. What was your most successful ad campaign? _____
_____

16. When was it? _____

17. How did you measure its success? _____
_____

18. What was your least successful ad campaign? _____
_____

19. When was it? _____

20. How did you measure its failure? _____
_____

21. What is your employee turnover rate? _____

22. How are new employees trained? _____
_____

23. What is the major strength of your present training program? _____

24. What is its major weakness? _____

25. What major obstacles impede your sales force? _____
_____
_____
_____

26. Do you perceive that a motivational or sales promotional video would help remove one or more of these obstacles?

    [a] Yes    [b] No

27. Have you seen one or more such videotapes?

    [a] Yes       [b] No

28. May we make a presentation of our ideas to you and your staff at no obligation to you?

    [a] Yes       [b] No

29. What is a convenient date and time for the presentation? _____

**Figure 1-3 (cont.)** Questionnaire for evaluating media needs.

by subject every article published in popular magazines, newspapers, and journals. Going to the library is an action, as well. Libraries are equipped to stimulate good research practices. You really feel like you're doing the job when you hit the library. In addition, there is a growing number of computer services throughout the country that provide users with access to a wide variety of specific research topics. If you have a personal computer and a modem, you can join one or more of these services and conduct in-depth research from the comfort of your own desk. Check with your local computer dealer to find out what is available in your area, or subscribe to one or more of the computer magazines that serve this field and that advertise computerized research networks and services. If you don't have an Internet provider, get one immediately—and use it daily.

Every time you make a sales call, think of it as a battle of wits. Solid information and your own personality are the only weapons you have. Make sure that you are armed with both when you begin.

## Meeting with the Client

After you have gained both access to and the confidence of clients, it is time to let them explain the needs of the company. After your initial skillful presentation, they will be ready to talk. Let them do so. What you are actually doing is leading the client down the path to a project that you have already conceived. In the example here, for example, you are trying to sell a training tape. Never forget the point of your mission.

Devise a questionnaire like the one illustrated in Figure 1–3. Use it as a consulting form that enables the client to open up to you. Have the questionnaire printed with a self-duplicating second so you can leave a copy with the client when you leave. If you have a laptop with a printer attachment, so much the better. Use them. This informational meeting is, of course, offered to the client with no obligation. You hope, though, that by the time you have finished your six-step procedure, you will have locked up a contract! But don't act as if your life depends on it. That is the fastest tip-off to the client that you're desperate, and it's a fast way to be shown the door.

Accentuate the positive as you fill out the questionnaire. Keep the client answering your questions in the affirmative by phrasing statements this way: "It's true that you have a high turnover rate with your housekeeping staff, isn't it?" Follow by asking, "And I'm sure you'd like to be able to reduce the costs of training new people, wouldn't you?" You can count on a positive response to that one from almost everyone!

By the time you reach the end of your presentation, the client will be so used to saying yes to you that in most cases you'll also get the desired response when you drop the bomb: "Since we're in total agreement on your need for a high-quality training tape, there's no reason we shouldn't sign a contract and get it done." There will be more about this aspect of the sales presentation when we discuss closing the deal later in this chapter. At this point—thanks to your research, your friendly and timely fact-finding mission with the client, the information you have garnered from the questionnaire, and a solid feel for the potential amount of money the client has to spend on your project—you're ready to return to the office for the next step.

# Writing the Proposal

There are no pat formulas for proposal writing. The best advice runs along the lines of what high school teachers still tell students about doing a term paper:

Tell 'em what you're gonna tell 'em
Tell 'em
Tell 'em what you told 'em

In Appendix C, you'll find two sample proposals, one for a motorcycle company and another for a major manufacturer of heavy-duty equipment. Both are representative of standard proposals.

The key thing to remember is to be concise and to the point. You are not writing a book, a technical article, or a script. Use many action words, and write as if you're doing the project were a foregone conclusion. At this stage, what you are really doing is putting on paper what has already been discussed in your first meeting with the client. The following is a general outline that you can use until you develop an individual style of your own.

## Proposal Outline

### Title Page
For the title page, use your letterhead. A little less than halfway down the page, write the title of the project you have in mind. About three-quarters of the way down the page, on the left margin, list the client's name, your name, and the date.

### Page 1
Using no more than one page, state your case. Tell the client specifically what you propose to do. Your first paragraph to the hotel manager should say something like this:

> We propose to do a training videotape to assist Jones Hotels in training its housekeeping staff. The tape will demonstrate all aspects of the housekeeping tasks, focusing on the unique approaches that make Jones Hotels the exemplar of good service. The tape will be used by your in-house trainers to reduce the amount of time they spend in this high-turnover area of your business. In line with the proven effectiveness of audiovisual training aids, the tape will help make your housekeepers more thorough and more efficient than ever.

Flesh out the rest of the page with the data you have collected in your research and on which you and the client have already agreed. Once more, try to keep the client thinking positively. Do not, at this stage of the game, include new information or some outlandish idea that occurs to you while you're writing. It is imperative that this written proposal be the essence of the contractual agreement that you will make at the end of the process. Lay the foundation for your project, and then leave it alone.

### Pages 2 and 3
On these pages, lay out in very specific terms what your project will entail. Get to the point quickly, and be concise. By this time, you will have outlined the script on paper; from this outline, write a treatment—a description of your script in paragraph form. For Jones Hotels, the first portion of your treatment might look something like this:

> Our production opens with an introduction by Harold Jones, president of Jones Hotels. Mr. Jones will explain that the housekeeping staff is the key to the entire operation, since the reputation of the hotel is one of personal service. We find that having top management appear in this capacity gives employees a positive feeling of being cared about and not being treated as peons. Following Mr. Jones's introduction, we will feature Harriet Smith, director of housekeeping, who will explain that the tape will teach new staff members the secrets that have made Jones Hotels such a desirable stopover for guests here in our city. She will show a chart listing all the areas to be covered in the production.
>
> The video will be filmed at Jones Hotel for authenticity. Each training segment will be no more than five minutes long, with cutbacks to Ms. Smith for quick review between segments. We will provide printed review forms that ask questions taken from the text of the video presentation. These may be retained by the trainees and used for refreshers on the job.

Depending on the length of the project, this section of your proposal will take about two pages. Under no circumstances should you use more than three pages to tell your story; otherwise, your reader may lose interest. As Shakespeare had Polonius say, "Since brevity is the soul of wit, . . . I will be brief." Think about Ernest Hemingway, too. Write in short, declarative sentences. Use small, familiar words. Don't try to impress the client with the number of jawbreakers you can stuff into a phrase.

### Page 4

Here you might wish to include a sample page of the script. Laypeople are frequently impressed when they see the script form; it makes them feel like insiders in a business that has glamour and excitement. (Don't tell them that's why you're including it.) Explain that you have included a sample page of the script to show them how it is going to look on paper. Remember that proper script format is imperative to the professionals who will be making your video with you. It is equally important to present a professional script to the client.

An enormously helpful tool for all writer-producers is a fine writing program for your computer from Screenplay Systems called Movie Magic Screenwriter. Earlier versions were a bit cumbersome to use, but version 3.0 and higher is extremely friendly. Screenplay formatting is as simple as hitting the Tab and Enter keys. The software allows you to write in every script format, including multimedia, and features spell check, a thesaurus, and drag-and-drop editing. The printout looks like a first-rate script. Test-drive the software for free at http://www.screenplay.com to see if it is for you. It runs about $250.

If you elect not to show your client a sample page of the script, this page of your presentation can be used to further discuss your treatment. Be sure to explain to the client that you are fully prepared to begin writing the script upon contract approval.

### Page 5

To make a decision, businesspeople need to see the bottom line. And this is where you present it in the form of a Production Budget Summary. Figure 1–4 shows a sample. *Caution:* You will arrive at the summary figures on your cover form through a complex budgeting process that we will examine in detail in the next section of

this chapter, along with a dynamic computer program that will assist you in film and video budgeting. The detailed figures from this longer process are generally not shown to the client. They reveal proprietary information about your company, your costs, and your profit margins that you should keep strictly confidential. Don't be cajoled or bullied by clients who demand to see all of your figures.

### Page 6

This is your conclusion page. Use it to "tell 'em what you told 'em." You should always end on a positive note, like this:

> We are very excited about working on this project with Jones Hotels. We know that your housekeeping staff will enjoy our presentation and that you will enjoy the considerable cost savings it will bring to your operation. We look forward to a long and happy association with you.

Figure 1–5 is an example of a successful proposal that sold a project idea to a major manufacturer. (See Appendix C for additional proposal samples.)

## General Tips

Finally, here are a few tips about proposal writing that you should keep close at hand:

- As you write your proposal, remember that this is the document that your client will keep after you have gone. It is a primary selling tool.
- When it comes time to deliver the final product, you are going to be held to whatever you say in this document. Make sure you can deliver what you say you can.
- Use positive language. Do not use phrases like, "We think" or "We believe." Instead, say, "We will," "We do," "We are," and so on. Any hesitancy or negativity that appears in the language or style of your proposal will exert a subtle but real effect on your clients as they pore over the document.
- While being as positive as possible, avoid hyperbole. Don't blow your own

"Cry Me A River"

ASSOCIATION OF INDEPENDENT COMMERCIAL EDITORS POSTPRODUCTION COST SUMMARY

Bid Date:
Postproduction Co:   Lost Planet Editorial, Ltd.
Address:   725 Arizona #304, Santa Monica, CA 90401
Telephone:   310•395•9298
Business Coordinator:   Kim Sprouse
Editor:   Keith, Mark, Lee
Job:
Production Co:
Address:
Telephone:
Contact:
Director:
Fax:

Company:   Bradley University
Address: Dept. of Comm. & Fine Arts, Peoria, Il
Telephone:   309•677•2973
Client:
Product:
Agency Job#:
Project Coordinator:   Bob Jacobs
Agency Business Mgr:
Agency Creative Dir:
Agency Writer:
Agency Art Director:

Fax:   309•677•3750

**Commercial Identification**

| Title:     "Cry Me A River" | 60:00 | *THIS BID IS COST PLUS.* |
|---|---|---|
| | | |
| | | *EDIT DATES SUBJECT TO AVAILABILITY.* |
| | | |
| | | *PLEASE NOTE THAT EDITORIAL WORK* |
| | | *CANNOT COMMENCE BEFORE RECEIPT OF* |
| | | *FIRST HALF OF EDITORIAL FEE.* |

**SUMMARY OF ESTIMATED POSTPRODUCTION COSTS**

| | | ESTIMATE | ACTUAL |
|---|---|---|---|
| **1000 Prep** | **Total A** | $0 | |
| **2000 Sound** | **Total B** | $11,950 | |
| **3000 Opticals** | **Total C** | $0 | |
| **4000 Laboratory** | **Total D** | $0 | |
| **5000 Videotape** | **Total E** | $43,500 | |
| **6000 Misc** | **Total F** | $750 | |
| **SUB-TOTAL** | **SUB-TOTAL** | $56,200 | |
| | | | |
| **6500 Mark-up:  10%** | | $5,620 | |
| **7000 Travel/Equipment** | **Total G** | $16,250 | |
| **8000 Creative Fee/Labor** | **Total H** | $23,000 | |
| | | | |
| **9000 Total** | **TOTAL** | $101,070 | |
| **9100 Sales Tax** | | | |
| | | | |
| **9500 Grand Total** | **GRAND TOTAL** | $101,070 | |

Page 1

**Figure 1-4** Sample production budget summary.

"Cry Me A River"

**1000 Prep**

| | | | | |
|---|---|---|---|---|
| Sync Dailies | | | $0 | |
| Screening room | | | $0 | |
| Code Dailies | | | $0 | |
| Stock Footage + fee | | | $0 | |
| Video dailies are provided by the production company. | | | $0 | |
| | | Sub-Total A: | $0 | |

**2000 Sound**

| | | | | |
|---|---|---|---|---|
| Narration Recording | | | $0 | |
| Dialogue Replacement | | | $0 | |
| Sound Prep/Avid | | | $0 | |
| Sound Effects Pro Disk | | | $0 | |
| Sound Effects Transfers | | | $1,100 | |
| Transfers+Stock | | | $800 | |
| Scratch Mix | (Included in Avid time) | | $0 | |
| Mix Lay-Up | 5 | | $2,250 | |
| Final Mix | 13 | | $5,850 | |
| D2 Rental | | | $800 | |
| Video Sound Transfers | | | $650 | |
| Video Sound Mix | | | $0 | |
| Video Sound Stock | | | $500 | |
| Audio Relay/Retrack | | | $0 | |
| | | | $0 | |
| | | | $0 | |
| | | Sub-Total B: | $11,950 | |

**3000 Opticals**

| | | | | |
|---|---|---|---|---|
| Artwork | | | $0 | |
| Projections | | | $0 | |
| Title Prep+Photography | | | $0 | |
| Matte Prep+Photography | | | $0 | |
| Color Stand Photography | | | $0 | |
| Rotoscoping | | | $0 | |
| Interpositive | | | $0 | |
| Tape to Tape Manipulation | | | $0 | |
| Optical Testing | | | $0 | |
| Pre-Opticals | | | $0 | |
| Optical Negative/Effects | | | $0 | |
| Duping/Blow-ups (Blk&W) | | | $0 | |
| Animation | | | $0 | |
| | | | $0 | |
| | | Sub-Total C: | $0 | |

**Figure 1–4 (cont.)**  Sample production budget summary.

"Cry Me A River"

**4000 Laboratory**

| | | | | |
|---|---|---|---|---|
| Negative Cutting | | | $0 | |
| Negative Develop+Print | | | $0 | |
| Reprints | | | $0 | |
| Reversal Dupes | | | $0 | |
| Optical Track Processing | | | $0 | |
| Answer Print 35mm | | | $0 | |
| Answer Print 16mm | | | $0 | |
| 35mm Proj./Dup. Element | | | $0 | |
| 16mm Proj./Dup. Element | | | $0 | |
| Release Print 35mm | | | $0 | |
| Release Print 16mm | | | $0 | |
| Print Breakdown | | | $0 | |
| | | | $0 | |
| | | **Sub-Total D:** | **$0** | |

**5000 Videotape**

| | | | | |
|---|---|---|---|---|
| Work Pix to Cassette (inc. st) | | | $0 | |
| Film to Tape w/color Corr. to D2 | | | $0 | |
|   Pin Registered Gate | | | $0 | |
|   Electronic Pin Registering | | | $0 | |
| Additional Machines | | | $0 | |
| Ultimatte | | | $0 | |
| Tape to Tape w/ Color Corr. | 16 | | $9,200 | |
| Dub of Dailies | | | $4,500 | |
| Dubs/Dub Stock | | | $2,000 | |
| Dubs to D2 for Slo-Mo / Dub to D1 | | | $1,500 | |
| Off-line Edit (Avid) | (See Room/Equipment Rental) | | $0 | |
| Off-line Edit (Case System) | | | $0 | |
| Avid Rough Cut Layoffs | | | $500 | |
| Video Layout/EDL | | | $0 | |
| On-line Edit to D2 | 24 | | $18,000 | |
| Additional Machines | | | $0 | |
| Digital Effects Equipment-Kaleidoscope | | | $0 | |
| Digital Effects Equipment-Abekus | | | $0 | |
| Digital Effects Equipment-ADO | | | $0 | |
| Composite Effects System/Henry | 6 | | $5,400 | |
| Additional Machines | | | $200 | |
| Character Generator | 3 | | $600 | |
| Color Camera | | | $0 | |
| B/W Camera | | | $0 | |
| | | | $0 | |
| Tape Stock + Reels | | | $800 | |
| Generic Master | | | $0 | |
| Edited Master | | | $150 | |
| Protection Master/Pr. Dupe | | | $150 | |
| | | | $0 | |
| Finished Cassettes | | | $500 | |
| Tape to Film Transfer | | | $0 | |
| | | | $0 | |
| | | **Sub-Total E:** | **$43,500** | |

Page 3

**Figure 1–4 (cont.)**  Sample production budget summary.

"Cry Me A River"

**6000 Miscellaneous**

| Deliveries + Messengers | | | $0 | |
|---|---|---|---|---|
| Shipping | | | $750 | |
| Editorial Supplies | | | $0 | |
| Long Distance Telephone | | | $0 | |
| Working Meals in Facilities | | | $0 | |
| | | Sub-Total F: | $750 | |

**7000 Travel**

| Airfare | | | $0 | |
|---|---|---|---|---|
| Per Diem | | | $0 | |
| Room/Equipment Rental (Avid) | 6.5 | weeks | $16,250 | |
| | | | $0 | |
| | | | $0 | |
| | | Sub-Total G: | $16,250 | |

**8000 Creative Fee/Labor**

| Editor  (5 Weeks for Prep & Editorial/1.5 Week for Post)  6.5 | weeks | | $13,000 | |
|---|---|---|---|---|
| Editor Overtime: | | | $0 | |
| After 10 hrs: $300/hr. | | | $0 | |
| Saturday: $300/hr. | | | $0 | |
| Sunday: $400/hr. | | | $0 | |
| Assistant Editor (1 assist. for 6.5 weeks/2 assist. for 3.5 weeks) | | | $10,000 | |
| Assistant Editor Overtime: | | | $0 | |
| After 10 hrs: $75/hr. | | | $0 | |
| Saturday: $75/hr. | | | $0 | |
| Sunday: $100/hr. | | | $0 | |
| | | Sub-Total H: | $23,000 | |

Page 4

**Figure 1–4 (cont.)**  Sample production budget summary.

horn. This does not mean that you should engage in false modesty. The late actor Walter Brennan said it quite well as a character in *The Guns of Will Sonnett*: "No brag. Just fact."

- This tip may seem obvious, but it needs to be stressed. Proposals should always be printed on a laser-quality printer, should be double-spaced, and should include page numbers. If your only typewriter is an antique Remington handed down to you by Grandpa, engage the services of a professional with a word processor and a printer. Better still, take the manuscript to a printer to have it finished, and get enough duplicate copies so that your client can pass them around to colleagues. A few dollars spent on making your printed work look top-notch will pay dividends in the end.

- Always submit your proposal in an attractive binder. A three-ring plastic binder will do, but most printers and many photocopy service stores offer even snappier covers. You might want to have a number of proposal covers printed with your company name and logo on the front for a classy, professional look. Let your good taste—and your pocketbook—be your final guide.

# THE RIGHT WAY TO DO IT!

Proposal for a video project

presented to

Caterpillar, Inc.
Technical Center, Building E
Peoria, IL 61656-1875

by

Bob Jacobs
Videomax, Ltd.

**Figure 1–5**  Training video proposal.

1.

## INTRODUCTION

You have expressed a need for a video production that will serve as a training aid for employees both here in Illinois and in Alabama. Specifically, you need to be able to train operators on proper techniques for both the operation and the maintenance of certain items of equipment used in spray coatings. It is fair to assume that such a video program might also be used as an intercorporate promotional tool. To that end, you need a piece that will sparkle with professional quality, capture the attention of a variety of viewers, and transmit the message clearly and forcefully to your audience, rather than merely documenting the prosaic surface vision of that work.

You understand that the medium of video is the most effective way to state your message, primarily because creative video can enhance that message. It can take what seems superficially to be dry and boring and make it seem colorful and intriguing. You have seen several samples of the type of video work that we produce, and you sense in that style the same elements you would like to see in your program. This includes our use of colorful lighting, close-up imagery, musical underscoring, stimulating editing pace, and personalization of concepts by having the story told by the people who do the work.

We have toured your facility and discussed the project in some depth. We can do the job for you this summer.

2.

## THE PROPOSAL

We will produce one high-quality, instructional video illustrating the proper methods for operating, servicing, and maintaining the equipment that is used in your spray coatings laboratory. We will go through a step-by-step process, using close-ups and graphics to highlight details. The length of the piece will be determined by the needs of the program. We anticipate that it will be no longer than 12 to 15 minutes.

We propose to begin the project immediately after an initial conference with you and your selected participants. After determining the featured players and the order in which you wish to proceed, we will develop a shooting schedule and begin taping segments. The postproduction phase follows shooting, with a completed program to be delivered by an agreed-upon date. We anticipate that the entire project will be completed within eight working weeks from the outset.

**Figure 1–5 (cont.)**  Training video proposal.

3.

## The Budget

To write, produce, direct, and deliver one finished Betacam SP edited master, between 6 and 10 minutes in length, with music, narration, graphics, live action, and on-camera interviews, and five VHS dubs suitable for viewing:

1. Writer/producer/director/editor                          $ 6,800
2. Production staff                                          $ 4,500
3. Materials and supplies (tape, shipping, music, etc.)     $ 2,328
   TOTAL                                                    $13,628

4.

## CONCLUSION

If this proposal is agreeable to you, please let me know so that we can get underway. I appreciate your confidence and look forward to working with you on this project.

All we need to commence principal photography is a purchase order from your organization, describing the project, made out to Bradley University and sent to the attention of Joan Wilhelm, Administrative Assistant, Slane College of Communication and Fine Arts, Bradley University, Peoria, IL 61625.

Please let me hear from you soon!

**Figure 1–5 (cont.)** Training video proposal.

# Preparing a Detailed Budget Breakdown

Budgeting a project is probably the toughest, most time-consuming part of producing. Ultimately, though, it is the most important, as well. After all, the budget determines your bottom line. Budgeting requires care and a keen, analytical mind. If the production is underbudgeted, you risk losing your shirt. If it is overbudgeted, you risk losing the client. Walking the balance beam between these two is the heart of successful producing. Budgeting is not a mysterious process, but it requires meticulous attention. Fortunately, there are some sensible and time-tested techniques that will assist you. The process of budgeting involves considering everything you can possibly think of . . . and then some! Recently, the process has been simplified with the development of software programs that deliver all of the insight of a major accounting firm right to your computer.

The Production Budget Summary form shown in Figure 1–4 is used by the Walt Disney Company for all of its film and television productions. In the example shown, the form is for the adult-themed feature division, Touchstone Pictures. This form and all of the others depicted in this book are available from Movie Magic Budgeting, a software program available from Screenplay Systems, Inc., in Burbank, California. Figure 1–4 is a reproduction of the two-page cover sheet for this rather lengthy and detailed set of forms, which guide you through the budgetary maze. Several of the categories listed on this form do not apply to smaller productions, but it is important for you to understand what goes into a major production. Movie Magic Budgeting was used for the most expensive movie ever produced, 1997's "Best Picture," *Titanic*. However, the program is so flexible that you can use it for a production of any size, including our hypothetical Jones Hotels training tape. This program will handle fringes/payroll taxes and subgroups, letting you estimate different possible scenarios, such as studio versus location or domestic versus foreign budgets, and store it all in a single spread-

sheet. It has a global feature that lets you build your own customized rate books. Entire accounts can be predesigned and stored in the Library for instant recall. There's also an optional Labor Rates program that gives you the hourly rates for every specialty category in every production center in the United States and Canada, including the cost of fringe benefits and union pensions.

The program is updated regularly, so you always have current rates on your computer. The Labor Rates feature appears right on the Budgeting Toolbar, and it covers all guilds and unions, including the Screen Actors Guild (SAG), the Directors Guild of America (DGA), the Writers Guild of America (WGA), the American Federation of Television and Radio Artists (AFTRA), the International Alliance of Theatrical Stage Employees (IATSE), the American Federation of Musicians (AFM), and the Teamsters. For a small company without an in-house accounting staff, this is a great investment—the cost is about $500. As a bonus, the program includes 25 industry-standard film, television, and video forms and a special function that enables you to make a custom budget form for your production company. Test-drive a fully functional demo at http://www.screenplay.com.

Let's take a detailed look at the forms reprinted in the appendix to this chapter. Items 31-00 through 41-00 are the above-the-line costs. Items 42-00 through 89-00 are the below-the-line costs. This arbitrary "line" separates the creative elements, such as talent and script, from the technical aspects of production.

As you read through these forms, you will notice that each category from the summary sheet is broken out into a number of subheadings and line items. In the case of our hotel training tape, it is quite unlikely that we would need all of the personnel listed in Category 44-00, Wardrobe, for example. The process of considering all of the possibilities in this manner will, however, sharpen your mind and bring out many things that you might otherwise have overlooked, only to surface later, when it could affect your bottom line. And by following the budgeting steps outlined here, when you do get ready for that miniseries or network television special, you'll be fully prepared to deal with a complex budget!

## Estimating Time

In looking at the budget forms, you'll see that they indicate a column for days, weeks, or quantity. Next to that is a column for the rate per day, per week, or per quantity. All you have to do is figure out how many days or weeks you will be needing your staff, supplies, and equipment and how much each category is going to cost. Add in a profit margin, and you have a budget total.

The process can be just as simple as it sounds. All it takes is a logical approach to the situation and a means for determining worth.

Step one in budgeting is figuring out the time needed for each category. The Script Breakdown form shown in Figure 1–6 is a sample from Screenplay Systems's Movie Magic Scheduling. With this software package, you can streamline the entire process of scheduling from script breakdown through detailed shooting schedule. The example printed here is from the classic feature film *It's a Wonderful Life*. As you go into production, this form becomes very detailed and is the bible for your preproduction planning. The script breakdown is a budgeting tool with which you go through the script page by page, scene by scene, and project all of your needs for the shoot. Using this tool, you can project to the quarter hour who and what you will need and where and when you'll need them. If you had a script at this point, the Script Breakdown would be your primary tool.

You do not have a script yet, however. The reason you do not is simple: You have not been paid to write it because you haven't sold the project. From time to time, you will present a script on spec, hoping to sell it. For now, we'll assume that you are playing it tough and are not going to go to the considerable expense in both time and effort to write a script until someone is paying you to do so.

What you do have instead of a script is a very good notion of what the script will be like when you do get around to writing it. The late Gene Roddenberry, creator and producer of the *Star Trek* television series, said, "Producers in television tend to be writers or writer types. Producing is just an extension of the storytelling process."[4] So we'll assume that you are that kind of producer and that you are going to be the writer. Without actually writing the script, you can draw on your research, your visit to the hotel, and your discussion with the client to do a quick outline of the project. From this outline, you can draw some conclusions that will allow you to use the Script Breakdown form to estimate a budget. Remember that it is only an estimate at this time.

To predict the number of days in the shoot (discussed further in Chapter 2), you must first have an idea of how many camera setups will be involved. Each time the camera and lights have to be moved, time is consumed. A good rule of thumb is 35 minutes per setup once the master scene has been lit. At this stage of planning, overestimate the number of setups unless you are very experienced or are so familiar with your crew that you know how fast the changes can be made. From this estimate, you'll have a fairly accurate idea of the number of hours; break this number down into days, and enter it on your Shooting Schedule. A typical shooting day is 10 hours. After 10 hours, you will normally have to pay overtime.

## Estimating Equipment and Extras

The next factor to include in your budget is the cost of all of the equipment you will need. If it is a relatively small shoot, you may not need much more than a camera with a variable-focal-length lens, a video-

**Breakdown  Sheet**

Sheet: **1** _____  I/E: _____  Set: _____  D/N: _____

Scenes: _____  Pages: _____

Synopsis: _____

Location: _____

Sequence: _____  Script Day: _____ Script Page: _____

Figure 1–6 Script breakdown form.

*smart ways to shoot amatuers*

cassette recorder (VCR), a microphone, and a three- or four-instrument lighting kit. [When using nonprofessional talent, even on a small shoot, you'll find that the addition of a second camera and operator will save time and trouble in postproduction.] Pros, of course, can repeat actions interminably for matching cuts in postproduction. Amateurs almost never can. The use of multiple cameras gives you real-time cuts on the action of the best performances.

Whatever equipment you will need must be spelled out thoroughly here. Some producers own the basics—a camera, VCR, light kit, and so forth. Many do not, simply because of the enormous investment involved. That is why rental equipment houses have spread from the major production centers like Los Angeles and New York into smaller markets. Rental houses are now located throughout the country.[5] All have free catalogs that you can obtain simply by calling or writing. Most houses have daily and weekly rates; the weekly rate is typically three or four times the daily rate. All of the rental firms ship anywhere in the country. You will have to know how much they charge for shipping as well as whether they charge you for the time the equipment is in transit.

In addition to equipment considerations, you must attempt to project all of the things you will need to complete the production. This stage of planning requires careful thought and attention to minute detail. Nonequipment requirements might include props, costumes, makeup, shipping boxes—everything that you, your cast, and your crew will have to use. Budgeting forms are very helpful here in organizing your thinking.

## Budgeting for People

Now you are ready to consider the next major budget item: people. Two categories of technicians and performers are available: union and nonunion. If your project is being prepared for national television broadcast, you have no choice but to hire a union cast and crew. There are two major

unions for technicians: the National Association of Broadcast Employees and Technicians (NABET) and the International Alliance of Theatrical Stage Employees. Video performers also have two unions or guilds: the Screen Actors Guild and the American Federation of Television and Radio Artists. The addresses and telephone numbers of these four unions are listed in Appendix A.

Major producers and production companies are signatories to the union or guild contracts and, as such, are committed to hiring only union or guild members. Violators can be penalized with fines and production halts. Even major studios tremble at the prospect of a union strike. Medium-sized to large independent signatories are well advised to stick to the book when dealing with unions.

If you are a signatory producer, the job of budgeting for your cast and crew is simplified. Each guild has a set of minimum pay scales, including fringe benefits and payment schedules for residuals, or repeat runs of the work. Any signatory can obtain copies of the guild or union rules, regulations, and fee schedules simply by writing for them. If you have Movie Magic Budgeting, the labor rates are included in the package that is upgraded each year. Touch a key, type in the category of employee, and the rates appear on your screen.

The unionization of the production industry is a controversial issue. Many people feel that the unions have acquired too much power and have set rates so high that they have driven producers out of the major centers of production. Others feel that the unions and guilds provide a valuable service by establishing a system of internal screening and testing of candidates, thereby guaranteeing that their members are highly qualified technicians.

Figuring the worth of nonunion personnel is a matter between you and them. A typical freelance rate for a competent videographer is $400 to $1,000 per day. Frequently, you can hire operators with their own cameras and VCRs for that amount. Remember that this person will be more responsible than anyone else for the final look of your piece, and therefore it may be foolish to scrimp on the videographer's fee.

The number of crew people you will need is entirely dependent on the size and scope of the project. Unless you are able and want to do some of the technical work yourself, a typical minimum crew (in addition to the producer) for a small to moderate production consists of a director, videographer, VCR operator/sound recordist, camera assistant/gaffer, grip, and script supervisor. If you are not familiar with all of these terms, you'll find helpful the brief descriptions that follow.

- A gaffer is an electrician. This is the person responsible for setting the lights, patching into power sources if necessary, and so on. Many videographers have long-standing relationships with gaffers who also double as camera assistants to pull focus, push dollies, and so on, in nonunion settings.
- A grip is a general helper who loads and unloads equipment, assists the gaffer, arranges the set, and so on. Grips do the heavy lifting and carrying. They are good with tools. Working without at least one grip on the set puts a major strain on everyone involved.
- The script supervisor is responsible for continuity, for noting changes and ensuring that the script is being shot as it was written. Script supervisors will also time shots with a stopwatch so that at the end of each day you will know about how long your project is turning out to be. You and the editor will use the script supervisor's notes in postproduction.

As your production develops, you will have to add additional categories of people from the Picture Budget Detail form. For the Jones Hotels shoot, we will assume that you can handle makeup, wardrobe, and so on yourself. However, if you don't feel competent in these areas, employ someone who is.

When you have figured the amount for cast and crew salaries, be sure to add on the following:

Meals—at least two a day (one hot); three if you go overtime
Coffee, juice, soft drinks, and snacks on the set
Travel expenses
Lodging, if necessary
Special dietary considerations (vegetarian, restricted sodium, etc.)
Liability insurance for all personnel and equipment

As an independent producer, in some cases you may not have to compute withholding income taxes, worker's compensation insurance, or Social Security taxes because your freelancers do not work for your company. You employ people on a per-project contractual basis as independent craftspeople who are solely responsible for reporting their own wages to the Internal Revenue Service. Chapters 3 and 6 discuss these and other contractual considerations in more detail.

## Budgeting for Yourself

When you have arrived at cost figures on a daily or weekly rate for the crew and cast, direct your attention to yourself. The producer is, of course, entitled to a fee for each production over and above the profit margin that you will include for your company. Many novice producers forget this important factor or figure that they will pay themselves out of the profit. If you are going to stay in business, remember that the business itself needs to be paid on each project. This profit is what will sustain the business and you through periods during which there is no work. Count on having such periods.

There is no fixed formula for determining a fair profit margin for your company. Because they do a lot of continuing business, some producers can operate on a profit of as little as 5 to 10 percent of the total of each production budget. Others, if the client can afford it, have a built-in profit factor of 50 percent of the total production budget. Profit ultimately depends on your needs, your client's pocketbook, and your conscience. Remember, though, that your company is not like a grocery chain that can operate on a 2 to 5 percent overall profit margin because it sells stuff every single day in large volume. Your profit margin has to be larger simply because the company may not be working every day, every week, or every month, but it's overhead must continue to be paid.

After estimating time and equipment and budgeting for staff and profit, it is time to move to the second phase of preparing a detailed budget: projecting finishing costs and unexpected costs.

## Finishing Costs

Finishing costs cover postproduction and completion. You will have to estimate how many minutes or hours of tape you will end up with and approximately what the shooting ratio will be. A typical shooting ratio for a tape similar to the Jones Hotels tape is 10:1. This means that you will shoot 10 minutes of tape for every 1 that makes it to the final product. If you have projected a 10-minute finished tape, you'll be editing it down from 100 minutes of raw footage. Shooting ratios can easily run much higher than this. Unbelievably, many national directors regularly shoot 50,000 to 100,000 feet of 35mm film for a 30-second spot commercial that will end up using just 45 feet of film.

You will do your first edit off-line. This is the stage in which you make a rough cut and log the footage numbers to guide the final cuts. The final edit at an on-line facility will be very expensive. For example, you can find off-line editing at fees ranging from $200 to $400 per hour, whereas on-line fees run from $600 to more than $2,000 per hour. Estimating postproduction time is, therefore, critically important.[6] A postproduction budget estimate for a one-hour musical program submitted by Lost Planet Editorial, Ltd., in Santa Monica, California, appears later in this chapter.

Music is your final postproduction consideration. A number of stock libraries provide music that you pay for on a "needle-drop" basis.[7] Original music is preferable,

of course, because it can be composed and performed to meet the specific needs of your production. There is a growing number of audio production studios that specialize in original scoring. Whether you use stock music or original scores will probably depend on your budget limitations, but either type of music will contribute a professional polish to any video production. In this age, music has become a vital and integral part of production. Clients are sophisticated visually and aurally now, and they expect top-quality sound in their projects. If you live in a college town, you may be able to enlist the help of graduate students or even faculty in the music department to both score and perform compositions for your videos for a very modest financial consideration. It doesn't hurt to make a phone call or, better yet, a personal visit to these potential resources and introduce the concept of professional exposure for their work.

## Budgeting for the Unexpected

When you have tabulated all of the costs on your budget form, you will come to the block marked "Contingency." All producers overlook some small detail in the budgeting process. Even if you haven't overlooked anything, an unforeseen emergency is likely to arise during the production. Your lead actor could get sick and miss a day or two of shooting. Your videographer could quit and have to be replaced. A crucial piece of equipment could break down and have to be replaced. The mayonnaise on the potato salad at lunch could go bad and take down your whole crew with diarrhea for a week. Your shoot could be rained out for days on end. Remember Murphy's Law. These are some of the reasons for the contingency fund. It is a built-in "fudge factor" that insures the project against the unexpected. The typical contingency runs from 20 percent to a high-risk guesstimate of 40 percent of the total budget.Tally it in at this point to give you the grand total.

When you have completed this process, you have done everything possible to estimate honestly the real production cost. Use the completed budget summary forms through each phase of the production, striving at all times to bring the project in at no more than the figures slated for each category and, if you are good and lucky, under budget. There is nothing in the world that a client appreci-ates more than a producer returning, along with the final tape, a reduced claim by the amount that a project came in under budget. This simple act of honesty will assure you of years of repeat business and a great reputation that will spread through the industry. It is also just plain ethical.

## Demonstrating Your Cost-Effectiveness

At your presentation meeting with clients, lay the budget summary top sheet before them. For a project like the Jones Hotels training tape, the figure might typically run between $35,000 and $50,000. In many cases, this sum may represent a consider-able savings compared to the annual costs of training programs in wages and time. If so, you are well on your way to wrapping up the deal.

On the other hand, the cost of the video project may be more than the company is already spending on training. Your job in this case will be to convince the client that the effectiveness of the training aid will enhance the quality of training. It might, for example, make the trainer's job simpler because the trainees will have access to the tape for reviewing on their own. Per-haps the fact that Mr. Jones has provided his staff with this state-of-the-art training aid will make his people think more highly of him, of themselves, and of Jones Hotels.

Because you know that your product is top quality and that it will help your cli-ents and their businesses in spite of the cost, you can resort to the emotional sales technique with a clear conscience. If you can't justify the product in your own mind after research and budgeting, it is better to tell the client this and withdraw from the project. Your honesty will win their respect and may pay off in other jobs down the line. Businesspeople are not stu-pid. If you buffalo them this time, you may sell them this project. But you will never sell them another thing as long as you live once they catch on. Repeat business and word-of-mouth publicity are the lifeblood of the independent producer. Therefore, a few minutes of real soul-searching at this stage of the game is crucial.

## Making an Effective Presentation— "The Dog and Pony Show"

An effective presentation is a selling tool that can be as important as the actual pro-posal or the bottom line of the budget. Thus it is imperative that you learn the techniques and know the tips that set a mediocre presentation apart from an excellent one.

The quite respectable, quite necessary, and generally final sales pitch made to a client is called "The Dog and Pony Show" by those in the business. When making this final sales pitch, pull out all the stops and use all of your powers of showman-ship, positive thinking, and persuasion to convince the client to buy your deal. So institutionalized has this performance become that we call it the D&P. Although you may be a very good video producer with a bookshelf full of Peabody or Emmy Awards, and the idea you're sell-ing may be able to save the client mil-lions of dollars if it is implemented, none of this matters unless you have a solid D&P to sell it all to the client. This pre-sentation is your only chance to convince the client that you are the one person for the job. Following are some elements of a good D&P.

## Setting the Stage

The impression you make at the D&P has to be a lasting one. No matter how casually you may be received by the client, consider this a formal occasion. Dress for it. The client may sit at the table in shirtsleeves, but you must keep your best suit and polished business shoes on. It's an antique saying, but write it on your forehead so you see it every morning before venturing out in the real world: "If you look good, you feel good. If you feel good, you are good!" Yes, it's cornball. But it works.

Adopt the salesperson's technique of practicing your speech in front of a mirror. Rehearsal is the secret of making presentations seem to be spontaneous, just as if you were putting on a play. Know all of your facts and figures without having to fumble through sheaves of paper to find them. Tell your client how long the presentation will take at the outset, and be sure to stick to your time frame.

Although the D&P speech is prepared formally, make it sound as if it's coming off the top of your head. Spontaneity and a casual delivery put people at ease. Allow time at the end for questions, but try to be so thorough that there are few, if any.

Take charge of the presentation and maintain it. Although it is the client's time and place, it is your moment. Be polite, cordial, and friendly, and don't forget to inject a sense of humor into the proceedings. An occasional self-deprecating joke does wonders for the client's nurturing instincts.

Remember, too, that you are in the audiovisual business. Make good use of charts, slides, graphs, audio recordings, and presentation software if you can. These allow the client to see your efficiency and your command of the medium you represent.

## The Demo Reel

The demonstration reel, or demo reel, is your major sales tool. It is quite simply a compilation of your best work to date, assembled on one tape. Show it to the prospective client to prove that you know what you're doing. A smooth and impressive demo reel isn't just thrown together. It requires careful thought and preparation. Here are some suggestions for assembling a demo reel that shines:

- *Keep it short.* This is a demo reel, not an epic extravaganza. Keep it no longer than 5 to 10 minutes, which is about the length of time any busy executive can be expected to sit still and pay attention. If you do mainly industrial or training tapes, select brief sections from two or three that show your best creativity. If you do spot TV commercials, choose a few of your best :30s and :60s to showcase here.
- *Orchestrate it.* Treat the demo reel as if it were a complete production. Use musical segues between sections to create a sense of flow. If portions of the reel need to be explained, use a narrator. Begin with a title, and end with tasteful graphics using your company logo. You might even want to run a short credit roll at the end over some triumphal music to show that you aren't working alone. Credits impress clients and leave them with the feeling of having seen a show rather than a demonstration. It's also about the only time you will be able to use credits in this business!
- *Tailor the demo reel to fit the client.* If you're going to be a generalist, then make more than one demo reel. You may have won awards for your industrial work, but an industrial reel is practically worthless to a fast-food client.
- *Tailor it to suit the need.* Advertising agencies, especially, tend to pigeonhole producers and directors. If you have a reputation with an agency for doing excellent airline work, for example, you can count on not being called to produce its spots for a hotel chain. Therefore, develop a series of demo reels for each of the major areas in which you intend to work. If you just haven't done enough to make separate reels, then show as much diversity as possible on the one reel you put together.

• *Show it off.* Normally, you will do the D&P at the client's place of business. You may be making your presentation in an office or a conference room, which means that the kind of equipment you use to show your demo reel is critical. It should be portable, simple to set up, and easy to use.

With recent advances in the quality and compactness of 1/2-inch-format VCRs, many producers are showing demo reels on VHS. These "home market" consumer machines are very compact and able to withstand the abuse of frequent moves. Many come with stereo sound capability for superb audio quality. The monitor should be the largest screen practicable. Usually, more than one person will be viewing your tape, and you will want the screen to be commanding. A number of large-screen monitors are available. Make sure that the one you choose is aligned and working properly before the showing. Nothing can kill your demo reel—and your sale—quicker than having to make excuses for a fuzzy, unregistered picture.

If the client is coming to your office, make sure that you have a tasteful screening room. A wide variety of very large video projection units is available. By adding high-quality speakers, pretty common video can look and sound very impressive. And after all, impressing the client is what the demo reel is all about.

## The Handouts

During the course of the D&P, you will hand out copies of the proposal, including the budget. Be sure you know how many people will be at the presentation so you can have copies for everyone. Have the proposal bound as discussed earlier in this chapter. A nice touch is to have the name of each individual at the presentation printed on the cover. You can do this yourself with press-on letters or with a typed self-adhesive label. This personal touch makes each individual feel important. It also suggests that you really care about the account.

Give those present time to read the proposal. You might wish to read through it formally so that each person can follow along. At the conclusion of the reading,

---

1. Did the presentation answer all of your questions about this production? [    ] Yes  [    ] No

2. Did the quality of the demo reel meet your expectations? [    ] Yes  [    ] No

3. On a scale of 1 to 10 please indicate your response to the demo reel.

4. Were all staff members needed to make the decision present? [    ] Yes  [    ] No

5. If not, would you like a second presentation to brief them? [    ] Yes  [    ] No

6. If so, when?_____.

7. We will be making our decision to proceed with production in _____ days.

8. We have the following questions about the production based on issues raised after the presentation:

_____

_____

_____

_____

**Figure 1-7** Questionnaire for soliciting client response.

open the session to questions and answers. If you've done your job well and presented a package in line with the client's budget limitations, the main question you should anticipate is, "When do we start?"

Give the client and each of the others present a copy of your brochure with a business card attached. Again, this makes the people at the presentation feel as if you have taken a personal interest in them. Make a brief statement to each person, calling each one by name. For example, "Laura, it's been a pleasure meeting you. Here is a pamphlet for you to keep. Don't hesitate to call if you have any questions. We're looking forward to working with you."

Finally, print up a brief questionnaire to solicit the client's response to the presentation. Explain that you do this to test yourself, not the client. Make it simple for the client to fill out, and include a stamped, self-addressed envelope. Figure 1–7 shows a sample questionnaire for clients. Based on your knowledge of the client's business, invent a series of questions designed to appeal to the client. The questionnaire is obviously a leading one; its purpose is to make your clients comfortable and involved so that they lack any reason to turn the project down.

# Closing the Deal

No matter how well you have presented your case, don't expect a decision on the spot. In most cases, you are asking clients to commit to an expenditure of tens of thousands of dollars. If this is the client's first venture into video production, the prospect is also a little strange and frightening. The client will need some time to think it over; how much time is somewhat up to you.

During your presentation, firmly suggest that you can't wait forever to get rolling. You have budgeted this project based on several factors, including the current price of equipment, videotape, and so on. These figures can change without notice. Your budget is also contingent on the availability of certain talent, both on- and off-camera. Explain these factors to the client. Finally, you can schedule only so much of your time for this one project; there are others waiting in the wings. Businesspeople will certainly understand these considerations. Don't overstate things; don't even exaggerate, but act like the progressive, positive, success-oriented professional you want to be. Attitude counts for a lot, especially during this phase of the proceedings. Act like a winner, and you're likely to become one.

There is a phenomenon known as "cooling off" that takes place in potential buy-

ers. In the heat of a good sales pitch, people may sign a contract to buy an expensive car or a resort condominium, even if they really can't afford it. The longer your clients have to think over a major purchase like a video production, the more likely they are to pass on it. Check your own memory for times when you've been talked right up to the brink of a large purchase, only to walk away to think it over. Chances are that if you did your thinking for more than 48 hours, you did not make the purchase. That's why many states have passed laws mandating a cooling-off period. These laws give clients the right to cancel contracts for a fixed period of time following the sale.

Your clients will experience this cooling-off if you give them more than a few days to decide. In our business, five working days are generally enough for anyone to make a yes-or-no decision. This time frame allows for review of the project at all levels necessary. During those five days, you can perform follow-up maneuvers to help the client make a favorable decision.

## Follow-up Actions

First, send a letter to arrive the day after the presentation. This is a simple exercise in good manners. Thank the client for giving you the time and opportunity to make the presentation. Tell clients how enjoyable it was for you to meet the staff and with what pleasure you are looking forward to working with them on the project. Write this letter as if the project is definitely going to proceed. Keep it positive and cordial. Use phrases like "When we begin production," instead of "If we begin production." Always plant positive suggestions. These help keep the client pointed toward the actuality of going ahead.

Next, evaluate your performance at the D&P. Some producers tape the entire presentation on a small, concealable audio recorder (check to make sure this practice is legal in your state.) Playing it back gives them insight into their own strengths and weaknesses. It also lets them hear the audience's reactions for a second time, which can be helpful in preparing for questions that may arise. Anything that jumps out at you—an awkward pause, a pointed jab you missed at the time, a strained comment from anyone in your audience—may call for spin control, requiring a follow-up informational phone call, for example. Two days after the D&P, make that call. Using the information from your playback, you might impress the client by referring back to one or two areas of concern expressed at the meeting. If the people you speak to have not decided by this point, inform them that you will phone back on Friday, say, at a specific time to receive the go-ahead.

If the answer does not come on Friday, press politely but firmly for reasons why. If your prospects need the weekend to decide, that's fine, but on Monday you must have the final word. If you don't receive it then, forget about this client and move on. You have encountered one of the biggest frustrations of this—or any other—business. You have done your best, but the client won't move. If the client is recalcitrant, in fact, drop the deadweight and walk away to pitch someone else. It's terribly hard to do that sometimes, after all the effort and talent you've expended. Do it

anyway. Get over it, and go on to the next project, and the next.

## Negotiations

You will sometimes encounter a client who is a horse trader. This person has an innate need to haggle over the cost of everything. No matter how carefully you have constructed a case for your budget, this client won't go for it unless you make some concessions. Other clients have absolutely fixed financial limitations that prevent them from buying your product at the price you've quoted, even though they may want the production very much. With both of these types, you must be prepared to negotiate.

The word *negotiate* means "to compromise." You give up something; the client gives up something. It is true give-and-take, at the end of which you reach an equitable agreement and the production proceeds.

Anticipating the need to negotiate on price, many producers build into their budgets an additional "fudge factor." This percentage varies from 2 percent to as much as 10 percent. This practice bothers many people from an ethical standpoint. If the client accepts without negotiation the budget you have proposed, you've made an additional windfall profit. Although this may make you happy, it can backfire if word gets out to the industry that you are a rip-off artist or that you will haggle like a used car salesperson with a bad wig. Not a good image to get stuck with.

A better tactic—one that will help maintain your good reputation in what is in fact a fairly small, close-knit business— is to prepare an alternative budget. Demonstrate to the client that you can cut costs, but in so doing, you will also be eliminating certain positive production values. For example, you might handle the haggler this way: "Mr. Jones, I understand that you want a high-quality piece here, and our budget has provided for that quality. I really can't cut back on the essentials, but we could make the piece shorter if you like. Every day we cut out of the schedule saves you X dollars, as you can see. We might also be able to reduce the cost somewhat by eliminating the music or changing it from an original composition to something from a stock music library." Be able to make your case in specific terms. Point out exactly what the reduction in cost will mean to the finished product. A negotiation has to be an open and honest exchange of viewpoints on both sides. Each party must be willing to give and take.

Only as a last resort should you consider reducing your fair profit margin on the project. If landing the account might mean a great deal more work down the line from this client, it may be wise to reduce your profit on this one project to get the contract. Make clear, however, your reason for backing down, and let the client know in no uncertain terms that this is a one-time deal.

## Expectations

Selling, which is really what we've been discussing here, is a numbers game. The more sales calls you make, the higher the volume of business you can expect to do. This business is not like owning a shoe store or a taco stand. Foot traffic is important for a retailer at the local shopping mall. It is not important to the independent producer. You have to get out of the store and hustle up the prospects. They won't come to you until you land them the first time and convince them that your production company is their best friend.

No matter how well you prepare and present a D&P, don't expect it to result in an automatic sale every time. Avoid blaming yourself for failed prospects. Even the people at the very top cannot and do not expect to sell every idea they have. The biggest frustration you will encounter as an independent producer is knowing in your heart that the project you've proposed to clients is good for them and the best thing available and that the price is rock-bottom, yet they won't buy it. There is just no accounting in the end for what motivates all people. That's why selling is a fine art, not a science. And that's why the producer has to be very self-sufficient emotionally.

Learn to expect and accept rejection, and do not let it turn you into a cynic. The times the sale does go through—when the client shakes your hand and signs the contract—are among life's real peak experiences for the independent producer. And in the long run, they will more than make up for the failures.

## Summary

This chapter introduced one method you can use to achieve one of the most important functions in independent business: finding a client and making a sale. Knowing how to sell your idea and how to present the specifics of your proposal is an important asset for the independent producer. Only when you become well established will clients come to you; in the meantime, you must seek them out and know how to sell your product.

## Notes

1. Comments from Saul Turtletaub and the other Hollywood producers quoted in the remainder of this book are taken from a series of taped interviews conducted by the author each January, beginning in 1980 and continuing to the present, as part of his ongoing college teaching. He conducts an annual seminar in commercial film and television in Southern California. This quote is taken from an interview conducted in January 1984.

2.  You can find a list of most of the major trade associations in America in *The Encyclopedia of Associations* (Detroit: Gale Research, 1995).

3.  Joel Schumacher, interview with the author, January 1982.

4.  Gene Roddenberry, interview with the author, January 1982.

5.  For a complete list of video equipment dealers, see *The Video Register 1996* (White Plains, NY: Knowledge Industry Publications, 1996).

6.  A number of books on postproduction are available from Focal Press.

7.  For a list of music and sound-effects libraries, as well as contact information for celebrities, services, networks, and so on, see *The Hollywood Reporter Studio Blu-Book Directory* (Hollywood, CA: Verdugo Press, annual). Also see *LA 411*, the Professional Reference guide for Television and Music Video Production, P.O. Box 480495, Los Angeles, CA 90048, (213) 460-6304.

# Appendix to Chapter 1

Project  Title:  Untitled

*Filename: Disney Form*

Project Number:                                    Revision Number:

Notes:

| File  Information: | | Budget  Data: | |
| --- | --- | --- | --- |
| Budget Form: | Disney97 | Total Categories: | 48 |
| Creation Date: | AUG 19, 1997 | Total Accounts: | 781 |
| Modified Date: | AUG 19, 1997 | Total Details: | 0 |
| Modified Time: | 11:29:06 AM | Total Fringes: | 16 |
| | | Total Globals: | 64 |
| | | Total Subgroups: | 8 |

**Appendix Page 1**    Picture budget detail. (Forms reproduced with the permission of Screenplay Systems, Inc.)

TOUCHSTONE   PICTURES

DIRECTOR:                                    START  DATE:
PRODUCERS:                                   FINISH  DATE:
                                             SHOOT:
WRITER:                                      HOLIDAYS:
SCRIPT:                                      POST:
CO-PROD/UPM:                                 BUDGET  DATE:
UNIONS:                                      BUDGET  FILE:

| Acct# | Category  Title | Page | Total |
|-------|-----------------|------|-------|
| 31-00 | STORY RIGHTS | 1 | $0 |
| 32-00 | WRITER | 1 | $0 |
| 33-00 | SCENARIO MISCELLANEOUS | 2 | $0 |
| 36-00 | PRODUCER | 3 | $0 |
| 37-00 | DIRECTOR | 4 | $0 |
| 38-00 | CAST | 6 | $0 |
| 39-00 | BITS & STUNTS | 7 | $0 |
| 41-00 | ATL TRAVEL & LIVING | 8 | $0 |
| | TOTAL   ABOVE-THE-LINE | | $0 |
| 42-00 | EXTRAS & STANDINS | 10 | $0 |
| 43-00 | PRODUCTION STAFF | 11 | $0 |
| 44-00 | WARDROBE | 13 | $0 |
| 45-00 | MAKEUP & HAIRDRESSING | 15 | $0 |
| 47-00 | CAMERA | 16 | $0 |
| 48-00 | PICTURE FILM/DAILIES | 18 | $0 |
| 49-00 | SET DRESSING | 18 | $0 |
| 50-00 | ACTION PROPS | 20 | $0 |
| 51-00 | ACTION PROPS - VEHICLES | 22 | $0 |
| 52-00 | CREATURES | 23 | $0 |
| 53-00 | SET DESIGNING | 24 | $0 |
| 54-00 | SET CONSTRUCTION | 25 | $0 |
| 55-00 | SET STRIKE | 27 | $0 |
| 56-00 | VIDEO | 28 | $0 |
| 57-00 | PRODUCTION SOUND | 28 | $0 |
| 58-00 | SET LIGHTING | 29 | $0 |
| 59-00 | SET OPERATION | 30 | $0 |
| 60-00 | FACILITIES | 32 | $0 |
| 61-00 | SPECIAL EFFECTS | 34 | $0 |
| 62-00 | TESTS | 36 | $0 |
| 63-00 | LOCATIONS | 36 | $0 |
| 64-00 | TRANSPORTATION | 38 | $0 |
| 65-00 | SECOND UNIT | 40 | $0 |
| 66-00 | AERIAL/BLSCREEN/SPCL UNIT | 41 | $0 |

**Appendix Page 2**   Picture budget detail. (Forms reproduced with the permission of Screenplay
                      Systems, Inc.)

| Acct# | Category Title | Page | Total |
|---|---|---|---|
| 67-00 | PLATE UNIT | 44 | $0 |
| 69-00 | BTL TRAVEL & LIVING | 45 | $0 |
| | SHOOTING PERIOD | | $0 |
| 70-00 | VISUAL EFFECTS | 45 | $0 |
| 71-00 | PROJECTION | 47 | $0 |
| 72-00 | EDITING | 47 | $0 |
| 73-00 | TITLES | 49 | $0 |
| 74-00 | MUSIC | 49 | $0 |
| 76-00 | POST-PRODUCTION SOUND | 51 | $0 |
| 78-00 | PREVIEW EXPENSES | 52 | $0 |
| 79-00 | FILM LAB EXPENSE | 53 | $0 |
| 80-00 | PURCHASE FILM FOOTAGE | 54 | $0 |
| 82-00 | POST-PRODUCTION RESHOOTS | 55 | $0 |
| | TOTAL COMPLETION PERIOD | | $0 |
| 85-00 | INSURANCE & MEDICAL | 56 | $0 |
| 87-00 | PUBLICITY | 56 | $0 |
| 88-00 | MISC. UNCLASSIFED EXPENSES | 57 | $0 |
| 89-00 | CERTIFICATES & ROYALTIES | 58 | $0 |
| | TOTAL OTHER | | $0 |
| | TOTAL ABOVE-THE-LINE | | $0 |
| | TOTAL BELOW-THE-LINE | | $0 |
| | TOTAL ABOVE & BELOW-THE-LINE | | $0 |
| | GRAND TOTAL | | $0 |

## Fringe Breakdown Summary

| Fringe | Description | % | Units | Cutoff | Total |
|---|---|---|---|---|---|
| IA-STUDIO | | 41.0% | | 0 | 0 |
| FICA | | 6.2% | | 61,200 | 0 |
| Fringe_1 | | 1.45% | | 0 | 0 |
| FU/SU-LA | | 6.2% | | 7,000 | 0 |
| BTL W/C | | 2.29% | | 0 | 0 |
| OFFICE W/C | | 0.66% | | 0 | 0 |
| SAG/DIR/1sT W/C | | 2.29% | | 15,600 | 0 |
| WGA/DGA | | 12.5% | | 200,000 | 0 |
| P&H&W-SAG | | 13.3% | | 200,000 | 0 |
| P&H&W&V-DGA/... | | 20.719% | | 200,000 | 0 |
| FU/SU-CHI | | 7.6% | | 9,000 | 0 |
| UNION XTRAS | | 38.64% | | 0 | 0 |
| NONU EXTRAS | | 28.14% | | 0 | 0 |
| AFM | | 32.0% | | 0 | 0 |
| LN OUT-NO AFF | | 14.0% | | 0 | 0 |
| P/R-FRNGS/NO CUT | | 16.14% | | 0 | 0 |
| ALL FRINGES | | | | | 0 |

**Appendix Page 3**   Picture budget detail. (Forms reproduced with the permission of Screenplay Systems, Inc.)

### Fringe Table

#### Percentage Fringes

| Percentage Fringe | Description | ID | % | Cutoff | Total |
|---|---|---|---|---|---|
| IA-STUDIO | | | 41.0% | 0 | 0 |
| FICA | | | 6.2% | 61,200 | 0 |
| Fringe_1 | | | 1.45% | 0 | 0 |
| FU/SU-LA | | | 6.2% | 7,000 | 0 |
| BTL W/C | | | 2.29% | 0 | 0 |
| OFFICE W/C | | | 0.66% | 0 | 0 |
| SAG/DIR/1sT W/C | | | 2.29% | 15,600 | 0 |
| WGA/DGA | | | 12.5% | 200,000 | 0 |
| P&H&W-SAG | | | 13.3% | 200,000 | 0 |
| P&H&W&V-DGA/BTL | | | 20.719% | 200,000 | 0 |
| FU/SU-CHI | | | 7.6% | 9,000 | 0 |
| UNION XTRAS | | | 38.64% | 0 | 0 |
| NONU EXTRAS | | | 28.14% | 0 | 0 |
| AFM | | | 32.0% | 0 | 0 |
| LN OUT-NO AFF | | | 14.0% | 0 | 0 |
| P/R-FRNGS/NO CUT | | | 16.14% | 0 | 0 |

#### Flat Fringes

| Flat Fringe | Description | ID | Rate | Units | Cutoff | Total |
|---|---|---|---|---|---|---|

**Appendix Page 4** Picture budget detail. (Forms reproduced with the permission of Screenplay Systems, Inc.)

Global Report

Default status for global display: Display by value

| D | Name | Description | Equation | Units | P | Value |
|---|---|---|---|---|---|---|
| ☐ | P1LA | | 12 | | | 12 |
| ☐ | XTRAS | | 1750 | | | 1,750 |
| ☐ | LOCWKS | | LOCDYS/5 | | | 9 |
| ☐ | LOCDYS | | 45 | | | 45 |
| ☐ | STGWKS | | STGDYS/5 | | | 0.6 |
| ☐ | STGDYS | | 3 | | | 3 |
| ☐ | WKSLA | | (LOCDYS+STGDYS)/5 | | | 9.6 |
| ☐ | DYSLA | | LOCDYS+STGDYS | | | 48 |
| ☐ | L10 | | 11*5 | | | 55 |
| ☐ | L12 | | 14.25*5 | | | 71.25 |
| ☐ | L125 | | 15.25*5 | | | 76.25 |
| ☐ | L13 | | 16.25*5 | | | 81.25 |
| ☐ | L135 | | 17.25*5 | | | 86.25 |
| ☐ | L14 | | 17.5*5 | | | 87.5 |
| ☐ | L145 | | 18.75*5 | | | 93.75 |
| ☐ | D145 | | 18.75 | | | 18.75 |
| ☐ | Q | | XTRAS-UXTRS | | | 1,723 |
| ☐ | UXTRS | | 27 | | | 27 |
| ☐ | HOLDYS | | 2 | | | 2 |
| ☐ | HOLWKS | | 0.4 | | | 0.4 |
| ☐ | RNTLWKS | | 10 | | | 10 |
| ☐ | SNDYS | | 10 | | | 10 |
| ☐ | SNWKS | | SNDYS/5 | | | 2 |
| ☐ | HOLWK | | 0.4 | | | 0.4 |
| ☐ | PREPHOL | | 0.4 | | | 0.4 |
| ☐ | F10 | | 11*5 | | | 55 |
| ☐ | F11 | | 12.5*5 | | | 62.5 |
| ☐ | F12 | | 14.25*5 | | | 71.25 |
| ☐ | F125 | | 15.25*5 | | | 76.25 |
| ☐ | F13 | | 16.25*5 | | | 81.25 |
| ☐ | F135 | | 17.25*5 | | | 86.25 |
| ☐ | TF145 | | 18.75*5 | | | 93.75 |
| ☐ | S10 | | 11*5+16.5+4 | | | 75.5 |
| ☐ | S11 | | 12.5*5+16.5+4 | | | 83.0 |
| ☐ | S12 | | 14*5+18+4 | | | 92 |
| ☐ | S125 | | 14.75*5+18.75+4 | | | 96.50 |
| ☐ | S13 | | 15.5*5+19.5+4 | | | 101.0 |
| ☐ | S135 | | 16.25*5+20.25+4 | | | 105.50 |
| ☐ | TS14 | | 17.5*5+21.5+4 | | | 113.0 |
| ☐ | D8 | | 8 | | | 8 |

**Appendix Page 5**    Picture budget detail. (Forms reproduced with the permission of Screenplay Systems, Inc.)

Global  Report

| D | Name | Description | Equation | Units | P | Value |
|---|------|-------------|----------|-------|---|-------|
| ☐ | D10 | | 11 | | | 11 |
| ☐ | D12 | | 14.25 | | | 14.25 |
| ☐ | D125 | | 15.25 | | | 15.25 |
| ☐ | D13 | | 16.25 | | | 16.25 |
| ☐ | D14 | | 18.75 | | | 18.75 |
| ☐ | D15 | | 14 | | | 14 |
| ☐ | D16 | | 20 | | | 20 |
| ☐ | D17 | | 15 | | | 15 |
| ☐ | LA125 | | 15.25*5+4+4 | | | 84.25 |
| ☐ | LA10 | | 11*5+4+4 | | | 63 |
| ☐ | LA13 | | 16.25*5+4+4 | | | 89.25 |
| ☐ | HOLD | | 2 | | | 2 |
| ☐ | HOLW | | 0.4 | | | 0.4 |
| ☐ | STEADI | | 10 | | | 10 |
| ☐ | BCAM | | 20 | | | 20 |
| ☐ | DEVELOP2 | | FILM2*0.9 | | | 3,375.0 |
| ☐ | FILM2 | | 3750 | | | 3,750 |
| ☐ | FILM | | 5000 | | | 5,000 |
| ☐ | DEVELOP | | FILM*0.9 | | | 4,500.0 |
| ☐ | PRINT | | FILM*0.65 | | | 3,250.00 |
| ☐ | POST | | 22 | | | 22 |
| ☐ | PRINT2 | | 3750*0.65 | | | 2,437.50 |
| ☐ | OldGlobal_63 | was 'CAN$' | 0.85 | | | 0.85 |
| ☐ | CCAM | | 10 | | | 10 |

Subgroups  Report

Default status for all unmarked lines: Include
When there is a status conflict, always: Exclude

| Name | Description | ID | Status | Lines | Total |
|------|-------------|----|--------|-------|-------|
| LOC 1 | | | Included | 0 | $0 |
| LOC 2 | | | Included | 0 | $0 |
| WRAP LOC 1 | | | Excluded | 0 | $0 |
| LA P/S/W | | | Included | 0 | $0 |
| HIDE | | | Excluded | 0 | $0 |
| TRAVEL DAYS | | | Excluded | 0 | $0 |
| ATL HIDE | | | Included | 0 | $0 |
| Subgroup_1 | | | Included | 0 | $0 |

**Appendix Page 6**   Picture budget detail. (Forms reproduced with the permission of Screenplay Systems, Inc.)

Currency   Report

| Key | Country | Currency | Rate | Sample + | Sample - |
|-----|---------|----------|------|----------|----------|
| U | United States | Dollar | 1 | $1,234 | ($1,234) |

Units   Report

| Key | Unit | Units | Rate   Conversion | Number | Hours |
|-----|------|-------|-------------------|--------|-------|
| A | Allow | Allow | One "Allow" equals... | No | Hours |
| D | Day | Days | One "Day" equals... | 12 | Hours |
| W | Week | Weeks | One "Week" equals... | 60 | Hours |
| F | Flat | Flat | One "Flat" equals... | No | Hours |
| H | Hour | Hours | One "Hour" equals... | 1 | Hours |
| M | Month | Months | One "Month" equals... | 240 | Hours |

**Appendix Page 7**    Picture budget detail. (Forms reproduced with the permission of Screenplay Systems, Inc.)

# 2

# Managing People and Productions

In Chapter 1, you learned that independent producers must be successful salespeople first. But once the project is sold, whether it's a pilot for a new television series or a 30-second commercial for a local retail store, the producer puts on a brand-new hat. At this point, the producer becomes a manager.

Good management requires skill, tact, a firm knowledge of what motivates human beings to do things, and a fine sense of organization. Whether you are managing a shoe store or a production company, certain basic principles of management apply.

In most businesses, managers accept the axiom "The customer is always right." As an independent producer, however, your "customer" is your client, and because clients are usually unfamiliar with the idiosyncrasies of video production, they cannot be expected to be "right" all the time. This paradox presents a set of unusual problems. This chapter will examine effective ways of handling some of these delicate situations.

The independent producer's job differs from managerial positions in other businesses. The producer walks a thin line between satisfying two disparate types of people. The client, as one type, is generally a pragmatic, bottom-line-oriented businessperson who is used to a certain set of predictable and common behavior patterns in employees and customers alike. The producer has to know how to recognize and to maneuver within those parameters.

The other type of person in our field includes those who work in the artistic and technical crafts: the cast and crew. These folks are of a different cut altogether. They are creative, and creative people often have special needs and require greater understanding on the part of the manager. We will go into some detail on dealing with the production people later in this chapter. For now, let's consider the fundamentals of management that apply across the board.

## Basic Management in Review

Two primary theories of management are commonly accepted today. Both probe

the process of drawing productivity from employees, but the means for achieving productivity differ. For the purposes of this overview, I will refer to the two schools of thought as "traditionalist" and "behavioralist." In very simple terms, traditionalists manage by directive, whereas behavioralists manage by objective, with a stress on teamwork and empowering the individual performer.

A traditionalist manager makes decisions and passes them along to the workers in the form of directives, orders, and quotas. The system relies on rewarding extra output with bonuses and other incentives. Behavioralists put more emphasis on creating a positive environment and letting the workers feel that they have a say in the decision-making process. Employees are given the chance to set goals or objectives for themselves, rather than having them imposed from above by the manager.[1]

There is no one "best" way to manage. Many producers, in fact, use elements of both techniques, plus much creative "winging it," depending on their personality. Some producers, for example, are involved in every step of the game from initial idea to the final sound mix. They are on the set giving advice and suggestions to the director, the sound technician, and everyone else within earshot. Other producers are content to make the big decisions, hire experts for each of the key crew positions, and then get out of the way and let them do their jobs. We'll discuss these two approaches later.

Regardless of what your approach to leadership will be, there are areas in which both the traditional and the behavioral methods of management agree. The following discussion coalesces these forms into some purely practical advice.

## The Human Touch

You don't need to be a psychoanalyst to understand the basic motivations of other people. No matter what our station in life, our ethnic or racial derivation, our gender or religion, we all share a common humanity. As a producer-manager, you must remember this simple fact above all others. At work, you are dealing with an individual—a person, not a number on a budget form. Each of us needs to feel important and bright and well meaning. And while there is no doubt of the biological fact that intelligence comes in different degrees, no one likes to be thought of as, or treated as if they were, stupid.

The first rule of good management, then, is to treat your workers like human beings. That simple, old-fashioned golden rule is the number one practice of good management. Leadership is always proven by example rather than dictate. If you expect your crew to be cheerful and easygoing, then you must be the same. If you expect others to work overtime, then you must set the example by being the first to arrive and the last to leave the set or the office. You seldom have to go beyond your own instincts to know what to do with employees; *insight* is the key word. If possible, draw from your own experience. If you have ever worked under a manager who treated employees poorly, who micromanaged every move, who treated you like you were a moron, then you know that this type of management style breeds contempt and nonproductivity in the end.

Don't repeat this mistake.

## Communication

Although a video production needs a spot at which "the buck stops," it remains a communal project. Everyone involved should have a chance to give you some input. Listening to your employees is not only good for their self-esteem, but it may save you a good deal of grief down the line. No one person, even a great producer, is expected to be perfect or to have thought out all of the ramifications of a given situation. Employees are often closer to the problem than you are. They can see what you might have missed. Therefore, good communication on the job is imperative, and good communication means listening as well as talking.

Good communication from you to your employees requires clarity, conciseness, and a cordial delivery—whether written or spoken—so the employees know what you expect. Good communication also means effective listening on your part. There are three types of listening:

Listening for information
Listening critically (evaluating persuasive messages)
Listening for feelings

Your employees will tell you a lot about how they are feeling—and therefore what you might be able to anticipate in terms of developing problems—if you give them the chance. And this means that you have to be more than a passive receptor. You have to be proactive.

Don't expect your employees to take the initiative. As producer, you're the boss, so it's up to you to solicit employee input. You can do this in regular meetings or simply by dropping by a worker's desk and saying, "Allison, would you have a look at this proposal and let me know what you think of it?" And when Allison lets you know what she thinks, give her thoughts some real consideration. She may have spotted a flaw or come up with a new angle that you overlooked. If she hasn't, at least you have treated her as a valuable team member and have earned her respect.[1]

## The Good Word

Almost every person on this planet responds to praise. We seek approval, we need it, and hardly any of us receive enough. If we do our job satisfactorily, we receive a paycheck, and many managers think that's all that's required. A paycheck may not be sufficient, however. Look inward to find the value of a pat on the back, a good word, a simple thank-you for a task well done. The Academy Awards, the Emmy Awards, the Peabody Awards, the Nobel Prize—all of these are nothing more than formal pats on the back from peers. These awards share a common characteristic and one that is crucial to effective management: public praise.

If Allison comes up with something you use in the proposal, be sure to tell everyone in the office. Reward her in public with sincere thanks for her help. This will do several things for the morale of your employees. First, they'll know that you're prepared both to seek and then to acknowledge their help. Second, they'll know that you do not regard yourself as infallible. Finally, it will spur them to work harder and be helpful and not to settle for a mediocre performance. The toughest part about this area of management is that producers do not get any pats on the back themselves because they are on the highest rung of the ladder. As a producer, you will "give" constantly but "get" practically never. If you can't handle this simple fact, if you need constant reassurance yourself, then do *not* become a producer!

## The Reprimand

From time to time, employees make errors. Sometimes, the mistake is simply a bad judgment call. Sometimes, it is due to a bad attitude or just plain carelessness. Whatever the cause, the producer as manager has to deal with the consequences.

Because we have all grown up in a social milieu of reward and punishment, we expect that we will be reprimanded when we do something wrong. Many managers have the most difficult time of all disciplining an employee. They put it off, ignore the problem, redo the job themselves—anything to avoid a confrontation. This ostrichlike behavior is extremely bad for the team. Other employees will know that the error has not been acknowledged or dealt with, and their morale will suffer. It's just as important for a manager to address a problem quickly and effectively as it is to reward good work in the same way. Leadership means that you are expected to lead, not follow.

The first rule of reprimand is the inverse of the first rule of praise. Always criticize an employee in private. And never take action while you are angry. Cool off before you make things much worse by losing your temper in front of the staff. And, however difficult face-to-face confrontation may be for you, do *not* fall into the easy out of "flaming" the employee with a vicious e-mail message. Nothing is more cowardly or brutal than hiding behind a computer while you berate a fellow human being.

Call the offender into your office, or find a spot where the two of you cannot be seen or heard by others. Remember that you are not dealing with a child, but another adult. Speak to the person frankly and from the heart. Do not accuse; instead, question the situation. Lay out your case in specific terms: "John, I just found out that the order for the light kits for the Jones Hotels shoot was not placed. Now we're in a bind. This was your responsibility. Can you tell me what happened?"

By opening up the dialogue in this non-aggressive manner, you clear the way for John to explain the error without putting him on the defensive. He may open your eyes to a procedural problem of which you weren't aware. For example, he might say, "I couldn't place the order without a purchase request, and accounting hasn't given me one yet."

If it's John's responsibility to do the ordering and he's having trouble with someone in another area, you need to know about it. You also must tell John that he should have notified you sooner about the situation if he couldn't handle it himself. If he just plain forgot to do the ordering, you need to let him know that you are not happy with his performance and that he must take action to prevent it from recurring.

Whatever the cause of the situation, you have to remain calm and cool. Losing your temper, shouting, and making threats are not productive. Such behavior puts the recipient on the defensive and usually ends poorly. It is your job to keep the conversation rational.

Most employees feel bad about causing or being part of a problem; therefore, assume that employees want to make amends. Turn this negative moment into a positive one by making employees feel as though they can be a part of the solution. If you ask John for suggestions on how to rectify the situation, more than likely he will leave your office feeling chastened but positive about continuing the work. This does not mean that you can just slough off the problem. You must certainly make employees aware of the seriousness of their errors and the fact that you can't accept continued work of this quality from them. However, you can also, with some consideration for their feelings and a subli-mation of your temper and frustration, turn them around so they can get on with the job. After all, that is what you want: the job completed.

## The Challenge

If you give your employees a specific set of tasks to accomplish in an orderly and timely manner, they will probably do just that. They will probably also decide that you don't expect them to do anything above and beyond those specifics. To reap the most from employees, an effective man-ager must learn how to present challenges. Most people fall into an inertial laziness if they don't feel challenged slightly beyond their abilities. They will become bored and complacent, neither of which is good for building a dynamic business.

As a producer-manager, you walk an extremely fine line here. You can't over-challenge employees by setting goals that no one could be expected to accomplish. That will simply frustrate and ultimately destroy your staff. What you must be able to do is recognize the full potential of each employee by paying attention to what is going on. Encourage employees to move into other areas of a project, rather than directing them to do more "busy work." If John, for example, has done all of his ordering and paperwork for the day and you find that he has time on his hands, you might encourage him to help Julie in accounting, or you might ask him to work on a new procedure for ordering to present at the next staff meeting.

It is important that employees develop a sense that nothing in your business is cast in concrete. Let them know that you are receptive to new suggestions and that you have established a policy of rewarding extra achievement. Those things alone present a challenge to anyone who wants to excel. Establishing an Employee of the Month Award is one simple but effective way of recognizing exemplary work. And the reward can be as simple as a reserved parking spot in the company lot or a free dinner for two at a nice restaurant in your town.

## Ensuring Consistency

Nothing will destroy the spirit of a team working toward a common goal more quickly than inconsistent leadership. You must do everything possible to present a consistent image. If you come into the office one morning all smiles and good cheer and the next day you show up looking like someone ate your porridge and set your house on fire, the staff will be on edge and not know what to expect from you. Everyone has an off day now and then. If you're feeling ill or depressed once in a while, it simply means you're human. But if you make a habit of exhibiting extreme mood or personality swings, you will find yourself going through good people by the score. If pressure makes you behave this way, that's another good signal that you just aren't cut out to be an independent producer or that you need to seek professional counseling to help you handle the pressure.

You must treat all of your employees equally. It is quite common for a manager to like one employee better than another. We're all humans, after all. If this turns into favoritism, however, it will spell disaster for your company's team spirit. If you fraternize with one of your employees, fraternize with them all. That means that if you take Phil and Alice to a ball game, you'd better be prepared to take the whole darn staff along with you!

To maintain a professional business image and to retain a camaraderie on your team, you must be seen as a boss who is fair, equitable, and just to everyone. Write a solid policy on sexual harassment, and make sure that everyone in the company gets a copy. Without going to absurd lengths of political correctness, it is important to maintain a cordial and professional working environment in which each team member, regardless of gender, sexual preference, race, or ethnicity, feels respected as a human being and valued as a colleague.

## Delegating Authority

As a producer-manager, you are ultimately responsible for everything. You can't delegate that responsibility to anyone else. What you can and must delegate, however, is authority. You simply can't do it all yourself. If you continually meddle in the jobs that have been assigned to your employees, looking over shoulders constantly, micromanaging their every move, you will make your employees feel like robots or children, and you don't want either of these working for you.

From the stock boy to your associate producer, everybody likes to feel a degree of autonomy on the job. John likes to know that the ordering department is all his; he doesn't want to have to check with you on every detail. It gives him a feeling of satisfaction and worth to do it himself; to feel that he alone is responsible. Once he knows what your policy is and what you expect from him, leave him alone to do his job. The only time you should step in is when he makes a mistake. Even then, as we've discussed, you should try to let him solve the problem himself.

## Recognizing Individual Needs

Finally, managers must recognize the uniqueness of individuals and realize that each employee has special needs. Some people require more positive reinforcement than others. Some require much structure on the job and appreciate specific task assignments. Other workers are self-starters, needing very little motivation from you. Some will want to cry on your shoulder now and then about personal problems, some will whine about seemingly inconsequential office politics, and some will take charge and relieve you of your burdens if you let them. It takes little more than a genuine interest in the welfare of your people to uncover these differences and to accommodate them in your management style. You will be confessor, counselor, teacher, parent, guru, and class clown, depending on the need and the time.

# Production Management

Production management is much more specific than general office management. Larger production companies take much of the load off the producer by hiring specialists in the field of production management. Most smaller companies cannot afford this luxury, however, and so it falls to the producer to do the jobs of the unit manager and the production manager for each project. All of this can be more stressful than necessary if the producer fails to understand that he or she is dealing with a large collection of creative people.

These "creative types" tend to be a little more zany than their counterparts in non-production businesses. With their innate nonconformity, they tend to have a different view of themselves as employees than do people working on an automobile assembly line, for instance—not a better view, just different. Recognizing that difference and responding to it are crucial.

For the most part, creative people are exceptionally intelligent, artistically gifted humans with unusual senses of humor. They don't like to be "pushed," but they will go to any length for the sake of the production once they feel that they are part of it, that they enjoy some "ownership." Although most of the management principles covered in this chapter certainly apply to production managers, these managers have to approach a creative crew with flexibility and a willingness to be tested incessantly. There are no pat ways to prepare anyone to be good at managing creative folks. The truth is that it's like having any talent. One can paint, or not; sing, or not; act, or not. You can't be taught to do those things unless you were born with talent. The same is true of creative management. You either have the talent or you go to work for an established bureaucracy.

The mechanics of production management, on the other hand, are relatively straightforward and have been codified over the years. By breaking the production unit into departments, each with its own head, the production manager has a system for reporting and accounting. And this process has been simplified and made accessible with the advent of a practical, friendly software program. Screenplay Systems, Inc., offers independent producers the same assistance available to major players like Warner Brothers, Stephen J. Cannell, and Chris Carter. Called Movie Magic Scheduling, it produced many of the forms used as illustrations in this book. With this computerized aid, you can do everything from script breakdowns to storyboarding to daily shooting schedules.

## The Production Schedule

A team can function well only when each member knows what to do, when to do it, and where to do it. This information is derived from the production schedule, which includes estimates of how long it will take to prepare, shoot, and complete the production. Because of the nature of creative projects, no schedule can be expected to survive intact from the moment it is created. Frequently, daily changes must be made as unforeseen problems arise on the set. Scheduling, therefore, is a continuing process throughout the production, and this process must begin with the script breakdown.

### The Script Breakdown

The script has two major components: the scene description and the dialogue or narration. The scene description is most important for the script breakdown. Figure 2–1 is a reproduction of the first page of a script for a 60-second television commercial. The subject of the commercial, a restaurant entertainment complex, was still under construction when the advertising campaign began. The client wanted to stimulate interest in the complex before it was finished in the hope that people would buy charter subscriptions to the private "key club." Figure 2–2 is the same script sample in split-page format. The process of production scheduling is the same regardless of the length of the script or its format.

*Extracting Information from the Scene Description*
From the scene description, you should be able to extract the following information: Which scene? Who? What? Where? When? Props needed? Costumes needed? Special effects? And so forth.

Figures 2–3 and 2–4 show the first page of the Fourdrinier script marked to demonstrate how you would go through every page of your script to identify each element for the breakdown. Notice that a line has been drawn between each scene, unless the scenes are numbered, as in the split-page format. Each person, whether a major character or background extra, has been circled, and essential props and costumes have been underlined. Directors also circle and underline items to indicate other important considerations, such as special effects and lighting requirements.

In the margins, the director has made notes about other elements of the scene that can be inferred even though they are not called for specifically. Your scriptwriter may not specify each little detail that will be necessary to create the atmosphere of the scene. You have to fill them in here, based on your scouting of the loca-

tion. After you have analyzed the entire script in this way, you are ready to move to the second phase of script breakdown.

*Drawing Up the Production Lists*
On separate sheets of paper, one for each production element, make simple lists of the required pieces. Make one list for each category (sets, cast, props, costumes, details, etc.). Figures 2–5 through 2–7 are examples of a few of the ready-made breakdown forms from Movie Magic Scheduling. Figures 2–5 and 2–6 are based on the Frank Capra classic, *It's a Wonderful Life.* The Chart of Accounts is a layout of all the account categories, with numbers, for a one-look glance. It is used by the accountant to help order the books.

A key element to remember in making up your set lists is that you will be scheduling all scenes shot on a certain set one after the other, even though they may appear at widely separated places in your script. For example, if the Fourdrinier spot ended at the paper mill, you would shoot the last scene immediately after shooting the first scene because you would be in the proper location. This is called "shooting out of sequence." When making your set list, you will list the set only once and include all of the scenes to be shot there.

The cast list has the names of the actors, followed by all of the scenes and sets in which they appear. The same is true of each of your other lists. The name of each prop, costume, and so on, is followed by a list of all the scenes in which it will be needed.

The detail list, sometimes called an "insert list," is prepared to track small bits that can be recorded at one time without keeping the entire cast and crew standing around waiting. These details become very important in postproduction, when your editor is stuck trying to make a cut because of a mismatch in screen direction or a jump of some sort that would be jarring. Inserts can also save you considerable grief if your piece is turning out to be too long and you need a place to get out of a long scene. An insert is shot to be used to jump ahead in the action in a master scene. A cutaway can also be used. An insert shows

**THE FILM AND VIDEO RANCH 3674 Knapp Street Road   Oshkosh, WI 54901**

Client: Como of Wisconsin                    FOURDRINIER SCRIPT
        4321 W. College Avenue
        Appleton, WI 54911                    60 second

INTERIOR- BERGSTROM PAPER COMPANY - FOURDRINIER MACHINE - DAY

ANGLE ON SPRAYER

We open on a deep gold mist. SNAPZOOM back to reveal the sprayer on the
Fourdrinier papermaking machine. The wet pulp races away on its screen. Lines
converge. On the SOUNDTRACK we HEAR FOURDRINIER JINGLE UP.

ANOTHER ANGLE

We see a ROLLER. The paper pulp whizzes around it lit with colored gels. GEARS
are seen in the foreground. They turn. The machine shakes in rhythm to the
music.

ANOTHER ANGLE

Another part of the machine. We see it through a tunnel. At the end of the
tunnel is the FOURDRINIER LOGO SUPERED. The shaking of the machine is
accentuated.

dissolve to

CU ACTOR

A handsome young exec-type. We SNAPZOOM back to reveal him walking between the
machines which dwarf him with their size. He gestures toward one of them.

<u>ACTOR</u>

        THAT'S THE RHYTHM OF A REVOLUTION. A REVOLUTION WHICH BEGAN
        IN 1874 WHEN THE FOURDRINIER BROTHERS REVOLUTIONIZED THE
        PAPER INDUSTRY WITH THIS MACHINE TO TURN WOOD PULP INTO
        PAPER.

soft cut to

ANGLE ON PAPER ROLL - END OF MACHINE

It is coming off the machine. ACTOR enters frame, tears off a strip of the paper
and we DOLLY IN FAST to the paper. On it is the FOURDRINIER LOGO.

<u>ACTOR</u>

    NOW, OVER A HUNDRED YEARS LATER, THERE'S A NEW FOURDRINIER

**Figure 2-1** Sample page of Fourdrinier script.

**THE FILM AND VIDEO RANCH** 3674 Knapp Street Road   Oshkosh, WI 54901

| | |
|---|---|
| Client: Como of Wisconsin<br>4321 W. College Avenue<br>Appleton, WI 54911 | FOURDRINIER SCRIPT<br><br>60 second |

| VIDEO | AUDIO |
|---|---|
| **1. INT. BERGSTROM PAPER CO.**<br>We open on a deep gold mist. SNAPZOOM back to reveal sprayer on Fourdrinier paper machine. The wet pulp races away on its conveyor screen. Lines converge. | (MUSIC UP- FOURDRINIER JINGLE) |
| **2. CU ROLLER**<br>The paper pulp whizzes around the roller lit with colored gels. Gears are seen F.G. turning. The machine shakes back and forth in rhythm to the tune. | |
| **3. ECU ANOTHER PIECE OF THE MACHINE**<br>We see it through a tunnel. At the end of it is a SUPER of the Fourdrinier logo. The shaking is accentuated. | |
| dissolve to | |
| **4. CU ACTOR**<br>He is a handsome young exec type. We SNAPZOOM back to reveal him walking between the machines which dwarf him. He gestures toward them. | <u>ACTOR</u><br>THAT'S THE RHYTHM OF A REVOLUTION. A REVOLUTION WHICH BEGAN IN 1874 WHEN THE FOURDRINIER BROTHERS REVOLUTIONIZED THE PAPER INDUSTRY WITH THIS MACHINE TO TURN WOOD PULP INTO PAPER. |
| soft cut to | |
| **5. MS PAPER ROLL**<br>It is coming off the end of the machine. ACTOR walks into frame, tears a strip of paper off. FAST DOLLY into the paper which has on it the LOGO | <u>ACTOR</u><br>NOW, OVER A HUNDRED YEARS LATER, THERE'S A NEW FOURDRINIER REVOLUTION IN NORTHEAST WISCONSIN. |

**Figure 2–2** Sample page of Fourdrinier script in split-page format.

a detail within the action, a cutaway cuts to some other part of the scene. In video news, these details or inserts are called "B-roll." Your editor will bless you for providing as many of them as possible.

*Filling in the Breakdown Sheets*
Using your lists, fill in the blanks on each scene's breakdown sheet (see Figure 2–5). Once you have done this, you will have a document for each location, telling you

THE FILM AND VIDEO RANCH 3674 Knapp Street Road   Oshkosh, WI 54901

---

Client: Como of Wisconsin                    FOURDRINIER SCRIPT
       4321 W. College Avenue
       Appleton, WI 54911                     60 second

---

INTERIOR- BERGSTROM PAPER COMPANY – FOURDRINIER MACHINE – DAY

ANGLE ON SPRAYER

We open on a deep gold mist. SNAPZOOM back to reveal the (sprayer) on the    *prime wide angle lens*
Fourdrinier (papermaking machine.) The wet pulp races away on its screen. Lines
converge. On the SOUNDTRACK we HEAR FOURDRINIER JINGLE UP.

---

ANOTHER ANGLE                                        *Check D.P. for colorations suggestions to make it dramatic*

We see a ROLLER. The paper pulp whizzes around it lit with (colored gels.) GEARS
are seen in the foreground. They turn. The machine shakes in rhythm to the
music.

---

ANOTHER ANGLE

Another part of the machine. We see it through a tunnel. At the end of the    *check w/music*
tunnel is the (FOURDRINIER LOGO) SUPERED. The shaking of the machine is
accentuated.                           *first three scenes at same location*

---

dissolve to    *Same machine as Sc.#1*

CU (ACTOR)               *check wardrobe for contemporary "look".*              *dolly + track*

A handsome young exec-type. We SNAPZOOM back to reveal him walking between the
machines which dwarf him with their size. He gestures toward one of them.   *(sync sound)*

                                ACTOR

           THAT'S THE RHYTHM OF A REVOLUTION. A REVOLUTION WHICH BEGAN
           IN 1874 WHEN THE FOURDRINIER BROTHERS REVOLUTIONIZED THE
           PAPER INDUSTRY WITH THIS MACHINE TO TURN WOOD PULP INTO
           PAPER.

     soft cut to

---

ANGLE ON PAPER ROLL - END OF MACHINE

     It is coming off the machine. (ACTOR) enters frame, tears off a strip of the paper,
     and we DOLLY IN FAST to the paper. On it is the (FOURDRINIER LOGO)
*far end of building*         *dolly + track*
                                ACTOR                            *(sync sound)*

           NOW, OVER A HUNDRED YEARS LATER, THERE'S A NEW FOURDRINIER

         *Check D.P. for BIG area lighting requirements*

**Figure 2–3** Fourdrinier script marked for breakdown.

---

how many pages of script will be shot there, the cast needed, the number of scenes, and details concerning props and wardrobe, effects, necessary construction materials, and music playback. With all of this information categorized and filed in a loose-leaf notebook to facilitate changes as they occur, you and your production staff are ready to move ahead.

### The Shooting Schedule
Based on your experience with previous shoots, you can tell approximately how many hours you will need for each page of

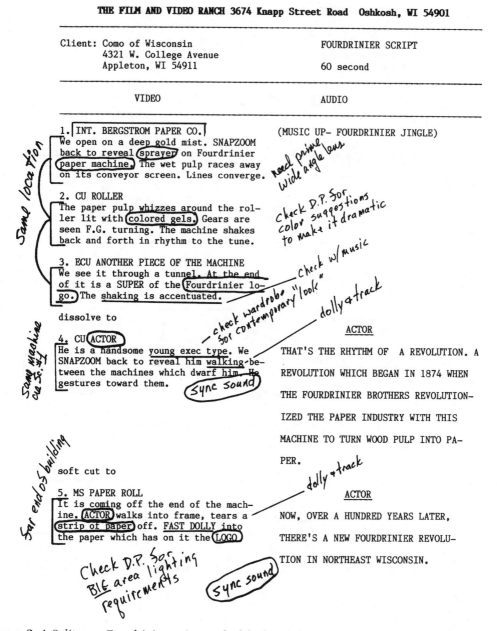

**Figure 2–4** Split-page Fourdrinier script marked for breakdown.

script. (If you haven't had a lot of experience, refer to the discussion of estimating time in Chapter 1.) Solicit input from the director and the videographer when you compose the shooting schedule because they will be essential in making that schedule work.

Many directors, for instance, require lots of rehearsal time for their actors. Some do a great number of takes so they can select the best ones in postproduction. Others pride themselves on spontaneity on the set, allowing the actors to improvise lines and situations. These considerations have a significant impact on the schedule.

**IT'S A WONDERFUL LIFE**        Page 3
**Breakdown Sheet**

Sheet: **22**     I/E: **EXT**    Set: **FRONT PORCH OF HOUSE**      D/N: **NIGHT**

Scenes: **22**                                           Pages:      **2/8**

Synopsis: **Grumpy old man watches George & Mary.**

Location:

Sequence: **Back Story**          Script Day: **1928**         Script Page: **39**

---

**Cast Members**
  37. Grumpy Old Man

**Set Dressing**
  Rocking Chair

**Figure 2–5** Script breakdown form. (Reproduced with permission of Screenplay Systems, Inc.)

The videographer, or director of photography (DP), also has a unique way of doing things. Some of these artist-technicians take a long time to decide on a lighting setup in order to make it perfect on the first take. Others, working with gaffers who seem to have an extra adrenal gland, delight in seeing how quickly they can achieve each setup.

There is no right or wrong way of directing a scene or lighting a set, of course. This is art, after all, not science. For the producer,

Scene # 33

Date:

## IT'S A WONDERFUL LIFE

Bkdown Page # 33

Script Page 60

Int/Ext: EXT

Breakdown Sheet

Page Count 2 1/8

Day/Night: NIGHT

Scene Description:    Violet tries picking up George.

Setting:    VIOLET BICK'S BEAUTY SHOP

Location:

Sequence: Back Story                                    Script Day:    1932

| Cast Members | Extras | Props |
|---|---|---|
| 1. George | 6 Onlookers | |
| 11. Violet | | |
| 44. Suitor #1 | | |
| 45. Suitor #2 | | |
| | **Stunts** | **Vehicles** |
| **Special Effects** | **Costumes** | **Makeup** |
| | George's coat | |
| | George's hat | |
| **Set Dressing** | **Greenery** | **Special Equipment** |

**Notes**

**Figure 2–5 (cont.)** Script breakdown form. (Reproduced with permission of Screenplay Systems, Inc.)

## Prop List for "IT'S A WONDERFUL LIFE"    Page 1

| ID | Name | Start | Finish | Total Days | Total Pages |
|----|------|-------|--------|------------|-------------|
| | "Bridal Suite" sign | 7/22/92 | 7/22/92 | 1 | 1 4/8 |
| | "Buffalo Gals" record | 7/30/92 | 8/7/92 | 7 | 4 4/8 |
| | "Tom Sawyer" book | 8/20/92 | 9/2/92 | 2 | 5 |
| | 10 Travel Posters | 7/22/92 | 7/22/92 | 1 | 1 4/8 |
| | 24 Bank Passbooks | 8/3/92 | 8/3/92 | 1 | 5/8 |
| | 3 Highballs | 8/7/92 | 8/7/92 | 1 | 3/8 |
| | 4 old rubber tires | 10/2/92 | 10/2/92 | 1 | 1/8 |
| | 4 Pies | 7/10/92 | 7/14/92 | 3 | 12 4/8 |
| | 6 Shovels | 10/5/92 | 10/5/92 | 1 | 1 2/8 |
| | Assorted Wrapped Gifts | 8/31/92 | 8/31/92 | 1 | 2/8 |
| | Bag of peanuts | 7/21/92 | 7/21/92 | 1 | 6/8 |
| | Banners and Bunting | 9/15/92 | 9/15/92 | 1 | 2/8 |
| | Banquet plates | 7/14/92 | 7/14/92 | 1 | 6 1/8 |
| | Bert's Watch | 7/6/92 | 7/6/92 | 1 | 1 4/8 |
| | Blueprints | 10/2/92 | 10/2/92 | 1 | 2/8 |
| | Bottle of champagne | 7/28/92 | 7/28/92 | 1 | 1 2/8 |
| | Bourbon bottle | 9/4/92 | 9/4/92 | 1 | 4 5/8 |
| | Bowl of Caviar | 7/30/92 | 7/30/92 | 1 | 4/8 |
| | Broom | 7/10/92 | 7/10/92 | 1 | 6 3/8 |
| | Bucket of ice | 7/30/92 | 7/30/92 | 1 | 4/8 |
| | Camera | 7/17/92 | 7/28/92 | 2 | 1 4/8 |
| | Carter's briefcase | 9/21/92 | 9/21/92 | 1 | 3 1/8 |
| | Cash register | 9/4/92 | 9/4/92 | 1 | 4 5/8 |
| | Champagne Bottle | 7/30/92 | 7/30/92 | 1 | 4/8 |
| | Character letter | 9/17/92 | 9/17/92 | 1 | 1 1/8 |
| | Chickens on a spit | 7/30/92 | 7/30/92 | 1 | 4/8 |
| | Christmas packages | 8/21/92 | 8/26/92 | 4 | 2 |
| | Christmas presents | 8/31/92 | 8/31/92 | 1 | 1/8 |
| | Cigar | 8/13/92 | 10/1/92 | 2 | 5 1/8 |
| | Cigar lighter | 7/13/92 | 9/29/92 | 2 | 3 7/8 |
| | Clothes basket full of money | 9/2/92 | 9/2/92 | 1 | 4 2/8 |
| | Coffee and Doughnuts | 10/2/92 | 10/2/92 | 1 | 2/8 |
| | Coffee pots of money | 9/2/92 | 9/2/92 | 1 | 4 2/8 |
| | Dance programs | 7/14/92 | 7/14/92 | 1 | 6 1/8 |
| | Deposit Slip | 9/16/92 | 9/16/92 | 1 | 2 1/8 |

**Figure 2–6** Prop list. (Reproduced with permission of Screenplay Systems, Inc.)

## Prop List for "IT'S A WONDERFUL LIFE"

| ID | Name | Start | Finish | Total Days | Total Pages |
|----|------|-------|--------|-----------|-------------|
| | Dictaphone | 8/14/92 | 8/14/92 | 1 | 1 3/8 |
| | Draft Papers | 10/2/92 | 10/2/92 | 1 | 2/8 |
| | Drawing Pad | 9/28/92 | 9/28/92 | 1 | 2 2/8 |
| | Easel | 8/3/92 | 8/7/92 | 5 | 3 1/8 |
| | Envelope of Money | 9/16/92 | 9/22/92 | 5 | 2 4/8 |
| | Fat roll of dollar bills | 7/28/92 | 7/28/92 | 1 | 1 2/8 |
| | Flash bulbs | 8/31/92 | 8/31/92 | 1 | 1 2/8 |
| | Flower | 9/14/92 | 9/14/92 | 1 | 1 4/8 |
| | Glass jar of notes | 9/2/92 | 9/2/92 | 1 | 4 2/8 |
| | Glass of Beer | 9/3/92 | 9/3/92 | 1 | 2 5/8 |
| | Glasses | 9/2/92 | 9/4/92 | 3 | 8 7/8 |
| | Gun | 8/20/92 | 8/28/92 | 7 | 3 |
| | handkerchief | 9/18/92 | 9/18/92 | 1 | 6/8 |
| | Ice cream | 9/29/92 | 9/30/92 | 2 | 3 5/8 |
| | Ice cream scoop | 9/29/92 | 9/29/92 | 1 | 3 4/8 |
| | Jar | 10/1/92 | 10/1/92 | 1 | 1 2/8 |
| | Large bank door lock and key | 7/16/92 | 7/16/92 | 1 | 3/8 |
| | Large Brown Bottle | 9/25/92 | 9/25/92 | 1 | 1 2/8 |
| | Large suitcase | 7/6/92 | 10/6/92 | 9 | 4 7/8 |
| | Legal papers | 7/9/92 | 7/16/92 | 6 | 6 |
| | Library books | 8/20/92 | 8/20/92 | 1 | 1 2/8 |
| | Library key | 8/20/92 | 8/20/92 | 1 | 1 2/8 |
| | Licorice shoelaces | 9/29/92 | 9/29/92 | 1 | 3 4/8 |
| | Liquor bottle | 8/3/92 | 10/1/92 | 8 | 7 6/8 |
| | Long black stocking with money | 9/2/92 | 9/2/92 | 1 | 4 2/8 |
| | Luggage | 7/23/92 | 7/23/92 | 1 | 2 7/8 |
| | Megaphone | 10/5/92 | 10/5/92 | 1 | 1 2/8 |
| | Mixing bowl of money | 9/2/92 | 9/2/92 | 1 | 4 2/8 |
| | Money | 9/17/92 | 9/17/92 | 1 | 1 1/8 |
| | Musical Instruments | 7/14/92 | 7/14/92 | 1 | 6 1/8 |
| | Newspapers (w/ Headline) | 9/15/92 | 9/22/92 | 6 | 6 6/8 |
| | Overnight bag | 7/15/92 | 7/15/92 | 1 | 2 2/8 |
| | PAcking Boxes | 7/30/92 | 7/30/92 | 1 | 4/8 |
| | Pad and Pencil | 8/31/92 | 8/31/92 | 1 | 2/8 |
| | Paper bag | 9/29/92 | 9/29/92 | 1 | 3 4/8 |

**Figure 2–6 (cont.)** Prop list. (Reproduced with permission of Screenplay Systems, Inc.)

Prop List for "IT'S A WONDERFUL LIFE"                                Page 3

| ID | Name | Start | Finish | Total Days | Total Pages |
|----|------|-------|--------|------------|-------------|
| | Pen | 9/28/92 | 9/28/92 | 1 | 2 2/8 |
| | phonograph | 7/30/92 | 8/7/92 | 7 | 4 4/8 |
| | Photographer's camera | 8/31/92 | 8/31/92 | 1 | 1 2/8 |
| | Poison capsules | 9/25/92 | 10/1/92 | 5 | 3 4/8 |
| | Popcorn | 7/23/92 | 7/23/92 | 1 | 2 7/8 |
| | Powder | 9/25/92 | 9/25/92 | 1 | 1 2/8 |
| | Prescription box | 9/25/92 | 10/1/92 | 5 | 3 4/8 |
| | Punch | 7/14/92 | 7/14/92 | 1 | 6 1/8 |
| | Punch Bowl & glasses | 7/14/92 | 9/2/92 | 2 | 10 3/8 |
| | Rice | 7/28/92 | 7/28/92 | 1 | 3/8 |
| | Rifle with Bayonet | 10/1/92 | 10/2/92 | 2 | 4/8 |
| | Rocks | 7/7/92 | 7/8/92 | 2 | 10 |
| | Seltzer bottle | 9/4/92 | 9/4/92 | 1 | 4 5/8 |
| | Silver bell ornament | 9/2/92 | 9/2/92 | 1 | 4 2/8 |
| | Sketch of George | 8/3/92 | 8/12/92 | 8 | 5 1/8 |
| | Spotlight on cab | 8/27/92 | 8/27/92 | 1 | 1 |
| | Telegram | 9/2/92 | 9/29/92 | 2 | 7 6/8 |
| | Telephone | 7/29/92 | 10/6/92 | 35 | 17 1/8 |
| | Toy Vacuum | 8/31/92 | 8/31/92 | 1 | 2/8 |
| | Trash Can | 9/25/92 | 9/25/92 | 1 | 1 2/8 |
| | Travel magazine | 9/29/92 | 9/29/92 | 1 | 3 4/8 |
| | tripod | 7/28/92 | 7/28/92 | 1 | 3/8 |
| | USO Cart | 10/2/92 | 10/2/92 | 1 | 2/8 |
| | Warrant | 8/31/92 | 8/31/92 | 1 | 1 2/8 |
| | Waste Paper Basket | 9/15/92 | 9/15/92 | 1 | 2/8 |
| | Wedding Cigars | 8/5/92 | 8/5/92 | 1 | 1 6/8 |
| | Wheelbarrow of scrap | 10/5/92 | 10/5/92 | 1 | 1/8 |
| | Wheelchair | 7/9/92 | 10/2/92 | 38 | 16 1/8 |
| | Whistle | 10/5/92 | 10/5/92 | 1 | 2/8 |
| | Wine | 9/2/92 | 9/2/92 | 1 | 4 2/8 |

**Figure 2–6 (cont.)** Prop list. (Reproduced with permission of Screenplay Systems, Inc.)

it is a matter of being able to work with creative people and allowing them as much freedom as the budget will permit. It is pure folly to create a shooting schedule that does not take into account the kinds of people who will be expected to follow it. A sample shooting schedule is shown in Figure 2–8.

When you have completed the shooting schedule, you finally have the documentation you need to do one other essential thing: predict the actual production budget, which could be estimated only roughly with the data in Chapter 1. Going through your budget estimate again at this

## Chart Of Accounts

| Acct# | Description | Acct# | Description | Acct# | Description |
|-------|-------------|-------|-------------|-------|-------------|
| | | 1100 | **Development** | | |
| 1101 | Story & Screenplay | 1102 | Producers Unit | 1103 | Directors Unit |
| 1104 | Budget Preparation | 1105 | Accounting | 1106 | Legal |
| 1107 | Office Overhead | 1108 | Transportation | 1109 | Research |
| 1110 | Travel/Living | 1111 | Additional Expenses | 1198 | Miscellaneous |
| 1199 | Fringe Benefits | | | | |
| | | 1200 | **Story & Other Rights** | | |
| 1201 | Story Rights Purchase | 1202 | Writers Fees | 1203 | Story Consultant/Editor |
| 1204 | Secretaries | 1205 | Research | 1206 | Typing |
| 1207 | Duplication | 1298 | Miscellaneous | 1299 | Fringe Benefits |
| | | 1300 | **Continuity & Treatment** | | |
| 1301 | Writers | 1302 | Research | 1303 | Typing |
| 1304 | Duplication | 1305 | Travel & Living | 1306 | Story Editor |
| 1307 | Consultants | 1308 | Legal Clearances | 1309 | Secretaries |
| 1310 | Office Expenses | 1311 | Entertainment | 1312 | Script Timing |
| 1398 | Miscellaneous | 1399 | Fringe Benefits | | |
| | | 1400 | **Producers Unit** | | |
| 1401 | Executive Producer | 1402 | Producer | 1403 | Co-Producer |
| 1404 | Line Producer | 1405 | Associate Producer | 1407 | Production Executive |
| 1408 | Secretaries | 1409 | Office Expenses | 1410 | Research |
| 1411 | Packaging Fee | 1498 | Miscellaneous | 1499 | Fringe Benefits |
| | | 1500 | **Directors Unit** | | |
| 1501 | Director | 1502 | Directors Assistant | 1503 | Choreographer |
| 1504 | Dialogue Coach | 1505 | Secretary | 1506 | Storyboard Artist |
| 1507 | Office Expenses | 1508 | Travel/Living | 1509 | Second Unit Director |
| 1598 | Miscellaneous | 1599 | Fringe Benefits | | |
| | | 1600 | **Talent** | | |
| 1601 | Principal Roles | 1602 | Supporting Roles | 1603 | Day Players |
| 1604 | Stunt Gaffer | 1605 | Assistant Stunt Gaffer | 1606 | Stunt Players |
| 1607 | Stunt Doubles | 1608 | Utility Stunt Players | 1609 | Casting Expenses |
| 1610 | Screen Tests | 1611 | Overtime/Turnaround | 1612 | Musicians |
| 1613 | Looping | 1614 | Second Run Residuals (TV) | 1615 | Welfare Worker/Teacher |
| 1616 | Rehearsal Expenses | 1617 | Contractuals | 1698 | Miscellaneous |
| 1699 | Fringe Benefits | | | | |
| | | 1700 | **A-T-L  Travel/Living** | | |
| 1701 | Hotels | 1702 | Travel | 1703 | Per Diem |
| 1704 | Car Rentals | 1705 | Misc. Expenses | | |
| | | 2100 | **Production Staff** | | |
| 2101 | Production Manager | 2102 | Unit Production Manager | 2103 | First Assistant Director |
| 2104 | 2nd Assistant Director | 2105 | 2nd 2nd Assistant | 2106 | Other Assistants |
| 2107 | DGA Trainees | 2108 | Production Associates | 2109 | Technical Adviser |
| 2110 | Production Coordinator | 2111 | Ass't Prod. Coord. | 2112 | Local Prod. Coord. |
| 2113 | Script Supervisor | 2114 | Production Auditor | 2115 | Ass't Production Auditor |
| 2116 | Payroll Secretary | 2117 | Local Auditor | 2118 | Location Manager |
| 2119 | Ass't Location Mgr | 2120 | Interpreters | 2121 | Government Rep. |
| 2122 | Censor | 2123 | Safety Officers | 2124 | Production Board/Budget |
| 2125 | Office Expenses | 2197 | Loss & Damage | 2198 | Miscellaneous |
| 2199 | Fringe Benefits | | | | |
| | | 2200 | **Art Direction** | | |
| 2201 | Production Designer | 2202 | Art Director | 2203 | Assistant Art Director |

**Figure 2–7** Chart of accounts. (Reproduced with permission of Screenplay Systems, Inc.)

Chart Of Accounts

| Acct# | Description | Acct# | Description | Acct# | Description |
|-------|-------------|-------|-------------|-------|-------------|
| | | 2200 | Art Direction (CONT'D) | | |
| 2204 | Set Designer | 2205 | Draftsman | 2206 | Graphic Designer |
| 2207 | Sketch Artist | 2208 | Storyboard Artist | 2209 | Models |
| 2210 | Set Estimator | 2211 | Blueprints | 2212 | Materials & Supplies |
| 2213 | Office Costs | 2214 | Secretaries | 2297 | Loss & Damage |
| 2298 | Miscellaneous | 2299 | Fringe Benefits | | |
| | | 2300 | Set Construction | | |
| 2301 | Construction Coordinator | 2302 | Construction Foreman | 2303 | Construction Labor |
| 2304 | Construction Materials | 2305 | Paint Department | 2306 | Carpenters |
| 2307 | Plumbers | 2308 | Electrical Fixtures Men | 2309 | Plasterers |
| 2310 | Labor Department | 2311 | First Aid | 2312 | Watchmen/Security |
| 2313 | Construction Space | 2314 | Tools | 2315 | Office Expenses |
| 2316 | Backings | 2317 | Trash Removal | 2318 | Construction Vehicles |
| 2319 | Special Equipment | 2320 | Scaffolding | 2321 | Striking |
| 2322 | Models | 2323 | Miniatures | 2324 | Construction Package Deal |
| 2397 | Loss & Damage | 2398 | Miscellaneous | | |
| | | 2400 | Set Decoration | | |
| 2401 | Set Decorator | 2402 | Lead Man | 2403 | Swing Gang |
| 2404 | Extra Men | 2405 | Local Labor | 2406 | Draper |
| 2407 | Drapery | 2408 | Carpet Man | 2409 | Carpets |
| 2410 | Fixture Man | 2411 | Fixtures | 2412 | Greensmen |
| 2413 | Greens | 2414 | Dressings Purchased | 2415 | Dressing Rentals |
| 2416 | Office Expenses | 2497 | Loss & Damage | 2498 | Miscellaneous |
| | | 2500 | Property Department | | |
| 2501 | Property Master | 2502 | Assistant Prop Master | 2503 | Buyer |
| 2504 | Local Hire | 2505 | Rentals | 2506 | Purchases |
| 2507 | Manufactures | 2508 | Animals | 2509 | Picture Vehicles |
| 2510 | Armorer | 2511 | Firearms | 2512 | Video Playback System |
| 2513 | Office Expenses | 2514 | Box Rentals | 2515 | Loss & Damage |
| 2598 | Miscellaneous | | | | |
| | | 2600 | Camera Operations | | |
| 2601 | Director of Photography | 2602 | Operator | 2603 | 1st Assistant Camera |
| 2604 | 2nd Assistant Camera | 2605 | Extra Operator | 2606 | Extra Assistants |
| 2607 | Extra Loader | 2608 | Steadicam Operator | 2609 | Steadicam Equipment |
| 2610 | Camera Package | 2611 | Special Rentals | 2612 | Purchases |
| 2613 | Video Assist | 2614 | Stillsman | 2615 | Still Equipment |
| 2616 | Shipping & Handling | 2617 | Process Department | 2697 | Loss & Damage |
| 2698 | Miscellaneous | | | | |
| | | 2700 | Electric Operations | | |
| 2701 | Chief Lighting Technician | 2702 | Best Boy | 2703 | Company Electricians |
| 2704 | Extra Electricians | 2705 | Local Hires | 2706 | Generator Operator |
| 2707 | Pre-rig Crew | 2708 | Strike Crew | 2709 | Generator Rental |
| 2710 | Equipment Rentals | 2711 | Musco Lights | 2712 | Purchases |
| 2713 | Power Charges | 2797 | Loss & Damage | 2798 | Miscellaneous |
| | | 2800 | Grip Operations | | |
| 2801 | Key Grip | 2802 | Second Grip | 2803 | Dolly Grip |
| 2804 | Crane Grip | 2805 | Crane Driver | 2806 | Company Grips |
| 2807 | Extra Grips | 2808 | Local Hires | 2809 | Rigging Crew |
| 2810 | Striking Crew | 2811 | Tent/Shelter Erection | 2812 | Grip Package |
| 2813 | Special Equipment | 2814 | Dolly Rental | 2815 | Equipment Purchase |
| 2816 | Crane | 2897 | Loss & Damage | 2898 | Miscellaneous |

**Figure 2–7 (cont.)** Chart of accounts. (Reproduced with permission of Screenplay Systems, Inc.)

## Chart Of Accounts

| Acct# | Description | Acct# | Description | Acct# | Description |
|-------|-------------|-------|-------------|-------|-------------|
|       |             | 2900  | **Production Sound** |   |   |
| 2901  | Production Mixer | 2902 | Boom Operator | 2903 | Cable Puller |
| 2904  | Utility Man | 2905 | Playback | 2906 | P.A. |
| 2907  | Sound Equipment | 2908 | Set Communications | 2909 | Special Equipment Rentals |
| 2910  | Purchases | 2997 | Loss & Damage | 2998 | Miscellaneous |
|       |             | 3000  | **Mechanical Effects** |   |   |
| 3001  | Key Man | 3002 | Assistant | 3003 | Extra Help |
| 3004  | Local Hires | 3005 | Rigging Crew | 3006 | Striking Crew |
| 3007  | Manufacturing | 3008 | Equipment Rental | 3009 | Material rental |
| 3010  | Purchases | 3011 | Shop Rental | 3012 | Firearms/Weapons |
| 3013  | Electronic Effects | 3014 | Explosions | 3015 | Permits |
| 3016  | Weather | 3017 | Office Expenses | 3097 | Loss & Damage |
| 3098  | Miscellaneous |   |   |   |   |
|       |             | 3100  | **Special Visual Effects** |   |   |
| 3101  | Rear Projection | 3102 | Front Projection | 3103 | Holography |
| 3104  | Optical Effects | 3105 | Mattes | 3106 | Glass Shots |
| 3107  | Rotoscope Photography | 3108 | FX Shop | 3109 | Introvision |
| 3110  | Miniatures | 3111 | Office Expenses | 3197 | Loss & Damage |
| 3198  | Miscellaneous |   |   |   |   |
|       |             | 3200  | **Set Operations** |   |   |
| 3201  | Set Carpenter | 3202 | Standby Painter | 3203 | Greens Department |
| 3204  | Craft Service | 3205 | First Aid | 3206 | Set Security |
| 3207  | Set Firemen | 3208 | Office Expenses | 3209 | Weather Service |
| 3210  | Portable Bathrooms | 3211 | Courtesy Payments | 3297 | Loss & Damage |
| 3298  | Miscellaneous |   |   |   |   |
|       |             | 3300  | **Wardrobe Department** |   |   |
| 3301  | Costume Designer | 3302 | Assistant Designer | 3303 | Men's Costumer |
| 3304  | Assistant Men's Costumer | 3305 | Extra Men's Costumers | 3306 | Local Hires |
| 3307  | Ladies' Costumers | 3308 | Ass't. Ladies' Costumer | 3309 | Extra Ladies' Costumers |
| 3310  | Local Hires | 3311 | Seamstresses | 3312 | Manufacture |
| 3313  | Rentals | 3314 | Purchases | 3315 | Alterations |
| 3316  | Cleaning | 3317 | Office | 3397 | Loss & Damage |
| 3398  | Miscellaneous |   |   |   |   |
|       |             | 3400  | **Makeup & Hair Department** |   |   |
| 3401  | Head Makeup Artist | 3402 | Assistant Makeup Artist | 3403 | Extra Makeup Artists |
| 3404  | Local Hires | 3405 | Body Makeup Artists | 3406 | Head Hair Stylist |
| 3407  | Assistant Hair Stylist | 3408 | Extra Hair Stylists | 3409 | Local Hires |
| 3410  | Makeup Supplies | 3411 | Hair Supplies | 3412 | Wigs/Hairpieces |
| 3413  | Special Makeup Design | 3414 | Prosthetics | 3415 | Special Appliances |
| 3416  | Rentals | 3497 | Loss & Damage | 3498 | Miscellaneous |
|       |             | 3500  | **Location Department** |   |   |
| 3501  | Survey Costs | 3502 | Travel Costs | 3503 | Per Diem |
| 3504  | Lodging | 3505 | Meals | 3506 | Caterer |
| 3507  | Guards/Watchmen | 3508 | Police | 3509 | Firemen |
| 3510  | Local Contact | 3511 | Government Representative | 3512 | Site Rentals |
| 3513  | Location Offices | 3514 | Crew Mileage | 3515 | Shipping |
| 3516  | Customs Brokerage | 3517 | Passports/Visas | 3518 | Editing Facilities |
| 3519  | Dailies Screenings | 3520 | Heating/Air Conditioning | 3521 | Location Weather Service |
| 3597  | Loss & Damage | 3598 | Miscellaneous |   |   |
|       |             | 3600  | **Transportation Department** |   |   |
| 3601  | Transportation Coord. | 3602 | Transportation Captain | 3603 | Dispatcher |

**Figure 2–7 (cont.)** Chart of accounts. (Reproduced with permission of Screenplay Systems, Inc.)

## Chart Of Accounts

| Acct# | Description | Acct# | Description | Acct# | Description |
|---|---|---|---|---|---|
| | | 3600 | Transportation Department (CONT'D) | | |
| 3604 | Mechanic | 3605 | Drivers | 3606 | Picture Vehicles |
| 3607 | Production Vehicles | 3608 | Personnel Vehicles | 3609 | Self-drive Rentals |
| 3610 | Pickup/Delivery Charges | 3611 | Gas/Oil/Maintenance | 3612 | Trucks to Location |
| 3613 | Vehicle Preparation | 3614 | Special Equipment | 3615 | Stunt Vehicles |
| 3616 | Office Expenses | 3697 | Loss & Damage | 3698 | Miscellaneous |
| | | 3700 | Videotape Department | | |
| 3701 | Playback Operator | 3702 | Playback Assistant | 3703 | Video Playback Package |
| 3704 | Teleprompters | 3705 | Production Unit | 3706 | Video Display |
| 3707 | Video RawStock | 3797 | Loss & Damage | 3798 | Miscellaneous |
| | | 3800 | Studio Facilities | | |
| 3801 | Rehearsal Stages | 3802 | Shooting Stages | 3803 | Back Lot/Ranch |
| 3804 | Electric Power | 3805 | Heating/Air Conditioning | 3806 | Studio Charges |
| 3807 | Office Charges | 3808 | Construction Charges | 3809 | Storage Space |
| 3810 | Dressing Rooms | 3897 | Loss & Damages | 3898 | Miscellaneous |
| | | 3900 | Atmosphere | | |
| 3901 | General Extras | 3902 | Stand-ins | 3903 | Silent Bits |
| 3904 | Minors | 3905 | Welfare Workers/Teachers | 3906 | Dancers/Singers |
| 3907 | Sideline Musicians | 3908 | Interviews | 3909 | Wardrobe Fittings |
| 3910 | Wardrobe Allowance | 3911 | Car Rentals | 3912 | Extras Casting |
| 3913 | Crowd Controllers | 3914 | Payroll Service | 3997 | Loss & Damage |
| 3998 | Miscellaneous | | | | |
| | | 4000 | Production Film & Lab | | |
| 4001 | Production Raw Stock | 4002 | Production Develop | 4003 | Print |
| 4004 | Sound | 4005 | Projection | 4006 | Videocassettes |
| 4007 | Video Format Transfers | | | | |
| | | 4100 | Tests | | |
| 4101 | Screen Tests | 4102 | Makeup Tests | 4103 | Wardrobe Tests |
| 4104 | Camera Tests | | | | |
| | | 4200 | Second Unit | | |
| 4201 | Crew | 4202 | Equipment | 4203 | Locations |
| 4204 | Transportation | 4205 | Film/Lab | | |
| | | 5100 | Editing | | |
| 5101 | Post Prod'n Supervisor | 5102 | Editor | 5103 | Assistant Editor |
| 5104 | Extra Editors | 5105 | Extra Assistants | 5106 | Apprentice Editor |
| 5107 | Music Editor | 5108 | Sound FX Editor | 5109 | ADR Editor |
| 5110 | Supplemental Assistants | 5111 | Extra Apprentices | 5112 | Secretaries |
| 5113 | Editing Rooms/Rentals | 5114 | Editing Supplies | 5115 | Storage |
| 5116 | Coding | 5117 | Projection | 5118 | Continuity |
| 5119 | Librarian | 5120 | Videocassettes | 5121 | Electronic Editing |
| 5122 | Travel/Living | 5123 | Office Expenses | 5197 | Loss & Damage |
| 5198 | Miscellaneous | | | | |
| | | 5200 | Post-Production Film/Lab | | |
| 5201 | Reprints | 5202 | Color Master Positive | 5203 | Duplicate Negatives |
| 5204 | Develop Optical Negative | 5205 | Negative Cutting | 5206 | Answer Prints |
| 5207 | Release Prints | 5208 | Stock Footage | 5298 | Miscellaneous |
| | | 5300 | Post-Production Sound | | |
| 5301 | Music Scoring Stage | 5302 | Music Dubb-Down Stage | 5303 | ADR Stage |
| 5304 | Foley Stage | 5305 | Sound Effects | 5306 | Temp Dubbs |
| 5307 | Rehearse Stage | 5308 | Pre-Dubb | 5309 | 1st Combine Dubb |

**Figure 2–7 (cont.)** Chart of accounts. (Reproduced with permission of Screenplay Systems, Inc.)

# IT'S A WONDERFUL LIFE

Shooting Schedule

Page 1

---

## SHOOT DAY #1 -- Mon, Jul 6

Scene #24          **EXT - BAILEY BUILDINGS AND LOAN SIGN OVER ENTRANCE - DAY**          1/8 Pgs.
                   *Establishing Bldg. & Loan sign.*

**Set Dressing**
Bldg. & Loan Sign

---

Scene #18          **EXT - MAIN STREET - DAY**          1 4/8 Pgs.
                   *George takes a cab ride.*

**Cast Members**          **Props**                    **Vehicles**
  1. George                   Bert's Watch                 Bert's Motorcycle
  7. Ernie                    Large suitcase               Ernie's Cab
  8. Bert                                                  Stunt car
  11. Violet

**Extras**
  Elderly Man

**Stunts**
  Car screechs to a stop
  Stunt driver

---

Scene #22          **EXT - FRONT PORCH OF HOUSE - NIGHT**          2/8 Pgs.
                   *Grumpy old man watches George & Mary.*

**Cast Members**
  37. Grumpy Old Man

**Set Dressing**
Rocking Chair

---

### END OF DAY #1 - 1 7/8 Total Pages

---

## SHOOT DAY #2 -- Tue, Jul 7

Scene #23          **EXT - STREET - NIGHT**          3 5/8 Pgs.
                   *George and Mary make a wish.*

**Cast Members**          **Props**                    **Vehicles**
  1. George                   Rocks                        Bailey's car
  2. Mary                 **Special Effects**          **Set Dressing**
  3. Harry                    Breaking glass               Rocking Chair
  4. Uncle Billy                                       **Costumes**
  37. Grumpy Old Man                                       Bathrobe
                         **Greenery**                      Jersey & football pants
                             Hydrangea bush                Wet clothes

---

**Figure 2–8** Shooting schedule. (Reproduced with permission of Screenplay Systems, Inc.)

**IT'S A WONDERFUL LIFE**

Shooting Schedule

**END OF DAY #2 - 3 5/8 Total Pages**

## SHOOT DAY #3 -- Wed, Jul 8

Scene #21          **EXT - TREE-LINED RESIDENTIAL STREET - NIGHT**                    6 3/8 Pgs.

*George and Mary's moonlight walk*

| **Cast Members** | **Props** | |
| --- | --- | --- |
| 1. George | Rocks | |
| 2. Mary | **Special Effects** | **Costumes** |
| | Breaking glass | Bathrobe |
| | | Jersey & football pants |
| | | Wet clothes |

**END OF DAY #3 - 6 3/8 Total Pages**

## SHOOT DAY #4 -- Thu, Jul 9

Scene #25          **INT - BAILEY BUILDING AND LOAN OFFICE - DAY**                    4 2/8 Pgs.

*B & L Directors meeting.*

| **Cast Members** | **Props** | |
| --- | --- | --- |
| 1. George | Legal papers | |
| 4. Uncle Billy | Wheelchair | **Costumes** |
| 5. Mr. Potter | | George's coat |
| 21. Goon | | |
| 34. Dr. Campbell | | |
| 41. Lawyer | | |
| 42. Real Estate Salesman | | |
| 43. Insurance Agent | | |

**END OF DAY #4 - 4 2/8 Total Pages**

## SHOOT DAY #5 -- Fri, Jul 10

Scene #19          **INT - BAILEY DINING ROOM - NIGHT**                    6 3/8 Pgs.

*Dinner at the Baileys'.*

| **Cast Members** | **Props** | |
| --- | --- | --- |
| 1. George | 4 Pies | **Set Dressing** |
| 3. Harry | Broom | Dining Room Set |
| 12. Ma Bailey | | Dishes |
| 16. Annie | | |
| 17. Peter Bailey | | |

**Figure 2–8 (cont.)** Shooting schedule. (Reproduced with permission of Screenplay Systems, Inc.)

# IT'S A WONDERFUL LIFE
Shooting Schedule

---

**END OF DAY #5 - 6 3/8 Total Pages**

## SHOOT DAY #6 -- Mon, Jul 13

Scene #16     **INT - GOWER'S DRUGSTORE - DAY**     3/8 Pgs.
*George re-visits drugstore.*

**Cast Members**     **Props**
1. George
6. Mr. Gower      Cigar lighter        **Set Dressing**
                Large suitcase       Candy counter
**Extras**                                  Juke Box
    12 Highschool Kids                   Soda fountain
    3 Soda Jerks

---

**END OF DAY #6 - 3/8 Total Pages**

## SHOOT DAY #7 -- Tue, Jul 14

Scene #20     **INT - HIGH SCHOOL GYM - NIGHT**     6 1/8 Pgs.
*George and Mary at High School Dance*

**Cast Members**     **Props**
1. George
2. Mary          4 Pies
3. Harry         Banquet plates
11. Violet        Dance programs
23. Marty       Musical Instruments
24. Sam Wainwright    Punch
27. Freddie      Punch Bowl & glasses
36. Principal    **Special Effects**
40. Mickey        Opening Dance Floor

**Extras**
    100 High School Students
    3 Dance Judges
    Orchestra
    Orchestra Leader
    School Faculty

**Stunts**
    Falls into swimming pool

---

**END OF DAY #7 - 6 1/8 Total Pages**

**Figure 2–8 (cont.)** Shooting schedule. (Reproduced with permission of Screenplay Systems, Inc.)

point will give you a very real approximation of costs by the day and, in some cases, by the hour.

It is wise to remember that talent is usually the most expensive item in your budget. If, for example, major celebrities will perform in your production, you may have to pay them several thousand dollars a day. In that case, it is best to make your shooting schedule fit around the time you have budgeted for your stars. Shoot all the scenes involving them, cut them loose from the payroll, and then go back and shoot all the scenes using less expensive talent according to the one-set rule. The one-set rule is where you shoot all the scenes from the script that take place on a given set at one time, even if they are out of sequence in the script.

You can apply this same budget consideration if you have a particularly expensive piece of equipment to rent—a helicopter, Steadicam, or Tyler Mount, for instance. At $10,000 a day for a helicopter, you would obviously schedule all of your aerial sequences to be shot on the same day. Whether the most expensive item per day is people or equipment, strive to schedule it for the least number of days.

A final note about your shooting schedule explains in part the rather large contingency factor that has to be programmed into any production. Unless you live and work exclusively in the Southwest, you must take the weather into account for exterior shooting. It is best to schedule all of the exteriors first if possible. And always have an interior set as a backup location when you have scheduled exteriors. Nothing can be more frustrating—or more expensive—than watching a cast and crew scheduled for a sunny exterior stand around under umbrellas waiting for the rain or snow to stop! Always have a fallback position, and then back that one up, as well!

## Preproduction Planning

The paper planning is now done. At this point, you should call together all of your department heads to begin preproduction planning, the process most frequently overlooked or underdone by the novice. Seasoned professionals, however, recognize that preproduction planning is the heart and soul of a successful operation.

Preproduction planning, known as "prepro" in the industry jargon, can make the production run like a precision machine. Lack of it can destroy you before you begin. In prepro, you and your department heads do all of the organizing that will carry the company forward to delivery of the final product to the client. You will have daily production meetings from this point on through production (called the "shooting phase" or "principal photography").

The heads of the following departments must be present at the production meetings: directing, art, camera, sound, makeup and costumes, transportation, and, of course, production. In very small operations, one person may have to do more than one job. The duties of each department are described below.

### Directing

The directing department consists of the director and at least one assistant director (AD). The function of the first AD, curiously, has very little to do with directing. He or she is really more of a producer's functionary, acting as the liaison or buffer between the director and the producer, the director and the technical crew, and the director and virtually all problems that could distract him or her from the creative task of bringing the script to life. First ADs grow up to be producers, not directors, oddly enough.

First ADs are responsible for revising the shooting schedule as changing requirements dictate. They make up a Daily Call Sheet that lists everybody and everything needed for the day's shoot, along with information on the time and place where everybody and everything should be. First ADs also make and distribute daily work orders, which list all of the technical requirements for each day. Figures 2–9 and 2–10 show sample forms that the first AD will fill out.

The first AD also makes and compiles Daily Production Reports. From these reports, the AD puts together the Daily Log, which is a summary of each element of each day's shooting. An example is shown in Figure 2–11. Using this form, the producer can make exact records of times and costs, which will be of tremendous assistance when budgeting for succeeding productions as well as for keeping on track during this one.

During the prepro phase of your project, the first AD prepares all of these forms while doing everything possible to meet demands for help from the director. A good first AD is the second most important member of the team. This position

SHOOT DAY **1**

## CALL SHEET
## SHOOTING CALL _____ UNIT

*Due To Extreme Fire Hazard, Please Be Careful Smoking. Use Butt Cans.*

PICTURE **IT'S A WONDERFUL LIFE**     NO. **541**    DIRECTOR **Frank Capra**

SHOOTING CALL _____ DATE **Mon, Jul 6**

ART DIRECTOR

SET DRESSER

| PAGES | SET DESCRIPTION | SC. NO. | D/N | LOCATION |
|---|---|---|---|---|
| | EXT BAILEY BUILDINGS AND LOAN SIGN | 24 | DAY | |
| | EXT MAIN STREET | 18 | DAY | |
| | EXT FRONT PORCH OF HOUSE | 22 | NIGHT | |

CONDITIONS:       COVER SET:

| CAST AND BITS | | CHARACTER AND WARDROBE | HAIRDRESSING | MAKEUP | ON SET |
|---|---|---|---|---|---|
| 1 | James Stewart | George | | | |
| 7 | Frank Faylen | Ernie | | | |
| 8 | Ward Bond | Bert | | | |
| 11 | Gloria Grahame | Violet | | | |
| 37 | | Grumpy Old Man | | | |

| ATMOSPHERE AND STAND-INS | THRU GATE | REPORT TO | READY ON SET |
|---|---|---|---|
| Elderly Man | | | |

TOTAL EXTRAS: 1

**Figure 2–9** Call sheet. (Reproduced with permission of Screenplay Systems, Inc.)

usually deserves a helper, the second assistant director, to do much of the actual legwork. Meanwhile, the director will be casting talent, scouting locations, planning camera shots, rehearsing talent (whenever the budget will allow for this luxury), discussing camera and lighting requirements with the DP, and working closely with the art department.

The script supervisor works for the first AD and the production manager on large shoots and is almost more impor-

tant than anyone else on the set. This detail-oriented job is frequently overlooked, but errors in keeping great records of exactly what is shot can sink the ship in postproduction. Script supervision requires careful attention to every minute of action on the set. The script supervisor records any changes to the script that are made by the director or the actors and keeps the director informed all the while about what has been shot and what is left to be shot.

SHOOT DAY **2** _____
**CALL SHEET**
**S H O O T I N G   C A L L** _____ UNIT

*Due To Extreme Fire Hazard, Please Be Careful Smoking.  Use Butt Cans.*
PICTURE  IT'S A WONDERFUL LIFE _____ NO. **541** _____ DIRECTOR **Frank Capra** _____

SHOOTING CALL _____
DATE **Tue, Jul 7** _____
ART DIRECTOR
SET DRESSER

| PAGES | SET DESCRIPTION | SC. NO. | D/N | LOCATION |
|---|---|---|---|---|
| | EXT  STREET | 23 | NIGHT | |

CONDITIONS:                                    COVER SET:

| CAST AND BITS | | CHARACTER AND WARDROBE | HAIRDRESSING | MAKEUP | ON SET |
|---|---|---|---|---|---|
| 1 | James Stewart | George | | | |
| 2 | Donna Reed | Mary | | | |
| 3 | | Harry | | | |
| 4 | Thomas Mitchell | Uncle Billy | | | |
| 37 | | Grumpy Old Man | | | |

| ATMOSPHERE AND STAND-INS | THRU GATE | REPORT TO | READY ON SET |
|---|---|---|---|
| | | | |

**Figure 2–9 (cont.)** Call sheet. (Reproduced with permission of Screenplay Systems, Inc.)

*Art*

During preproduction planning, the art department works on the storyboard with the director. Each major scene is broken down into drawings showing camera position and the major action to be included in the frame. The space below the drawing contains captions from the dialogue or narration and notes from the art director and the director. The storyboard simplifies the instructions given to the camera and lighting crew, the actors, and everyone else who is involved on the set. It also solidifies the director's thinking and gives the client a clear idea of what to expect on the screen.

Storyboards are guideposts at the outset of the production. The drawings are not indelible images; the director might see something better during the shoot. But without this blueprint from which to begin, each scene, each day's shooting, can be a nightmare of trying to decide where to place the camera and what to shoot. All the while, your budget will be trickling away by the hour. If you can't afford a real artist

SHOOT DAY **3**

**CALL SHEET**
**S H O O T I N G   C A L L** _____ UNIT

*Due To Extreme Fire Hazard, Please Be Careful Smoking. Use Butt Cans.*

PICTURE  IT'S A WONDERFUL LIFE                    NO. 541        DIRECTOR  Frank Capra

SHOOTING CALL _____     DATE **Wed, Jul 8**
ART DIRECTOR
SET DRESSER

| PAGES | SET DESCRIPTION | SC. NO. | D/N | LOCATION |
|---|---|---|---|---|
|  | EXT  TREE-LINED RESIDENTIAL STREET | 21 | NIGHT |  |

CONDITIONS:                                         COVER SET:

| CAST AND BITS | CHARACTER AND WARDROBE | HAIRDRESSING | MAKEUP | ON SET |
|---|---|---|---|---|
| 1    James Stewart | George |  |  |  |
| 2    Donna Reed | Mary |  |  |  |

| ATMOSPHERE AND STAND-INS | THRU GATE | REPORT TO | READY ON SET |
|---|---|---|---|
|  |  |  |  |

**Figure 2–9 (cont.)** Call sheet. (Reproduced with permission of Screenplay Systems, Inc.)

to do your storyboard, do it yourself with stick figures if nothing else. Visualizing how each scene is going to look is a fundamental tool in any professional production. Figure 2–12 illustrates a good storyboard format. The art department is also responsible for such practical things as designing and building sets, dressing (rearranging and decorating) existing locations that are going to be used as sets during the shoot, and coordinating literally all of the visual elements with the director and the DP.

*Camera*

The DP is in charge of the camera department and is ultimately responsible for all of the technical crew, aside from sound. This includes the grips (whose foreman is the key grip), the gaffer, and all who work for them. In a large-scale operation, this is what the minimum camera crew consists of and what they do:

- *Director of photography:* designs the lighting setups, chooses the camera

# IT'S A WONDERFUL LIFE
## Cast List

| Name | Start | Finish | Total Days | Tot. Pages | Pay |
|------|-------|--------|-----------|-----------|-----|
| 1. George | 7/6/92 | 10/6/92 | 67 Days | 146 1/8 Pgs. | $0 Day |

SCENES: 18, 23, 21, 25, 19, 16, 20, 15, 52, 50, 26, 30, 31, 28, 32, 66, 34, 36, 29, 33, 35, 38, 51, 49, 47, 54, 56, 58, 60, 62, 65, 68, 70, 42, 46, 44, 53, 63, 64, 39, 41, 74, 76, 72, 78, 80, 79, 152, 162, 135, 137, 158, 133, 163, 154, 147, 148, 153, 155, 156, 160, 129, 141, 143, 159, 132, 134, 144, 145, 139, 161, 136, 156, 146, 149, 151, 166, 169, 119, 120, 121,122, 124, 126, , 150, 123, 171, 131, 140, 142, 164, 128, 167, 168, 170, 138, 118, 125, 104, 117, 115, 113, 116, 114, 112, 106, 81, 85, 4, 8, 14, 12, 10, 5, 7, 11, 9, 6, 98, 97, 3, 99, 17

SETS: MAIN STREET, STREET, TREE-LINED RESIDENTIAL STREET, BAILEY BUILDING AND LOAN OFFICE, BAILEY DINING ROOM, GOWER'S DRUGSTORE, HIGH SCHOOL GYM, LUGGAGE SHOP, BUILDING AND LOAN, OUTER OFFICE  BLDG. AND LOAN, FRONT PORCH -- BAILEY HOME, HOUSE, RAILROAD STATION, MAIN STREET BEDFORD FALLS, OLD GRANVILLE HOUSE, RESIDENTIAL STREET, TRAIN, VIOLET BICK'S BEAUTY SHOP, BEDROOM WINDOW -- HATCH HOME, DOORWAY, CAB, ERNIE'S CAB, FRONT HALL BAILEY HOME, GEORGE'S OFFICE, GRANVILLE HOUSE, HALL, HALLWAY, HATCH HALL, PARLOR, MARTINI'S NEW HOUSE, SLUM STREET BEDFORD FALLS, STREET IN BAILEY PARK, BEDROOM -- GEORGE AND MARY'S HOUSE, POTTER'S OFFICE, BAILEY HOME, BEDFORD FALLS EMPORIUM, BRIDGE AT RAILING, BRIDGE OVER RIVER, BUILDING AND LOAN OFFICES, CEMETERY, GEORGE'S HOUSE, LIBRARY, NICK'S BAR, RESIDENTIAL STREET, RIVER, THEATRE, TOLL HOUSE ON BRIDGE, BLUE MOON, ENTRANCE HALL, GEORGE'S LIVING ROOM, HALLWAY GEORGE'S HOUSE, KITCHEN, LIVING ROOM, MARTINI'S BAR, POTTER'S OFFICE IN BANK, STAIRS, UNCLE BILLY'S LIVING ROOM, ZUZU'S BEDROOM, BEDFORD FALLS STREET -- WINTER, DOORWAY TO UNCLE BILLY'S OFFICE, OUTER OFFICE, BACK ROOM DRUGSTORE, BAILEY'S PRIVATE OFFICE, DRUGSTORE, PRESCRIPTION ROOM OF DRUGSTORE, RATION OFFICE, FROZEN RIVER AND HILL

| Name | Start | Finish | Total Days | Tot. Pages | Pay |
|------|-------|--------|-----------|-----------|-----|
| 2. Mary | 7/7/92 | 10/2/92 | 56 Days | 54 5/8 Pgs. | $0 Day |

SCENES: 23, 21, 20, 50, 36, 35, 38, 51, 49, 47, 68, 70, 42, 46, 44, 37, 63, 39, 41, 74, 76, 72, 78, 80, 155, 156, 156, 166, 169, 119, 120, 121,122, 124, 126, , 123, 171, 167, 168, 170, 84, 83, 5, 7, 13, 88

SETS: STREET, TREE-LINED RESIDENTIAL STREET, HIGH SCHOOL GYM, BUILDING AND LOAN, BEDROOM WINDOW -- HATCH HOME, DOORWAY, CAB, ERNIE'S CAB, FRONT HALL BAILEY HOME, GRANVILLE HOUSE, HALL, HALLWAY, HATCH HALL, HATCH HOME, OUTER OFFICE - BLDG. AND LOAN, PARLOR, MARTINI'S NEW HOUSE, SLUM STREET BEDFORD FALLS, STREET IN BAILEY PARK, BEDROOM -- GEORGE AND MARY'S HOUSE, LIBRARY, BLUE MOON, ENTRANCE HALL, GEORGE'S LIVING ROOM, KITCHEN, LIVING ROOM, STAIRS, SITTING ROOM, DRUGSTORE, FRONT ROOM DRUGSTORE, TRAIN IN RAILROAD STATION

| Name | Start | Finish | Total Days | Tot. Pages | Pay |
|------|-------|--------|-----------|-----------|-----|
| 3. Harry | 7/7/92 | 10/5/92 | 40 Days | 29 7/8 Pgs. | $0 Day |

SCENES: 23, 19, 20, 30, 31, 29, 47, 171, 104, 95, 3

SETS: STREET, BAILEY DINING ROOM, HIGH SCHOOL GYM, FRONT PORCH -- BAILEY HOME, HOUSE, TRAIN, FRONT HALL BAILEY HOME, LIVING ROOM, BEDFORD FALLS STREET -- WINTER, READY ROOM ON AIRCRAFT CARRIER, FROZEN RIVER AND HILL

| Name | Start | Finish | Total Days | Tot. Pages | Pay |
|------|-------|--------|-----------|-----------|-----|
| 4. Uncle Billy | 7/7/92 | 10/6/92 | 48 Days | 32 3/8 Pgs. | $0 Day |

SCENES: 23, 25, 26, 30, 28, 29, 54, 56, 58, 60, 62, 53, 64, 123, 171, 118, 117, 111, 105, 109, 107, 115, 112, 9, 91, 17

SETS: STREET, BAILEY BUILDING AND LOAN OFFICE, OUTER OFFICE - BLDG. AND LOAN, FRONT PORCH -- BAILEY HOME, RAILROAD STATION, TRAIN, GEORGE'S OFFICE, KITCHEN, LIVING ROOM, UNCLE BILLY'S LIVING ROOM, MAIN STREET BEDFORD FALLS, BANK, DOORWAY TO UNCLE BILLY'S OFFICE, STREET IN BEDFORD FALLS

| Name | Start | Finish | Total Days | Tot. Pages | Pay |
|------|-------|--------|-----------|-----------|-----|
| 5. Mr. Potter | 7/9/92 | 10/6/92 | 40 Days | 19 Pgs. | $0 Day |

SCENES: 25, 79, 77, 164, 128, 107, 108, 110, 4, 10, 90, 55, 57, 59, 61

SETS: BAILEY BUILDING AND LOAN OFFICE, POTTER'S OFFICE, POTTER'S OFFICE IN BANK, BANK, MAIN STREET BEDFORD FALLS, BAILEY'S PRIVATE OFFICE, DRAFT BOARD OFFICE, POTTER'S LIBRARY

**Figure 2–10** Cast list. (Reproduced with permission of Screenplay Systems, Inc.)

"IT'S A WONDERFUL LIFE"                                                                         Page 1

| July | 6 | 7 | 8 | 9 | 10 | 11 | 12 | 13 | 14 | 15 | 16 | 17 | 18 |
|---|---|---|---|---|---|---|---|---|---|---|---|---|---|
| Day of Week: | M | Tu | W | Th | F | Sa | Su | M | Tu | W | Th | F | Sa |
| Shooting Days: | 1 | 2 | 3 | 4 | 5 | | | 6 | 7 | 8 | 9 | 10 | |
| 1.  George | SW | W | W | W | W | | | W | W | W | W | W | |
| 2.  Mary | | SW | W | H | H | | | H | W | H | W | H | |
| 3.  Harry | | SW | H | H | W | | | H | W | H | H | W | |
| 4.  Uncle Billy | | SW | H | W | H | | | H | H | H | W | W | |
| 5.  Mr. Potter | | | | SWWD | | | | | | | | | |
| 6.  Mr. Gower | | | | | | | | SWWD | | | | | |
| 7.  Ernie | SW | H | H | H | H | | | H | H | H | W | H | |
| 8.  Bert | SWWD | | | | | | | | | | | | |
| 9.  Joe | | | | | | | | | | SWF | | | |
| 10. Clarence | | | | | | | | | | | | | |
| 11. Violet | SW | H | H | H | H | | | H | W | H | H | H | |
| 12. Ma Bailey | | | | | SW | | | H | H | H | H | W | |
| 13. Mrs. Hatch | | | | | | | | | | | | | |
| 14. Mr. Martini | | | | | | | | | | | | | |
| 15. Cousin Tilly | | | | | | | | | | | SW | WD | |
| 16. Annie | | | | | SWWD | | | | | | | | |
| 17. Peter Bailey | | | | | SW | | | H | H | H | H | WD | |
| 18. Cousin Eustace | | | | | | | | | | | SW | WD | |
| 19. Ruth | | | | | | | | | | | | SW | |
| 20. Pete Bailey | | | | | | | | | | | | | |
| 21. Goon | | | | SWWD | | | | | | | | | |
| 22. Carter | | | | | | | | | | | | | |
| 23. Marty | | | | | | | | | SWWD | | | | |
| 24. Sam Wainwright | | | | | | | | | SWWD | | | | |
| 25. Maria Martini | | | | | | | | | | | | | |
| 26. Ed | | | | | | | | | | | | | |
| 27. Freddie | | | | | | | | | SWF | | | | |
| 28. Nick | | | | | | | | | | | | | |
| 29. Tommy Bailey | | | | | | | | | | | | | |
| 30. Janie Bailey | | | | | | | | | | | | | |
| 31. Charlie | | | | | | | | | | | | | |
| 32. Tom | | | | | | | | | | | | | |
| 33. Zuzu Bailey | | | | | | | | | | | | | |
| 34. Dr. Campbell | | | | SW | H | | | H | H | H | WD | | |
| 35. Mr. Carter | | | | | | | | | | | | | |
| 36. Principal | | | | | | | | | SWWD | | | | |
| 37. Grumpy Old Man | SW | WF | | | | | | | | | | | |
| 38. Jane Wainwright | | | | | | | | | | | | | |
| 39. Tollkeeper | | | | | | | | | | | | | |
| 40. Mickey | | | | | | | | | SWF | | | | |
| 41. Lawyer | | | | SWF | | | | | | | | | |
| 42. Real Estate Salesman | | | | SWF | | | | | | | | | |
| 43. Insurance Agent | | | | SWF | | | | | | | | | |
| 44. Suitor #1 | | | | | | | | | | | | | |
| 45. Suitor #2 | | | | | | | | | | | | | |
| 46. Passerby | | | | | | | | | | SWF | | | |
| 47. Randall | | | | | | | | | | | | | |
| 48. Mrs. Thompson | | | | | | | | | | | | | |
| 49. Poster Man | | | | | | | | | | | | | |
| 50. Schultz | | | | | | | | | | | | | |
| 51. Mr. Reineman | | | | | | | | | | | | | |
| 52. Nurse | | | | | | | | | | | | | |
| 53. Bank Teller | | | | | | | | | | | | | |
| 54. Mr. Welch | | | | | | | | | | | | | |
| 55. Owner | | | | | | | | | | | | | |
| 56. Truck Driver | | | | | | | | | | | | | |
| 57. House Owner | | | | | | | | | | | | | |
| 58. Cop | | | | | | | | | | | | | |
| 59. Sheriff | | | | | | | | | | | | | |

**Figure 2–10 (cont.)** Cast list. (Reproduced with permission of Screenplay Systems, Inc.)

DAILY LOG                     Production F&VR-012-7 FOURDRINIER
Crew Call -9:00a.m.    Director- 9:00a.m.    Shooting -10:00a.m.

| | | |
|---|---|---|
| Sc 2-1 | 9:00-9:40 | Setup equipt. Lineup & light INT. BERGSTROM |
| | 9:40-9:55 | Place actor & background workers |
| | 9:55-10:04 | Director walks through w/talent |
| | 10:04-10:17 | Adjust lighting & practice dolly |
| | 10:17-10:25 | Shoot 1 take |
| | 10:25-10:30 | Shoot 2 takes |
| 3-1 | 10:30-11:00 | Move setup down the machine & relight |
| | 11:00-11:03 | Shoot 1 take |
| | 11:03-11:06 | Shoot 2 takes |
| 3a-1 | 11:06-11:25 | Blown circuit; rewire & run cable |
| | 11:25-11:30 | Shoot 1 take |
| | 11:30-11:42 | Adjust lights |
| | 11:42-11:45 | Shoot 2 takes |
| 4-1 | 11:45-12:02 | Relocate down the machine |
| | 12:02-12:22 | Adjust light & practice camera move |
| | 12:22-12:28 | Shoot 1 take |
| | 12:28-12:50 | Blown circuit; rerig & relight |
| | 12:50-12:55 | Shoot 2 takes |
| | 12:55-1:10 | Director decides on another shot. Move camera to top of machine. |
| | 1:10-1:15 | Shoot 1 take |
| | 1:15-1:20 | Shoot 2 takes |
| | 1:20-2:20 | Lunch at Valley Inn across street |
| | 2:20-3:20 | Shift all equipment to other end of factory relight and lineup |
| 5-1 | 3:20-4:00 | Director explains shot. Rehearse w/dolly. Humidity causes lens fog. Hair dryer obtained to clear fog during shot. |
| | 4:00-4:05 | Shoot 1 take |
| | 4:05-4:22 | Actor having trouble making move. Rerig lights and dolly track. |
| | 4:22-4:30 | Rehearse new move |
| | 4:30-4:34 | Shoot 1 take |
| | 4:34-4:40 | Adjust lights |
| | 4:40-4:44 | Shoot 2 takes |
| 6-1 | 4:44-5:00 | Move setup to end of machine |
| | 5:00-5:30 | Relight and practice fast dolly |
| | 5:30-5:45 | Rehearse talent w/camera move |
| | 5:45-5:46 | Shoot 1 take |
| | 5:46-5:55 | Adjust lights |
| | 5:55-5:56 | Shoot 1 take |
| | 5:56-6:00 | Rehearse move w/actor |
| | 6:00-6:12 | Shoot 4 takes |
| | 6:12-6:45 | Shoot inserts-4 takes |
| | 6:45-7:12 | Strike set & equipment |
| | 7:12 | Company dismissed w/ meal penalty |

**Figure 2-11** Daily log.

angles and lenses, coordinates with the director, and supervises the technical crew.

- *First camera operator:* operates the camera during the shoot.
- *First assistant camera operator (AC):* assists the operator in all functions, including taking distance measurements from camera to subject (called "spiking"), setting up the camera, taking light measurements and setting the correct f-stop, and pulling focus or zoom when necessary. The AC also keeps camera reports detailing exactly what was shot, logging time code numbers, and describing any problems with the shot. These forms are copied and passed along with the footage to the editor.

# Storyboard 8128

SCENE NO. 7

**PRODUCTION** *FOURDRINIER*

NO. *80-03* DATE *11-17-80*

DIRECTOR *Bob Jacobs* ARTIST *Same*

SCRIPT DATED *10-30-80* PAGE *2* OF *3*

SETUP NO. *27* SCRIPT PAGE NO. *2*

DIALOG AND/OR ACTION:
   ... *AND THIS WINE AND CHEESE CELLAR* ...

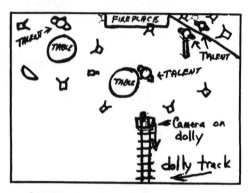

CAMERA PLACEMENT ON SET PLAN

*START C.U.*
*Dolly back to reveal*
*the entire room. LIGHTS*
*SUSPENDED ON GRID.*

SETUP NO. *27* SCRIPT PAGE NO. *2*

DIALOG AND/OR ACTION:
   ... *TO GIVE YOU BOTH AN INTIMATE CONVERSATION PLACE OF YOUR OWN* ...

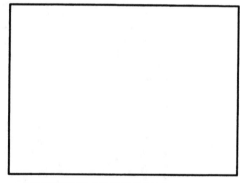

CAMERA PLACEMENT ON SET PLAN

*SAME*

**Figure 2–12** Storyboard.

- *Gaffer:* implements the instructions of the DP, rigs the lights and wiring on the set, patches into external power sources as necessary, and is directly responsible for all the electrical wiring on the set.
- *Key grip:* supervises the grip crew, does all of the practical moving of equipment for the shoot, and puts lighting and lighting control instruments in place at the direction of the gaffer.

During prepro, the camera department is very involved with locating all of the items that will be needed for production. Because most small production companies rarely own all of the equipment they will require, the DP and the producer need to have a line on all of the equipment rental houses. During prepro, you will go through the equipment catalogs with the DP and choose items based on the needs of the script and the storyboard.

Normally, you can and should trust the suggestions of your DP in technical matters. A wise producer, however, will be familiar with the technical end of the production. You won't have to know what a pigtail or a brute is, and you needn't change your perception of an octopus and a cookie as an ugly fish with eight arms and a flat, sweet thing with chocolate chips. But you should certainly know the difference between a three-chip and a two-chip video camera; between DVC PRO and Digital Betacam formats; and between top-of-the-line industrial and bottom-of-the-line broadcast-quality equipment so you don't get talked into using some toys that might be neat but unnecessary to Jones Hotels.

You should understand the elementary components of a grip truck to be able to determine whether you'll need an external generator on the set to handle the amperage of the lights you'll be using. Many technicians want to use the latest and best, when frequently the older and cheaper will do. Your DP must understand your budget limitations, so hold nothing back in your prepro discussions. Department heads are your full partners in the production, and they need to know the real parameters of the job.

### Sound

In most smaller video productions, the videotape recorder (VTR) operator also monitors and adjusts the audio levels and is, in effect, the sound recordist. This can work when the project requires only one actor wearing a lavalier microphone. If the sound recording is more complicated, however, one person is not sufficient.

Consider sound as an integral department of its own, and staff it with a recordist and a boom operator. The recordist records the audio track on the VTR, as well as on a backup audiotape deck, and does on-location mixing of various audio sources, including multiple microphones, to provide daily sound reports. The boom operator places microphones on the set and on the actors. When unidirectional (shotgun) or other kinds of microphones held overhead on a boom or "fish pole" are used, the boom operator physically holds the pole and directs the microphone at the actors.

As department head, the sound recordist, although only minimally involved in prepro, must be given the chance to estimate the amount and kinds of microphones, cables, tape, and so on, that will be required for the shoot. Many freelance recordists provide their own equipment and include it in their daily or weekly rate. As a rule of thumb, remember this: If what is being said on the set by your actors is important, don't trust the recording to an assistant cameraperson or VTR operator—hire an expert.

### Makeup and Costumes

Even if you will be using "real people"—such as the actual maids in our Jones Hotels training tape—you would be wise to have a costume and makeup coordinator. On smaller shoots, one person can frequently handle both jobs. This department is responsible for obtaining and applying makeup; buying or making clothing; taking measurements of the cast members; providing a sufficient number of identical costumes so that clothing can be changed if soiled or rumpled on the set; and attending to all of the details that will contribute to the look of your actors.

On major shoots, this department must sometimes begin work several weeks in advance of the actual production. In this case, you will need a head costumer, an assistant costumer, a men's dresser, a women's dresser, a hairstylist, a head makeup person, an assistant makeup person, and perhaps even a men's and a women's body makeup person!

### Transportation

The transportation captain is responsible for arranging for and providing the movement of people and things during your production. This person hires trucks and other vehicles to ensure the daily pickup and delivery of your talent to and from the set, arranges airline reservations for your cast and crew as necessary, and so on.

The transportation captain will need to see your shooting schedule as far in advance as possible to carry out this heady responsibility. Most production companies rent all of the necessary vehicles. If you are going to be on a remote location overnight, the transportation captain will also have to provide trailers or motor homes for the cast and crew to use as sleeping quarters as well as dressing and makeup rooms.

### Production

During the preproduction planning phase of the operation, you and your assistants will coordinate all of the details from the information provided by your department heads. Having approved, for example, the game plan of your DP, you will order the equipment from the rental houses, pay the bills, maintain accounting records, and more. A useful checklist at this stage is the Unit Manager's Worksheet, which is used daily during production.

On the worksheet, you'll find practically everything you'll need to think about and plan for. If you're shooting exteriors in a major city, for instance, you will need to know whether you will be required to obtain permits or licenses before shooting in public places. Whenever a camera crew shows up at a location like a city street or a park, their activity will likely attract a crowd. Either you or the police will have to provide crowd control. For that reason, many cities have established flat fees for the commercial use of public facilities—both interior and exterior. Fines for shooting without a permit are frequently rather steep. It pays, therefore, to make a call to your location's city hall to check on this kind of detail before an oversight pops up to ruin your otherwise swell day!

The production office also arranges for meals for the cast and crew. Generally, meals are brought to the shooting site to reduce downtime. Remember to find out if any cast or crew members have special dietary needs, and plan accordingly. A well-fed cast and crew is a happy one. On major Hollywood sound stages, craft services—the folks who provide the grub—is a high-priority item.

The production office coordinates everything that happens during preproduction and production; it brings together all of the details to make the project work. A first-class secretary in this office is essential.

As the project moves from prepro into principal photography, your planning and management should make the transition as smooth as possible. You have instilled in your department heads a feeling of camaraderie, and they know they have your total support. The pressure on you, however, doesn't let up for a second. The success or failure of the project, the making of a good product for your client, is completely your responsibility.

## Managing the Client

Whether your client is NBC or Jones Hotels, you will have creative control over the project. Stephen J. Cannell, a legendary producer behind a seemingly endless string of hit network shows like *The Rockford Files*, *The A-Team*, and others, has some insight into dealing with clients: "Network executives are, for the most part, businesspeople. They are accountants or MBAs. Now and then I get into, well, 'discussions' with them about a creative element in one of my shows. Now if it's 'Standards and Practices' or a thing like that, well, then they will have the final say. But if it's a matter of something I feel strongly about, like the characterization of this or that guy or the casting of this or that person, then I will try everything possible to have my own way. You have to remember that it is their money, but if they've hired me to do what I do creatively, then I want them to let me do my job.[2]

Some clients hire you and leave you completely alone to do your job. More frequently, however, clients feel that they should have input into the way things are done because they have put up the money. Naturally, clients have script approval. It is, after all, their story that you are telling. At the stage of script approval, you should be prepared to accede to reasonable requests for the insertion of this or that sequence, changes in dialogue and so on. You must also be able to argue for "the right and true" if you feel that the client is completely off base. Once you have hammered out the script and the clients have given their input and approved the thing, it becomes imperative that you be able to tell them, very diplomatically of course, to buzz off and let you get on with the production.

If your client shows up on the set every day, begins to interfere with the workings of your crew, starts telling the director what to shoot and how to shoot it, and wants to put family members in the scene, then you are in for trouble. This is when your integrity will be tested. If you don't care what your product looks like—if you're only in it for the money—then be sure that your cast and crew know that. Everybody can humor the client and walk away happy at the end.

If you do care about quality, then you will have to be fair and courteous but absolutely strong. Take your client to a private place, and say something like this: "Mr. Jones, this shoot is costing you $10,000 a day. I have your signature approving the script and the storyboard, and I've budgeted this thing down to the last penny based on that approval. Now if you're going to keep insisting on changes and interfering on the set like this, we're going to have to do a whole new budget. I know that you mean well, sir, but we are the professionals on the production end, and I'm going to have to ask you to let us do our jobs for you."

You can only hope that clients will be reasonable. Many clients and agency representatives actually contribute on the set by giving you fresh eyes and ears. Logic and tact will win the day for both of you in workable situations like this. But in extreme instances, rather than put yourself and your production people through a living nightmare, you must be prepared to either close down the project (returning the unused portion of the budget to the client with your best wishes), or grin and bear it through to the end. This decision will be the ultimate test of your integrity.

# Summary

Effective management is a creative process. It requires an awareness of human motivations and a love of working with people. Management also requires a keen mind for details and an ability to anticipate and organize. I hope that the forms and procedures outlined in this chapter will help producers who wish to manage their productions, staff, and clients with skill and effectiveness.

# Notes

1. For a good book on the behavioralist technique and other good books on basic management principles, see the bibliography.

2. Stephen J. Cannell, interview with the author, January 1993.

# 3

# The Independent Business: Setting Up Shop

The first two chapters of this book present and discuss information common to all producers, whether they work for a major corporation in-house or for an agency or as a supplier to one of the networks. This legion of very creative businesspeople is described in the trade as "work-for-hire."

This chapter is meant for those brave few who have made the decision, or are about to make the decision, to set out on their own, to grab for the gold ring as independent producers. These are the people for whom this book was conceived. If you're one of them, welcome to heady, exciting, dangerous waters filled with sharks waiting for the unwary. I hope the rest of this book will serve as your life preserver.

Deciding to go into business for yourself, to become the very symbol of free enterprise—the entrepreneur—is one of the most crucial moments in anyone's life. This is the ultimate adrenaline rush,

better than skydiving or bungee jumping for clearing the head and getting the heart racing. Above all, it means that you understand one simple but crucial thing about working for a living: You'll never get rich working for someone else. Anyone else.

It's true that many folks attain a nice level of comfort, perhaps contentment even, putting in time for someone else. But they will never know what it feels like to proclaim, as Leonardo DiCaprio's character shouted in the 1997 movie *Titanic,* "I'm the king of the world!" To know what Aaron Spelling and Stephen J. Cannell and Steven Bochko—and any of that other legion of small to large operators of production companies from coast to coast—feel as they fly on their own, you must take a chance. That thrill is reserved for the confident, the brave, the singular man or woman who takes it to the limit as "the boss."

## Making the Decision to Go Solo

When you stand on this precipice, you must consider several factors. You will give up security, regular paychecks, fringe ben-

efits, retirement plans, paid-for health care, and so on, along with the peace of mind that comes from having someone else worry about meeting the payroll. That is a huge leap of faith over the stony cliff of uncertainty.

There are a number of reasons why people take that jump into their own business. Hoping to make a lot of money is one reason. Another is the glamour and excitement in reaching for the great American dream. There are other reasons that will be explored later in this chapter. The ability to hold on to a dream is important. But there are also some very real character traits that these special people must have. This first part of this chapter provides food for thought about joining the ranks of the self-employed. Savor it slowly and with care.

## Entrepreneurship

An entrepreneur has to be a cross between a starry-eyed dreamer and a conservative capitalist. The dream part has to be so strong, so pervasive, and such a driving force that you cannot bear to do anything else for a living. This is the ultimate motivating force because it may have to sustain you through disillusionment and long-lasting hard times. If this urge, this dream, this fantasy isn't the most important thing in your life, if you don't feel that there is nothing else you'd rather be doing than heading up a company of your own, if you have the slightest doubt about your ability to endure pressure and to thrive in spite of contumely and criticism and doubt, then do not even think about stepping off that cliff into self-employment. Your parachute bag is empty. You will fall to your doom.

## The Bad News

The statistics regarding entrepreneurship are sobering. The Small Business Administration (SBA) indicated 10 years ago that only 67 percent of the 500,000 businesses a year that started up in America made it through their first year. Only 33 percent made it to five years, and a mere 20 percent hung on for a decade.[1] In the intervening years, the climate may have improved somewhat. According to a study done by Bruce A. Kirchoff, former chief economist for the SBA and then professor of entrepreneurship at the New Jersey Institute of Technology in 1993, only about 18 percent of new businesses fail during the first eight years. More than half of all start-ups make it more than eight years with their original owners or with new ones buying them out, and 28 percent of new outfits close down with no outstanding debts.[2] The risks are still high but not inordinate, according to this study.

According to creditors and business analysts, the primary reason for the failure rate, whichever you choose to believe, is ineffective management. The SBA offers advice in the next section about the kind of person who can get a business started and make it work.

## Assess Your Motivation

The SBA suggests that you think about why you want to own your own business and be certain that you want it badly enough to work long hours without knowing how much money you will earn. Past experience—especially as a manager—in a business like the one you wish to start can prove very helpful, and assets such as formal business training and extra money are a big plus on your side.

Despite the SBA's cautionary statistics, Uncle Sam wants you to make it in business. And he can provide some help, as described later in this chapter. But first, take a look at the characteristics that make up the personality type voted most likely to succeed. Then measure yourself honestly against this list. These are the qualities that make for a successful entrepreneur:

1. You are a self-starter. You do things on your own. Nobody has to tell you to get moving.

2. You actively like other people. You can get along with just about anybody.

3. You can lead people and get them to go along with your ideas and your momentum once you get started.

4. You enjoy responsibility. You seek it

out, take charge of things, and always see a project through to completion.

5.  You are a gifted organizer. You make a plan before you start a project, and you are usually the one to get things lined up when your group wants to do something.

6.  As a worker, you can keep going as long as you need to. You never mind working hard for something you want.

7.  You can make decisions in a hurry if you have to, and they usually turn out to be right. Not perfect, just right.

8.  Your word is your bond. You can always be trusted and never say things you don't mean.

9.  You have persistence. You stick to any job you've made up your mind to do, and you don't let anything stop you.

10. You are in top physical condition, and you never get run-down.

How do you compare to the SBA's assessment of personality types who are likely to make it in business for themselves? Notice that almost every one of these descriptions applies to the producer type discussed in previous chapters. If you see yourself in there, you're on track. If the types described look like aliens from another planet, take another path.

The conclusion here is simple. If you are currently a successful producer working for someone else and you have the drive and the capitalization, you have a good chance of succeeding on your own. However, you must assess your limitations as well as your motivation before you decide to go solo.

## Know Your Limitations

This section is about limitations. It is also about common sense—an essential attribute for those who wish to understand limitations. Caught up in the exhilaration of the moment, sometimes blinded by the light of our own derring-do, we can forget some basics—for example, paying attention to details, remembering who we are and where we came from and why we

went into business for ourselves. Some of the information and advice that follows is derived from the experiences of real people who learned these very real lessons the hard way—by going broke.

In a blind panic, with the monthly bills coming due again, when the one or two key sales that will put you over the hump are just hanging fire, you may be tempted to deal with one of the thousands of idiots who hover about the fringes of this business. Be prepared for them to pester you. They are like flies on horses, mosquitoes in a swamp. They are the ubiquitous gremlins hiding in the bushes, waiting to spring out and bite you when you least expect it. The problem is that they seem to be quite legitimate at first glance. If you make the error of taking a chance on them, however, they can break you before you know what's happened.

"They" are the dream merchants, the scam artists. I don't know where they hatch, but they are all over our business. They always have a million-dollar idea for a series, a made-for-TV movie, a special, or a hot new toy to sell with late-night, per-inquiry spot TV commercials. And for some reason you'll never comprehend, they choose to cut you in on it. All you have to do is join them in their madness, and they'll make you rich. They are wizards of deception, and you can't believe how good they are at it. Here are just two examples of what happened when otherwise sensible producers forgot the main limitation involved in their being in business: time.

Your time is precious. It flies on gossamer wings into the vapor. Don't waste it as these producers did. The most serious mistake a new producer can make when venturing out into the world of independent production is overextension. The names in these case studies have been changed, but the stories are true.

### Case 1

Frank was making good progress toward his goals as a producer. He had done work for a major corporation, and a long-term contract was in the offing. He had taken on a partner who was good at sales. Although accounts receivable were not actually overflowing, the future looked promising. A breakthrough was just around the corner.

Through an acquaintance of his sales partner, Harry, Frank met a prospect named John who had a small publishing business. Moderately successful at putting out a few do-it-yourself books and vanity novels, John had a dream. A very big one.

John had a wonderful Christmas story that he wanted to do as a TV special. He told Frank and Harry that he had backing to the tune of $1 million. All he needed from them were their production skills and access to some of their contacts in Hollywood. The script was being written, he assured them, by a top-notch screenwriter. Did they want in?

Now ask yourself, given the above, would *you* want in? Frank and Harry did. They ended up devoting nearly a year of their precious time to a project that never materialized. It was not a deliberate ruse, of course. John believed, as such people usually do, that saying something makes it so. He was in love with the story and knew that other people would be, too. A friend of a friend had, indeed, mentioned something about being able to come up with $1 million for the right project with the right cast at the right time. John simply had faith that it would all come together because he wanted it to happen so badly. So he misrepresented the actual deal to his newfound producers.

Here's what really went on. The screenwriter turned out to be John's brother in Saint Louis, who thought he was as good a writer as those "hacks" on TV. The story had been "borrowed" (without the publisher's permission) from a national magazine. Nobody had the rights to do it as a screenplay. The money guy turned out to be a middle-class stockbroker with an itch to break into Hollywood and enough personal debts to sink him at any moment. There was never backing of $1 million, as Frank and Harry found out when the stockbroker started to ask their Hollywood celebrity friends for money.

Frank and Harry wasted time on this asinine enterprise, jeopardized hard-won contacts in the business, and destroyed the confidence of a major distributor of syndicated television shows when the whole ship of fantasies sank. They also ended up losing the accounts they had and severing their partnership—all because they had been players in a fool's game. They jumped in without really qualifying the players because they forgot why they were in business.

They did not know their limitations. They did not know how to tell a legitimate deal from a pipe dream. They strayed outside the bounds of their goals and their real abilities. Neither man had any experience in producing major television movies, but they fell for John's flattery. It made them feel important.

In addition to exceeding their limitations, they forgot one other basic rule of business: Never do any work without a contract and a down payment. Also, when someone tells you that $1 million is in the bank for a major project, check to make sure it's there. The producer in the next story did, but he discovered a far more subtle limitation.

### Case 2

The producer's name was Bob, and his company was located in a small Midwestern town. He had moved to the Midwest from a successful career on the West Coast to escape the pressures that had given him a bleeding ulcer and a broken marriage. He decided in the middle of a commercial shoot in New York involving a scented douche product that he could surely find something better to do with his life than this.

He left the set. And he was followed from the shoot to his room in the Waldorf Astoria by the creative director of one of the top five ad agencies in the world. As he threw his clothes into a suitcase, the creative director asked in desperation, "What does it take to own you?" Bob drew himself up to his full six feet, two inches and said, "You haven't got enough."

On the way to Kennedy Airport, he wondered if maybe he should have thought of a figure. But he never looked back. Instead, he moved himself lock, stock, and lifestyle to the heartland.

Some of his reputation had preceded him into his tranquil hideaway. Because of this, his business was relatively easy to launch and to keep afloat at less than a blistering pace. Before he knew it, the slower pace of life and a hundred-year-old farmhouse had hooked him. Five and then 10 years went by. He lost the ulcer, along with all desire to return to life in the fast lane. He also lost the keen edge of his business sense, and this would end up costing him.

Bob had built a fine reputation in his community. His fees were reasonable, and the quality of his work was exceptional. He also gave back a lot to his community. He worked with kids at the local college to give them experience in the field and made a good many free public-service announcements for an assortment of non-profit local charities.

Bob became something of a regional folk hero, which didn't hurt his business. He also received some national attention in a couple of video and film publications for a project that was billed as the country's first community film. The project had been paid for by contributions from area businesses and public-spirited residents, much like a community theater production. This fact made the project newsworthy.

Shortly after the film's premiere, Bob was contacted by a young man. Dan had a script and a contact in New York. Jack, the New York contact, had $500,000 in cash to invest in making a low-budget, made-for-TV feature. He and Dan figured that the project could be done if Bob would lend his expertise and influence in the community and if he would help them get a start.

Bob was a little suspicious at first. Unlike Frank and Harry from the preceding case, he had no ambitions to make it in Hollywood. He had also learned to recognize and avoid pipe dreamers. He agreed, however, to meet Dan and Jack and talk it over. Jack flew out from New York. In three days of meetings, Bob probed for all the right answers and got them. Jack did, indeed, have the money. He also had the

key personnel: a director of photography and a director. He needed Bob's guidance and his amazing rapport with the people in town. With Bob's connections from the community project—which gave him free use of locations and access to experienced young people for minor roles and crew positions—Jack felt that they could make a movie with a million-dollar look for a fourth of the amount. Bob agreed. And since the writer was one of the students from the local college, it seemed a worthwhile effort to give a kid a break.

Because Jack wanted to produce, it was agreed that Bob would function as executive producer. It was his reputation and, in a very real way, his town. At the outset, Jack agreed that Bob would have the final say in everything. Jack was inexperienced at production and said that he was relying on Bob to be his mentor. "You'll actually produce it for me," he said. "I'll do all the legwork and learn from you."

After reaching an agreement on a fee for his services and receiving a down payment in cash, Bob gave the go-ahead, and the project began in a blaze of excitement and publicity. Bob arranged for donations of all sorts of equipment, up to and including company cars and a grip truck. He received discount rates on hotel accommodations and provided production offices for the New York crew. He obtained locations and free lunches from several cafés. He assembled a pool of free talent from which the director chose his cast.

Bob supplied office help and assistants for the producer and director, got a first-rate camera technician, and provided an accomplished art director who agreed to work for just a screen credit. These were only a few of his achievements. Two weeks into the project, however, things began to go very badly.

The man from the truck rental firm called Bob and said, "This friend of yours from New York is driving me crazy. He's been over here five times griping about the trucks. I've given him two now. What do you guys want for free? This is the last time I'll help you out, pal."

The woman who owned a Laundromat that was used as a location called Bob to ask him when he was going to replace her carpet. The crew had ripped it to pieces, and Jack had said that Bob would take care of it.

An elderly man whose house was used as a location wanted to know when Bob was going to repaint his house (as Jack had told him he would). The crew had painted the front door and entryway sky blue.

The list of oddities grew day by day.

Soon the flood of free and cheap help that Bob had provided began arriving in his office. The lines varied, but typically they ran something like this: "Bob, this Jack may be a friend of yours, but I can't work for him with that tyrannical attitude of his, so count me out."

When Bob tried to talk to Jack about the growing tide of complaints, the ruination of his good name, and the abuse of the town, he discovered that Jack was no longer rational and reasonable but instead had become a raving monster. He shouted obscenities, screaming that Bob was a "hick" who didn't know anything and that he'd "better shut up and keep out of the way."

Within a few weeks, Jack had alienated nearly every business and individual in town. He had fired or driven away all of the talent and technicians whom Bob had lined up. And in the end, he skipped town in the dead of night, leaving behind a stack of unpaid hotel and equipment bills, along with thousands of dollars of uninsured property damage for which Bob, to save his name, had to pay. Needless to say, the salary that was promised for Bob's services never materialized.

This solid, professional, experienced producer learned that there is a limitation to how much real control can be exercised over another adult. Once the project was under way and Jack had what he wanted, he simply rode roughshod over Bob, his company, and the community.

Again, the lesson is a simple one. If you spend your time, talent, and money establishing a base of respect for yourself in your community, keep it to yourself. And if you're a producer, stick to producing your own work. If you do venture into something of the sort we've talked about here, make sure you carry a big stick and get all your money up front!

You may be the most energetic person in the world. But as physicists are learning, there is only so much energy in the universe, and it does seem to be decreasing. It's called the theory of entropy. The energy you expend on pipe dreamers or on unproductive ideas is lost forever, and your construct will fall apart. Expend your energy wisely.

With these caveats as preamble, the following sections give some concrete suggestions for you to follow after you have made the decision to take the often frightening, but ultimately exhilarating, step out of the nest and into the rarefied air of real independence.

# Getting Started

There is nothing quite as exciting to the entrepreneur as taking action. Following the weeks and months of preparation and planning, comes the adrenaline rush of finding the place and opening the doors to your own business. Here's where the fun starts and the beginning ends.

## Choosing a Location

The first thing you need to do is choose a location for your production company. This decision involves some investigation into two major factors that will weigh on your chances for success: the marketplace and the competition.

### The Marketplace

If industrial and sales promotion productions are your specialty, you can't choose to set up shop in Two Guns, Arizona, or in the blissful wilderness of Idaho! You need to establish your business where your clients are. The U.S. Chamber of Commerce can help you research the location of large companies throughout the United States. The *Encyclopedia of Associations* gives the location of associations that serve all major businesses in the country; this can be very helpful in your planning. You'll also find on-line information on countless corporate and association Web sites.

You don't have to live in Minneapolis to land a production contract for 3M. But you should know that several production companies are in Minneapolis already and that they have a better chance of landing an account with this company than you do working from Trinidad, California, or Sidney, Nebraska. A little research time will pay off with lots of information about where the businesses are and who is there right now to service them.

Many people go into business for themselves hoping to be able to live somewhere other than Los Angeles, New York, or Chicago. Part of the beauty of the recent trend toward decentralization in America is that many producers are able to operate successfully from smaller communities, where both the cost of living and the cost of doing business are much less than in metropolitan areas. The Internet and the wonderful communication revolution that the computer has produced have enabled a broader definition of the workplace for a large number of such operations in America. No business can last long, however, if the owner has chosen sylvan tranquillity at the expense of being in close proximity to large-scale manufacturing and commerce if that is the business's market niche.

It is possible, for example, for a video production house to be located in the placid, quaintly Victorian Wisconsin town of Oshkosh. Milwaukee, a major marketplace, is only 80 miles to the south and is accessible by both air transportation and a major highway. The owner of the company also has sales opportunities in the corridor of commerce between Milwaukee and Green Bay, which houses major companies like Kimberly-Clark, Proctor & Gamble, and Mercury Marine, as well as

several major paper companies and a host of smaller manufacturers and merchants.

Assessing the real potential of an area is foremost in deciding where to locate. Once you've evaluated such factors as the number and nature of possible clients you will have to draw on in the area, you're ready to move on to other necessary considerations.

### The Competition

An old saying is that competition is the spice of life. It is also a very real factor in the potential longevity of an independent production house. Before you decide to join the ball game in Hollywood, for example, you should know that the Hollywood yellow pages list more than 200 independent video producers, starting with Ampersand Productions and ending with Yukon Pictures. In the greater Los Angeles area, including the relative tranquillity of Santa Monica, the list of production companies runs to more than 20 pages, 90 companies to the page, from A&R Group to Zona Productions. Consider all the firms, small to huge, in between. Assessing the competition is as important as understanding your own limitations.

Let's assume that you will eschew the Jacuzzi, the fast lane, and Frederick's of Hollywood because you recognize that the market in Southern California is saturated with competition. Here are some things you must do in any geographic area in which you choose to set up shop.

*Evaluating Your Competitors*
The first thing to do is to go through the phone book and find out how many other video producers there are in your immediate area and in any major metropolitan center nearby. Check for the number of local television stations, also, because most rely rather heavily on income generated from producing spot commercials and therefore must be considered competition. Launch a Web search, using Yahoo!, Lycos, or Infoseek or a yellow pages site and the subject "video production companies," and see what comes up. Follow the links, and in a short time you'll be printing out valu-

able information about the market saturation in your chosen region.

You need to know the present size of the market being serviced and estimate whether it will grow or decline so you can make a sensible guess at what percentage of that market you can take as your own. You need to know how the business volume of your competition stacks up year to year. Is it steady, increasing, or declining? Find out who the primary clients are and whether the producers rely on one or two major bread-and-butter accounts or whether they have a large number of smaller ones. Check on the size of their operations and sales forces. Do they have many salespeople out beating the bushes day after day, or are the owners-producers also the head salespeople? Check with the local Chamber of Commerce, the Better Business Bureau, and the state tax board to learn about the reputations and sales records of the competition.

Visit the physical plant of each competitor. You can tell quite a lot about a company by the way it looks. Does the company have an office, a receptionist, and a studio, or does the owner have an answering machine in the den of the house and a magnetic rubber sign on the side of an old Chevy van?

What are the strengths and weaknesses of the competition, based on your observations? Make a list of these, and then run through your own capabilities in comparison. For example, if one company has a large staff, an enormous facility, and therefore a whopping monthly overhead, you might position yourself by advertising that you can offer substantially lower fees for your services while delivering equal quality because your overhead is lower.

*Gathering the Information*
Gathering all of this information about your competition is a major research project, but there are a variety of ways to go about it. Company owners won't tell you the truth—if they tell you anything—about their operations if they know that you are going into competition with them. The best place to start your research, then, is in a community where you are not plan-

ning to locate. If you're honest and not overly pushy, most producers will be happy to give you tips about their business because they don't have to worry about your trying to take it away from them. So travel to another region to begin your research.

For the specifics about the competitors in your area, firsthand observation coupled with a little deviousness on your part can reward you with a great deal of factual data. You can, for example, call up a company and say that you are a prospective client, so you receive a sales pitch. This will certainly supply you with data about the operation and the pricing structure. After you've become a success, however, never allow yourself to be annoyed if the same thing happens to you!

If you feel brave and think that honesty is always the best policy, you can even go to a company and say exactly what you're doing. You may get all the answers you need, or you may get shown the door with this method. Individual owners will react to this approach in different ways. It's well to remember that Diogenes searches forever for an honest person.

*Positioning Yourself*
Whatever your method, researching your competition is an essential ingredient in the recipe for success. Only by knowing what others are doing, how they are doing it, and what they are charging for it can you determine how to position yourself and your service in your market area. In your own mind, as well as in the minds of your prospective clients, try to place yourself somewhere on the scale in between the very best and the very worst producers—in other words, the most expensive and the cheapest. You can always increase your rates as your reputation and number of clients grow. It's the basic law of supply and demand that sets the ultimate price.

## Deciding Where to Set Up Shop

After you have researched the competition, your next step is to choose a physical facility. There are a lot of options. Here are a few examples.

Stephen J. Cannell has an enormous modern glass tower on a corner of Hollywood Boulevard. His name in giant blue letters crowns this edifice and brags openly about his independent production success.

Videomax, Ltd., is in an old Victorian farmhouse in rural Illinois decorated in complete contrast to the high-tech nature of video production. From the outside, one would never guess that it was a production company at all. It looks like a nineteenth-century farm, complete with red barn, machine shed, stable, hay field, and John Deere tractor.

Metavision, a very successful producer of industrial programs and music videos, started on the top floor of a K-Mart store on Third Street in Los Angeles. Its window was hidden behind the letters *a-r-t* of the glowing department store sign, and the owners joked that they were "the art behind K-Mart." More about them later in this chapter.

Some mom-and-pop operations actually operate out of a spare room or a redone garage at home. And many such producers make a reasonable living.

### Identifying Your Needs

Your choice of a building should take into account several factors. To begin with, your facility will make an initial impression on clients. If you anticipate clients' visiting your place of business frequently, then the shop has to be an advertisement of sorts. You will spend a good deal more on rent and decorations for such an operation than if you decide to take the product to the client and keep your facility just for production and office work.

A production company is not a retail business dependent on foot traffic, lots of parking, and easy access from public transportation. Therefore, the decision of where to locate is much easier than if you were opening a shoe store or a camera shop. Because your overhead—monthly rent, insurance premiums, utilities, and so on—is a primary factor in whether you can expect to make it (as discussed later under

"Capitalizing the Business"), you can look off the beaten track for an adequate office.

Although you do not want to locate in a run-down area for quite obvious reasons, you might well find an old house for rent in a suitably zoned part of town. If so, you can conduct a small-volume operation with reasonable certainty that you won't be disturbing residential neighbors, and frequently you can find amazing bargains on long-term leasing of older houses. In many cities, downtown businesses are suffering because of the trend toward large shopping malls, and therefore you may be able to find good leasing bargains downtown. In some sections of the country, the urban shopping malls that supplanted the original downtowns have fallen on hard times as malls have moved out to strips along interstates and highways. Truly remarkable bargains in these places can be found in terms of large amounts of space for small amounts of money. Video Trend Associates in Oshkosh, Wisconsin, moved from its former location in a spare bedroom of its owner's home to the former Park Plaza Mall in the heart of town. The owner was able to rent enough space at a nominal fee to have a large studio, where he produced a celebrity athlete cooking show featuring the wife of all-pro Green Bay Packer defensive end Reggie White.

Spend some time driving around town, taking note of promising locations. Read the classified ads in your local papers, and call on several Realtors. Most important, be sure to check with the local zoning commission to ensure that you will be allowed to operate a service business from the place you choose.

The amount of square footage you will need is entirely dependent on the nature of your operation. If you think your business will require studio space, for example, then you have to consider ceiling height to enable the installation of a lighting grid. If you anticipate any studio lighting, the electrical wiring must be much greater than most commercial or residential properties are equipped to handle. The cost of rewiring will be a major overhead and operating budget factor. If you think your operation is going to require a studio, then you should investigate industrial buildings, such as former factories and warehouses.

### Practical Considerations

If your company is going to do most of its production on location, using rental studios when necessary, then your building decision is simplified. Many independent producers have no permanent full-time staff; they simply hire freelance technical help on a per-project basis. Others keep a regular staff in-house and on salary. Your operation will probably fall between the extremes possible on both ends of the scale. No matter where your operation fits in, here is a list to help you determine your physical requirements.

- *How much square footage will you need?* At a minimum, you should have enough space for a private office for yourself, a reception area, private working areas for each of the employees you anticipate hiring (or using frequently), a screening/conference room, and storage space for equipment, supplies, videotapes, and so on. Bear in mind that much of today's high-tech equipment, as well as those precious tapes, requires air conditioning and dehumidifying if you want to keep it in top shape.
- *What kind of parking is available?* You should make sure that the location has a parking lot or plenty of free and unlimited parking on the street for you, your employees, and clients. If you anticipate buying a van, a grip truck, or any other specialized vehicles, then you will also need to consider garage facilities for them.
- *What about remodeling?* It is unlikely that you will walk into a former store or old house and find it suited to production needs. When considering a lease arrangement, find out if the landlord is willing to remodel to suit your needs at no cost to you. The remodeling may become a bargaining chip for reducing your monthly rent if

you are handy and can do the work yourself. Don't be afraid to try a little old-fashioned horse trading or haggling here. Remember that you are going to be spending a considerable portion of your income on the physical facility and that you have the right and the obligation as a businessperson to try to get the best deal possible.

- *Why is this the right location for you?* This is the main question to answer for yourself. The worst thing you can do is to make do, thinking that you will move into the right place later on. A business has to project an image of stability, and staying at one location for a long time helps foster that image. Moreover, once you are in business, it is tremendously expensive to pick up the staff, the office furniture, the equipment, and so forth to make a move across town.

Take some time making your location decision. Don't rush into it in the excitement of getting started. A few extra days or weeks of waiting and doing some soul-searching and property searching can make your move a good one. Remember that you are going to be spending much more time at the business than you are at home, so you want the place to make you—as well as your employees and clients—feel good about being there.

## Finding Equipment Suppliers

The next step, now that you've assessed the marketplace and the competition and found a physical facility to suit your needs, is to take stock of your suppliers. Every businessperson needs to know what to get and how to get it at the best possible price. As an independent video producer, your requirements go beyond those of a retail business, which has to consider only stock, office supplies, and so on.

In your business, you must also consider a dizzying array of equipment coming out each year that is doing three things simultaneously: getting better in quality, getting lower in price, and making what preceded it the year before obsolete. Keeping up with technological innovations and suppliers in your field is one of your primary tasks.[3]

You can fill file cabinets with the literature and brochures that manufacturers and distributors are generally happy to send you on request. Even if you are not really in the market to buy anything, it is a vital part of your job as an independent producer to know what the technological innovators are doing to provide new and improved tools for your trade. Plan on attending the annual National Association of Broadcasters (NAB) convention in Las Vegas. It take place in April, and every manufacturer in the world puts on elaborate displays of existing devices and premieres the latest wave of futuristic toys.

Acquisition tools, usually a combination of camera and recorder, are becoming more and more miniaturized and less and less expensive. It is perfectly feasible for any producer on a very modest budget—for a total outlay of around $25,000 to $40,000—to own a good-quality, three-chip video camcorder, a simple-to-use, nonlinear editor, and a very satisfactory audio board with mixing and equalization capability. For less than the cost of many very ordinary automobiles, you can equip a business with production gear that is more than adequate for a great many small-market productions, such as news features, weddings, corporate and industrial training videos, depositions, and family histories. Beyond this level, the cost of owning the latest and best digital, broadcast-quality gear can run as high as your imagination and your ability to pay.

### Equipment Rentals

Even if you decide to own some production equipment, it is unlikely that you will go much beyond a few basic tools. It makes no sense for a producer who does only three or four major productions a year, filling in the remainder of the time with less complex and smaller projects, to own lots of expensive equipment that requires maintenance and that, when it is not being used in the field, represents a net loss.

Throughout the country, there are rental houses that have everything you need, from a second camera to a complete mobile production studio (as discussed in Chapter 1). Your production library should include the current catalog from each rental house; prices and availability usually change annually.

### Credit Accounts

You will want to establish a credit account with the primary rental house you choose, just as you will with all of your other suppliers. Most business credit accounts are payable 30 days after the billing date. In some cases, you will find 60- and 90-day payment schedules that allow you to collect on your accounts receivable before you have to pay your accounts due. Even if you have collected your money, it's wise to leave it in an interest-bearing account for as long as you can before paying it out to someone else!

A business's credit is absolutely essential to its success. Because video production equipment is so expensive and because this business has its share of fly-by-night operators who abuse the privilege of credit, it is not easy to get a credit account with a rental house. You will be required in most cases to provide the following:

Your personal credit history
Your business credit history, with three references from banks or other suppliers with whom you have accounts (this can be a catch-22 if you are just starting out)
Proof of insurance for the maximum value of all the equipment you intend to rent
A substantial cash deposit if you have no business credit history

Once you establish a credit account with your rental house, maintain it as arranged (of course, this axiom applies across the board to all of your suppliers). If your name ever pops up in a computer file because you skipped a bill, your future in this business may be in jeopardy. The world of production is really very small, in spite of the number of people in it. And a reputation is a terrible thing to waste.

### Expectations

If you are paying your bills on time, you can expect and demand that the equipment you rent be in top-notch condition and be available on time, every time. Have your technicians check each piece as it is unpacked to be sure that it operates as it should. If it doesn't, or if it didn't arrive when promised, call immediately and let the rental house know. Every good rental house wants you to be totally satisfied. If yours doesn't, choose another one.

A final note about renting: In most cities, you will also find office furnishings and machines available for rent or lease rather than purchase. Exercising this option can mean a major reduction in the amount of capital you will need up front to begin a business.

## Locating Technicians and Talent

Put simply, you can't make a video on your own. This is a group art form, a creative co-op. You need a stable source of people—actors, videographers, assistant directors, editors, recordists, and gaffers, for example—in order to produce. A final consideration when deciding on your location, then, is the availability of freelance technical people and talent.

### Technicians

There are regional business offices for the trade unions and guilds described in Chapter 1. If you are a union contract signatory, help for any project is only a phone call away. Don't overlook the colleges or universities in your area. Many schools these days have programs in video and multimedia production. Although students in these programs are not ready to perform as top-level technicians, they can be used as production assistants, assistant camera operators, computer graphic operators, and so forth. Their instructors, many of whom left the professional world to teach but who retain very high quality skills, are also

available to work, during summers and holidays in particular, for fees considerably lower than full-time freelancers. The local school's department of communication can be an incredible business asset right there in your community. Do not make the common mistake, however, of presenting "opportunities" to these folks that do not come with a paycheck attached. It's an insult to ask a professor who has paid dues over the years to work for Bozo Productions for free, as "an opportunity to get some real-world experience." It's equally asinine to expect that a student can give you professional quality results—for free or any other way. They are not professionals precisely because they are students. If they could make competent commercial videos, they would not be in school.

Considering all this, it is important that the place you choose to locate is close enough to the labor pool to make it profitable for you to pay transportation costs for every freelancer you will need. If the nearest reliable pool is several hundred miles away from your location but you believe that your choice is suitable in every other respect, then you should consider hiring a small, full-time technical staff.

Devise a current and projected personnel plan to help determine your labor needs. Consider what skills you have, what you will need, whether your employees will be salaried or hourly, and what the legal and financial ramifications will be in terms of withholding taxes, fringe benefits, and so on.

### Talent

As for talent, if you only want to do documentaries or industrial shoots featuring the actual people who work at the Land O' Lakes cheese factory or the Komatsu Dresser plant, for example, talent will not be a problem. If you look forward to doing television spot commercials or any other kind of production (like the Jones Hotels training video) with actors, then you need to know where to find talent.

As with technicians, if you are a union contract signatory, then your problems can be solved by contacting SAG, AFTRA, or the American Federation of Musicians at one of their regional business offices.

For nonunion productions, you may be able to find some talent agencies that book nonunion members. Because talent agencies are really employment agencies, most states require that they be licensed. Check the appropriate bureau in your state for its requirements. Because licenses are a matter of public record, you should easily be able to find a list of licensed talent agencies.

Another option is to check with local theater groups and college drama departments, where you just might be in for a happy surprise. Like their colleagues in the technical arts, many college drama teachers are professional actors who have given up the risk and uncertain pay for the security of the academy. The fact that these performers are not in Hollywood does not mean that they lack talent. Again, don't insult them by asking them to work for free.

Placing ads in some of the trade papers and periodicals will also help you build a file of available talent. Your ad might read something like this:

> Video production company seeking talent pool for commercials and other anticipated productions. Send composite photos and resume to: My Own Production Company, address and city.

### Freelance or Permanent Staff?

There are pros and cons to using both freelance technical talent and permanent staffers. Here are some considerations you might want to mull over before you decide which way to go.

Some people feel that freelancers are not as professionally competent as those technicians who work full-time for a company. In general, this is not the case. Many freelancers are, in fact, seasoned veterans who have become tired of the rat race and prefer to operate independently, picking and choosing their jobs and their schedules.

Sam Drummy, for example, is a four-time Emmy Award–winning videographer. After working full-time for NBC for a number of years, he chucked the security of corporate life to freelance. In his mid-forties, Sam works as many days a year as he likes, makes more money than he did with the network, and splits his time between his home in the Hollywood hills and the island of Hawaii.

Although Drummy's credentials are above average, there are thousands of highly skilled craftspeople who freelance in our industry. A good way to check the qualifications of a freelancer is to look at the person's list of credits and the ubiquitous demo reel that any real pro will be happy to show you.

One major advantage of hiring freelancers is relief from much of the paperwork and financial burden of full-time employees. A freelancer is an independent contractor. You do not need to withhold state or federal income tax or pay for fringe benefits, unemployment insurance, and so on (except in the case of union members, for whom you must pay into the guild or union fund). If you pay one person more than several hundred dollars in a single year, you are required to file a Form 1090 with the IRS. (See your accountant about the continuing changes to the tax code.) Another advantage to having a freelance staff comes during slack business times when you are not obligated to pay someone a salary to sit around the shop doing little, if anything.

A major disadvantage of using freelancers is that they are not always available when you want them. If you are scheduling a shoot, you may have to do so around the freelancers' previous bookings. If a project springs to life suddenly and you're used to working with a certain videographer who happens to be in Borneo that month, you'll have to settle for a different shooter.

To avoid delaying a shoot while you wait for the return of your itinerant freelancer, make a file from which you can draw several good people in each category. Sample the demo reels or other material from a large number of people, and keep data on the best prospects in your computer files. It is unlikely that all of them will be on assignment at the same time.

Full-time staffers are beneficial for a number of reasons. To begin with, it is easier to develop a familylike atmosphere with a permanent staff. If people feel that they are part of the group, working toward shared, long-range goals, you can expect them to work longer hours, sometimes not necessarily for extra pay. Because they are part of your team, involved in the day-to-day operations and expectations of the company, you can also expect to lead them into a consistent modus operandi and point of view—preferably your own.

Planning becomes easier when you have a core of dependable people on hand at all times. Because everyone is working for the good of the company and not just for their daily rate, you can share ideas and tasks and thus accomplish more.

Permanent staffers are more likely to make contributions of time and talent and ideas to promote the common cause, provided that you make them feel like integral parts of the company and not mere functionaries working for paychecks. An example of this attitude comes from one of the permanent staffers at Aaron Spelling Productions in Hollywood. "The only way someone's going to get a job here," he said, "is for one of us to die or retire. Aaron doesn't have a company; he has a family. And we're all part of it."[4] Certainly, this type of employee attitude contributes to the continuing phenomenal success of this independent producer.

In the final analysis, as with most producers, you will probably end up using a mix of freelance and permanent help. The beginning producer simply can't afford to take on a large staff. At the outset, you will use freelancers almost exclusively. As your company grows, take on permanent staff in the most vital areas. Your profit-and-loss sheet will dictate, to some extent, just how large your permanent core will become. Affordability is not the only criterion to consider, however. Here is one final story:

Theo Mayer and Peter Inova of Metavision experienced a very rapid surge of growth early in their history. From their humble beginnings (with $500 in capitali-

zation and an occasional freelancer), they soon found their company with 24 full-time employees.

"While we were making tons of money," Mayer said, "we were also working 18- to 24-hour days, seven days a week, and spending it all just to support the tremendous overhead we found ourselves with."[5]

Inova agreed. "Somewhere along the way we found that we'd forgotten why we wanted to be in business in the first place. We were doing jobs we didn't like, Theo was out pounding the streets every day bringing in more, and one day we just sat down and looked at each other and asked why we were doing this."[6]

"We went into business," Mayer concluded, "to do good, creative things, to have fun, and to take care of ourselves, our families, and our partners. We never dreamed of being responsible for 20 or 30 other people and their families along the line."[7]

In the late eighties, Mayer and Inova, caught in the paradox of too much success, fired most of Metavision's 24 permanent staff. They sold the bulk of the equipment they had purchased to support the large operation and returned to their original goals, taking on only as much work as they could handle personally, with freelance help as needed. As a result, they both grew artistically, and in different directions. During the nineties, they left K-Mart and moved to a new location out of the hustle and sham of Hollywood and into the hills of Burbank. There, slowly and methodically, they increased their business. Peter Inova submerged himself in computer animation and graphics, exploring the medium in its infancy and maturing with it. Mayer grew more and more into the business side of the merging technologies. The company swelled in the nineties with multimillion-dollar billings and projects so technically sophisticated that they had to invent new equipment.

The single entity of Metavision split into two: one lead by Theo Mayer inventing and selling hardware, the other pioneering new ways to merge the new technologies. Their most famous project to date is the Space Lounge at the Las Vegas Hilton Hotel, where visitors have been known to get motion sick so realistic is the effect of being in space—space conceived, invented, and projected by Peter Inova and his small team of computer geniuses. Metavision is today the oldest studio in Hollywood still owned by its founders.

## Registering and Licensing the Business

The regulation of small business varies from city to city, state to state, and business to business. In general, though, you can anticipate needing a business license from your city, town, or county.

At the state level, you will probably need to register under a fictitious name or "doing business as" law unless your full name appears in the title of the business. Most states will also require you to file for a sales-and-use tax number.

The issue of a name deserves some serious consideration. Your ego may want your name on the shingle out front, but think about the possible negative consequences. If the company goes belly up or has a calamitous life fraught with bad debt and worse publicity, you don't want your name to be associated with all that baggage. Generally, it is best to choose a fictitious name for the firm. The name should have something to do, even if indirectly, with what you do. It is currently fashionable for production and postproduction houses to call themselves bizarre names, like Lost Planet or Swell Pictures, and there is a practical reason for it. You want to adopt a name that is slightly whimsical or nondescriptive in conjunction with a word or phrase that is descriptive of the services provided. Videomax, Saddle Tramp Video, and Video-It are pretty good examples. They have a touch of whimsy but do not confuse the public about what they are.

The reason for a touch of lightness is quite practical. Service marks that are purely descriptive, such as Joe's Video Productions, cannot be protected legally from use by others unless it can be proved that the name has acquired a secondary meaning, which is nearly impossible for a new business. Once you settle on the right name, get an attorney to check with your state's office of the secretary of state to find out if anyone has chosen that name first. Do the same with the county clerk for each county in which you intend to do business.

Finally, contact the Internal Revenue Service for a federal employer's identification number and a "Going into Business Tax Kit." The latter is a free service from your friendly tax collector.

In some places around the country, you will find the business climate to be very hospitable, with a minimum of red tape to cut through. In other places, you will find the restrictions so frustrating that you may have to add psychotherapy bills to your overhead. In spite of what you may hear about "deregulation," some regulation still exists, and you will have to deal with governing bodies as you embark on your business venture. Although there is no rule that you must have a lawyer to go into business, it is very prudent to talk to one, and you are advised to do so at the outset. Interview several lawyers to find one with whom you are compatible because your relationship with him or her will probably be a long one. A lawyer can take care of many headaches, not only as you launch your business, but as you operate from day to day and year to year.

## Capitalizing the Business

A business should be able to keep its doors open for a minimum of one to two years from the date it starts without making one dime of profit. Undercapitalization is the number two reason for business failure, only a fraction behind poor management!

Acquiring capital and accounting for it are the final phases before opening the doors of your new business. All of the things you have done up to now will bear on the success (or failure) of your capitalization efforts. There are several sources to consider when looking for money. It's important to explore all of your options before deciding on the right one for you. Here are some sources:

- *Personal savings:* This is the primary source of capital for most new businesses.
- *Friends and relatives:* Many entrepreneurs look to private sources for capital. Often, money is loaned by friends and family interest free or at much less than the going rate. Remember that borrowing from friends can mean the end of the friendship should your deal go sour.
- *Banks and credit unions:* These are the most desirable sources of funding in this country. You must have a sound proposal and business plan before approaching a bank or credit union, however.
- *Venture capital firms:* These firms help expanding companies grow in exchange for equity or partial ownership.

Use the information you have compiled thus far to develop a business plan. Figure 3–1 is a worksheet from the SBA's *Checklist for Going into Business,* which will help you determine the amount of money you will need to start. Remember also that the SBA itself has a number of programs to help finance new and expanding small businesses. Contact the administration early on and often for help.

### Choosing the Right Legal Setup

The right type of capitalization depends on the type of business setup you choose. The three legal forms are sole proprietorship, partnership, and corporation. The form of business you pick depends on such things as your personal financial status, the number of employees you anticipate, the risk involved, and your tax situation. Consult your lawyer and accountant for advice on which form is best for you.

A sole proprietorship means that the full burden of capitalization and all of the risk are yours. A partnership can help you share these, but unless it is a limited partnership, you will give up sole control of your destiny. The standard corporate structure may make you accountable to a board of directors and can be frightfully restricting to your freedom, especially if you issue stock to the public.

There is now a setup called the Subchapter S corporation, which is designed for small businesses. This type of incorporation treats profits or losses by the corporation as ordinary income or loss to the individual stockholder. You find investors who need tax write-offs during a period when you are most likely to suffer losses. As you gain financial ground, you begin to buy back the stock. At any time, you are free to change to a regular corporate structure. One of the beauties of this arrangement is that in order for investors to keep their tax advantages, they must let you direct all the affairs of the business as you see fit.

Internal Revenue Service Code Section 1244 allows you, in this situation, to treat losses on the stock of a "small business corporation" as deductions against ordinary income. IRS publications 542, 544, and 550 have sections discussing this regulation. Because the rules for taking advantage of Subchapter S and 1244 are involved and very specific, read all of the publications and talk them over with a tax attorney before you decide.

### Possible Funding Sources

Aside from incorporation with stock offerings, there are four major sources of funding your business. You (or you and a partner) can (1) put up the money yourselves, or you can secure loans from (2) a bank, (3) the SBA, or (4) the Veterans Administration (VA).

According to University of Wisconsin business professor Richard Krueger, financing through a local bank is the most likely to succeed. Banks like to see local business starts because they help keep money in the area. This is especially true if your business enhances or stimulates other businesses in your area.

The SBA has money to loan, but the amount available is limited and can be affected by political factors from one administration to another. For the most part, the following remain constant:

| Estimated Monthly Expenses<br><br>Item | Your estimate of monthly expenses based on sales of<br>$ _____<br>per year | Your estimate of how much cash you need to start your business<br>(See column 3.) | What to put in column 2<br>(These figures are typical for one kind of business. You will have to decide how many months to allow for in your business.) |
|---|---|---|---|
| | Column 1 | Column 2 | Column 3 |
| Salary of owner-manager | $ | $ | 2 times column 1 |
| All other salaries and wages | | | 3 times column 1 |
| Rent | | | 3 times column 1 |
| Advertising | | | 3 times column 1 |
| Delivery expense | | | 3 times column 1 |
| Supplies | | | 3 times column 1 |
| Telephone and telegraph | | | 3 times column 1 |
| Other utilities | | | 3 times column 1 |
| Insurance | | | Payment required by insurance company |
| Taxes, including Social Security | | | 4 times column 1 |
| Interest | | | 3 times column 1 |
| Maintenance | | | 3 times column 1 |
| Legal and other professional fees | | | 3 times column 1 |
| Miscellaneous | | | 3 times column 1 |
| **Starting Costs You Have to Pay Only Once** | | | Leave column 2 blank |
| Fixtures and equipment | | | Fill in worksheet 3 and put the total here |
| Decorating and remodeling | | | Talk it over with a contractor |
| Installation of fixtures and equipment | | | Talk to suppliers from whom you buy these |
| Starting inventory | | | Suppliers will probably help you estimate this |
| Deposits with public utilities | | | Find out from utility companies |
| Legal and other professional fees | | | Lawyer, accountant, and so on |
| Licenses and permits | | | Find out from city offices what you have to have |
| Advertising and promotion for opening | | | Estimate what you'll use |
| Accounts receivable | | | What you need to buy more stock until credit customers pay |
| Cash | | | For unexpected expenses or losses, special purchases, etc. |
| Other | | | Make a separate list and enter total |
| **Total Estimated Cash You Need to Start** | | $ | Add up all the numbers in column 2 |

**Figure 3–1** Worksheet for estimating capital needed to start a small business. (Courtesy of the U.S. Small Business Administration.)

Loan guarantees are available through the SBA.

These loans are at market rate and can have terms of up to 25 years.

Loans can be at fixed or variable rates.

Loan funds can be used for most business purposes.

The SBA's financial assistance programs are delivered through commercial lenders, generally banks, which apply to the SBA. It's easy to access information about these loans and other programs at the SBA home page on the Internet (www.sba.gov).

Although the Veterans Administration has money to lend to qualified vets for business reasons, there are two myths about VA loans. The first myth is that loans are plentiful; the second is that they are easy to get. In fact, VA loans have some requirements that are often difficult to meet, such as the stipulation that you live on the site of your business. If you can operate out of a basement, spare room, or garage, investigate the VA opportunities in your area.[8]

There are other funding sources that are often overlooked by producers. For certain projects, you can get money from private foundations, as well as from state and local governments. The following publications catalog most of the major grants that might apply to you and your production company: *The Grants Register* (St. Martin's Press, 175 Fifth Avenue, New York, NY 10010); *The Foundation Directory* and *The Foundation Grants Index* (The Foundation Center, 888 Seventh Avenue, New York, NY 10106); and *The Gold Book* (The National Endowment for the Humanities, 1100 Pennsylvania Avenue, N.W., Washington, DC 20506).

Check with your state government for information on any grants and endowments that it administers. Nationwide, millions of dollars are given out annually for media projects, many of which you have seen on public television. There is no reason why you can't attract some of this money to fund worthwhile projects of your own. Writing proposals for grants is an art; many colleges offer classes in this spe-

cialty. Some granting institutions will give you copies of previously successful grant applications to use as a model for your own.

### Preparing the Presentation Package

Regardless of which money source you choose, you will have to make a presentation to the prospective lender. The following outline shows the format followed for a typical SBA-guaranteed bank loan:

**I.** Summary

**A.** Nature of the business. In this section, write a statement summarizing what your research of the market has shown. The full report will be in your business plan.

**B.** Amount and purpose of loan. Using the SBA worksheet in Figure 3–1, estimate how much it will cost to set up and operate your business for a year.

**C.** Repayment terms. Estimate a reasonable time and amount for repayment that will not cripple your operation.

**D.** Equity share of borrower (debt-equity ratio after loan). It is extremely unlikely that any lending institution will grant the entire amount. You will be expected to have up to one-half the total as your show of good faith. Equity in your business does not have to be cash. It can include any equipment or facilities that you have on hand. Signed contracts or letters of intent from clients or distributors may also be bankable equity.

**E.** Security or collateral. List here all of the equipment, including office furnishings, that you intend to purchase with the loan. Get market value estimates and quotes on these costs. You may also be required to put up some of your personal property as collateral, such as a second mortgage on your home. (Be very sure of your chances for success before going that far!)

**II.** Personal information

This information is provided for all corporate officers and directors and for any individuals owning 20 percent or more of the business.

  **A.** Education, work history, and business experience.

  **B.** Credit references. This includes your personal references (credit cards, automobile financing, etc.) as well as any business credit you have established.

  **C.** Income tax statements for the past three years.

  **D.** Personal financial statement. Your statement must not be more than 60 days old.[9]

**III.** Firm information (for whichever is applicable: A, B or C)

  **A.** New business.

    **1.** Business plan.

    **2.** Life and casualty insurance coverage.

    **3.** Lease or purchase agreement on facility.

    **4.** Partnership, corporation, or franchise papers if applicable.

  **B.** Business acquisition (buyout of existing firm).

    **1.** Information on acquisition.

    (a) Business history, including seller's name and reasons for sale.

    (b) Current balance sheet.

    (c) Current profit-and-loss statements.

    (d) Business federal income tax returns for the past three to five years.

    (e) Cash-flow statements for previous year.

    (f) Copy of sales agreement with breakdown of inventory, fixtures, equipment, licenses, goodwill, and other costs.

    (g) Description and dates of permits already acquired.

    (h) Lease or purchase agreement on facility.

    **2.** Business plan.

    **3.** Life and casualty insurance.

    **4.** Partnership, corporation, or franchise papers if applicable.

  **C.** Existing business expansion.

    **1.** Information on existing business.

    (a) Business history.

    (b) Current balance sheet.

    (c) Current profit-and-loss statements.

    (d) Cash-flow statements for previous year.

    (e) Federal income tax statements for last three to five years.

    (f) Lease agreement and permit data.

    **2.** Business plan.

    **3.** Life and casualty insurance.

    **4.** Partnership, corporation, or franchise papers if applicable.

**IV.** Projections

  **A.** Profit-and-loss projections (monthly, for one year) and explanation of projections.

  **B.** Cash-flow projections (monthly, for one year) and explanation of projections.

  **C.** Projected balance sheet (for one year after loan) and explanation of projections.

### The Five Cs

After you have prepared your loan package, take a critical look at yourself to see whether you match the typical good-risk candidate for a major loan. You can bet that your friendly neighborhood loan officer will, using the "five Cs":

- *Character:* If you have a history of being honest, have a good credit rating, are experienced in the field of video production, are ambitious, and communicate well, you are a person of good character.
- *Capital and collateral:* Your financial statement is your guide here.

- *Capacity:* Assess your expectations and the funding source you expect to use to repay the loan in a timely manner.
- *Conditions:* The conditions here are your health and the marketability of your products and services versus those of the competition.
- *Consequences:* Will the loan be truly productive? Can you demonstrate to the lender that both you and it will benefit in the long and short term?

If your self-assessment is honestly positive, then you have an excellent chance of convincing your banker to help make your production company a reality. Keep your expectations conservative, though. Any debt in business, just as in personal life, should be acquired cautiously. Too much can cripple you; too little may restrict your ability to function.

## Accounting and Record Keeping

Accounting and record keeping are often the weak links in an otherwise good operation. These two vital elements organize and control your business. It is essential to keep good records for these reasons:

To let you know if the business is making or losing money

To enable you to make solid management decisions

To obtain more financing

To comply with local, state, and federal laws and regulations

To make your case if you wish to sell the operation

Because accounting has become so specialized and experiences a constant stream of changing rules and legislation (especially in the tax area), the best thing to do is to put yourself in the hands of a competent accounting firm. Your accountant will provide you with a bookkeeping system or will provide regular monthly service, depending on your needs, and will be up to the minute on the law. Your accountant will also determine the best method for depreciating your fixed assets, show you how to keep every penny allowable by law from the tax collector, and worry about many of the details that would otherwise get in the way of your creativity.

At a minimum, your records will include cash receipts, cash disbursements, sales, purchases, payroll, equipment owned, equipment rented, inventory, accounts receivable, accounts payable, sales tax, and withholding tax for you and your employees.

You may be required to make quarterly tax statements in April, June, September, and January. You may also have to make a major payment to the IRS based on your estimated profit for the year if you are not on a tax withholding system.[10]

Once you have a good accountant, your role in accounting and record keeping will require little more than reconciling your bank statement monthly, depositing all income in a timely manner, and getting on with your work.

Be certain that you keep your personal records and accounts separate from those of the business. Failure to do so is an invitation to trouble. Remember that the business is not you; your salary—along with all of the other expenses—come out of the business. That's why you must program a profit margin for the company into every budget.

In 1974, the Commission on Federal Paperwork reported that small business in America was paying between $15 and $20 billion a year to fill out reports and forms. In the years since then, business has been somewhat relieved through a couple of acts and executive orders (see Figures 3–2 and 3–3).

In spite of all this, reporting remains a major annoyance as well as a sometimes costly endeavor. Find out what forms you will be required to file, and set up a calendar of report due dates so you know when they have to be completed. The bigger your operation, the more forms will be required. Check with your state for its requirements.

**Figure 3–2** SBA Rights to Regulatory Fairness.

## Overview of the Small Business Regulatory Enforcement Fairness Act of 1996

The Small Business Regulatory Enforcement Fairness Act (SBREFA) was enacted into law March 29, 1996.

The six key aspects of the legislation are as follows:

1 **Regulatory Compliance Simplification:** Federal agencies are required to develop comprehensive guidelines and a well-defined process to respond to small business inquiries on actions that businesses are required to take to comply with rules established by the agencies. These guidelines must be written in plain English.

2 **Equal Access to Justice Amendments:** Small businesses are given expanded authority to go to court to be awarded attorney's fees and costs when an agency has been found to be excessive in its enforcement of federal regulations.

3 **Congressional Review:** Congress is authorized to review each major rule promulgated before it can take effect.

4 **Regulatory Enforcement Reform of Penalties:** Within one year each agency shall establish a policy to provide for the

reduction and, in some circumstances, the waiver of civil penalties for violations of a regulation.

The final two key aspects most directly affect the U.S. Small Business Administration as follows:

5 **Small Business Advocacy Review Panels:** Before proposed rules are published, the Environmental Protection Agency and the Occupational Safety and Health Administration are required to establish government panels that receive input from affected small businesses and make public the panels' report as part of the record.

6 **Oversight of Regulatory Enforcement:** The SBA administrator must appoint a small business and agriculture regulatory-enforcement ombudsman and 10 small business regulatory fairness boards to comment on the enforcement activities of federal regulatory agencies. Small businesses are provided with a procedure to comment on the enforcement activity conducted by federal regulatory agencies. The national ombudsman must annually report to Congress on the findings.

## Your Rights to Fair Regulatory Enforcement

Federal agencies must establish a policy for the reduction or waiver of civil penalties for violation of a statutory or regulatory requirement. Agencies may consider ability to pay in determining penalty assessments. Policies or programs should contain the following conditions or exclusions:

- require the correction of a violation within a reasonable time,
- limit the applicability of violations discovered through small business participation in a compliance-assistance or audit program, and
- require a good-faith effort to comply with the law.

SBREFA makes certain that small businesses have a voice that will be heard by federal agencies as they go through the rule-making process. It also gives small businesses expanded opportunities to challenge an agency's final regulatory decision.

### Provision for Judicial Review

When small businesses believe a rule or regulation will adversely affect them, and the agency fails to meet its analysis and disclosure obligation under the Regulatory Flexibility Act (RFA) of 1980, they have the opportunity to seek review of an agency's compliance with the law.

The SBA's chief counsel for advocacy can become directly involved in appeals by filing amicus (friend of the court) briefs in the court proceedings brought about by the small business appealing the rule and violations of the RFA.

The chief counsel participates in the small business advocacy review panels and identifies the small entities that the panel should consult. The chief counsel also submits comments on agency proposals. These comments can be viewed on Advocacy's Home Page: http://www.sba.gov/ADVO. Concerns about proposed regulations should be addressed to the Chief Counsel of Advocacy; 409 3rd St., S.W., Suite 7800; Washington, DC 20416; or faxed to the Chief Counsel at (202) 205-6928.

## The Regional Fairness Boards

The SBA administrator is required to appoint 10 small business regulatory fairness boards. The boards are comprised of five small business owners. The 10 regional cities where they are based and the areas they cover are:

**Boston:** New England states,
**New York:** Mid Atlantic states,
**Philadelphia:** South Atlantic states,
**Atlanta:** Southeastern states,
**Chicago:** Midwestern states,
**Dallas:** Southern states,
**Kansas City:** Heartland states,
**Denver:** Rocky Mountain states,
**San Francisco:** Western states, and
**Seattle:** Northwestern states.

### The Regulatory Fairness Boards Will:

- receive a copy of your appraisal form,
- hold a follow-up meeting on your concern,
- report on significant enforcement issues, and
- reflect all concerns in their report to Congress.

### The Regulatory Fairness Boards Cannot:

- adjudicate your complaints directly, or
- reverse agency decisions.

Therefore, you should continue exercising your rights and exhausting every option you believe is in your best interest.

**Figure 3–2 (cont.)** SBA Rights to Regulatory Fairness.

## How to Register Your Concerns

Call **1-888-REG-FAIR** to obtain an appraisal form. If you have Internet capability, download the form from the SBA Home Page at **http://www.sba.gov/regfair.**

- A completed appraisal form will be reviewed by the national ombudsman and by the fairness board members in your region.
- The ombudsman may follow up with the agency, requesting an explanation of the enforcement action taken.

- The ombudsman will inform you, the business owner, and the appropriate regional fairness board of the agency's response.
- Public hearings may be held on issues that highlight significant regulatory problems or achievements of federal agencies.
- All comments received from small businesses will be reflected in the ombudsman and fairness boards' annual report to Congress.

## Major Developments Benefiting Small Business Related to Regulatory Compliance

### Chronology of the Last 20 Years

**1980 – Regulatory Flexibility Act of 1980**
The Regulatory Flexibility Act of 1980 requires each federal agency to analyze the effects of its regulations on small businesses.

**1981 – President Reagan's Executive Order**
President Reagan's Executive Order requires the Office of Management and Budget to review each new rule being promulgated to analyze the cost/benefit of that regulation.

**1993 – President Clinton's Executive Order and**
**1995 – Memorandum of Penalty Waiver**
President Clinton's Executive Order 12866 directed agencies to provide the public with meaningful participation in the regulatory process and laid the foundation for public involvement. The April 1995 Memorandum gives compliance officials more flexibility in dealing with small businesses and the authority to waive penalties and use enforcement discretion to help bring entities into compliance.

**1996 – Small Business Regulatory Enforcement**
**Fairness Act of 1996, P.L. 104-121**
The Small Business Regulatory Enforcement Fairness Act of 1996 was passed by Congress and signed into law by President Clinton on March 29, 1996. This law provides small businesses with new and meaningful ways to participate in the federal regulatory process. Specifically, it requires:

- agencies to develop written guidelines in plain English to help small businesses understand how to comply,
- Congress to review all major new rules,
- agencies to provide for the reduction and waiver of penalties imposed on small businesses,
- the creation of government small business advocacy panels to review rules proposed by EPA and OSHA and to consult with small businesses, and
- the creation of a national ombudsman and 10 regional fairness boards to monitor agency enforcement activities.

This law also provides small businesses with enhanced authority to go to court to challenge agency rules.

## How to Contact Major Agencies that Regulate Small Business & Agriculture Concerning SBREFA Issues

**Department of Agriculture** . . . . . . . . . . . . . . . .(202) 690-1516
**Department of Commerce** . . . . . . . . . . . . . . . .(202) 482-4144
**Department of Justice** . . . . . . . . . . . . . . . . . . . .(202) 514-0750
**Department of Labor** . . . . . . . . . . . . . . . . . . . . .(202) 219-9148
**Department of Transportation** . . . . . . . . . . . .(202) 366-4723

**Environmental Protection Agency** . . . . . . . . .(202) 260-5480
**Federal Energy Regulatory Commission** . . . .(202) 208-0004
**Internal Revenue Service** . . . . . . . . . . . . . . . . .(202) 622-4989
**Securities and Exchange Commission** . . . . . .(202) 942-2950
**SBA Office of the National Ombudsman** . . . .(312) 353-0880

*All of the SBA's programs and services are provided to the public on a nondiscriminatory basis.*

Federal Recycling Program    Printed on Recycled Paper

**Figure 3–2 (cont.)**   SBA Rights to Regulatory Fairness.

**U.S. Small Business Administration**
Office of the National Ombudsman
Mail Code:
409 Third Street, S.W.
Washington, DC 20416

Official Business
Penalty for Private Use, $300

# For information on your rights to regulatory fairness:

**Toll Free Number:**    **1-888-REG-FAIR**
                                    **(734-3247)**

**Website:**                **www.sba.gov/regfair**

CO-0055 (04/97)                    *Championing America's Entrepreneurs*

**Figure 3–2 (cont.)**  SBA Rights to Regulatory Fairness.

**Summary of the Ombudsman's Report to Congress**
**on**
**Regulatory Fairness**

**Introduction**

The Small Business Regulatory Enforcement Fairness Act of 1996 (SBREFA) was designed to foster a regulatory environment that is more responsive to small business. One very important goal of SBREFA is to let federal agencies know the full impact of their enforcement and compliance policies on small business. Armed with the knowledge of how their policies affect small business and the Administration's and Congress' commitment to reducing regulatory burdens, agencies will be able to accomplish their missions and support small business success.

The legislation assigned the Small Business Administration (SBA) the responsibility of creating a program through which small businesses could comment on the enforcement and compliance activities of the federal agencies that regulate them. To carry out this mission, the legislation gave the SBA Administrator the authority to appoint a National Ombudsman and ten Regional Regulatory Fairness Boards. The resulting program is called the Regulatory Fairness Program, or RegFair. SBA Administrator Aida Alvarez has made the implementation of the Regulatory Fairness Program a key part of the SBA's strategic plan.

In November of last year, the SBA Administrator appointed Peter Barca as National Ombudsman and 50 small business company owners to serve as regional Regulatory Fairness Board members. By February, the Regulatory Fairness Boards had been appropriately chartered, and the basic program tools had been created.

Over the past ten months, an enormous amount of time and energy has been spent implementing this new national program in a manner which was tailored to accommodate the unique needs of small business.

- A Federal Agency Appraisal Form was created to receive small business comments. The form was designed to be completed quickly, taking approximately ten minutes to complete.
- A structure was developed to facilitate the evaluation of federal agencies with regulatory authority over the nation's 22 million small businesses.
- Fairness Board members were prepared and educated about SBREFA. The planning meetings which ensued built a solid foundation that enabled the execution of ten major public regional Fairness Board Hearings.

By June, 1997, only eight months after the appointment of the Fairness Boards and the Ombudsman, the RegFair program was fully operational. The process for receiving comments has three goals; 1) simplicity for small businesses, 2) easy accessibility to Fairness Boards and the National Ombudsman, and 3) the process had to ensure that the Boards and the Ombudsman receive high quality feedback from small businesses on the regulatory environment.

Finally, two primary methods were created for small businesses to share their ideas, experiences and concerns with the regulatory enforcement environment: they can submit a Federal Agency Appraisal Form which can be filed confidentially or they can testify at public hearings.

**Figure 3–3** Summary of the Ombudsman's Report to Congress on Regulatory Fairness.

## Issues & Trends

Since the start of the program, the National Ombudsman and Fairness Board members convened ten regional public hearings across the country, in which over 100 small business owners representing a wide variety of small businesses, trade associations and industries offered testimony. Fairness Board members have met in planning sessions, and have held weekly conference calls with the National Ombudsman. These efforts enabled the Fairness Boards and National Ombudsman to collect a broad base of information with which to gain a good understanding of regulatory enforcement activities.

Additionally, over fifty small businesses filed completed Appraisal Forms in 1997. Of the fifty comments filed, SBREFA was applicable to 33, meaning they involved enforcement or compliance activity undertaken by a federal regulatory agency with regard to a small business.[1] The following shows an agency distribution of the comments.

| | | |
|---|---|---|
| Internal Revenue Service | 8 | |
| Environmental Protection Agency | 7 | |
| Federal Energy Regulatory Commission | 3 | |
| U.S. Department of Agriculture | 3 | |
| U.S. Department of Justice | 2 | |
| U.S. Department of Defense | 2 | |
| U.S. Department of Labor | 2 | |
| Small Business Administration | 2 | |
| Federal Communications Commission | 1 | |
| Food & Drug Administration | 1 | |
| Health Care Financing Administration | 1 | |
| U.S. Department of Transportation | 1 | |
| U.S. Post Office | 1 | |
| | | |
| Total | 34 | |

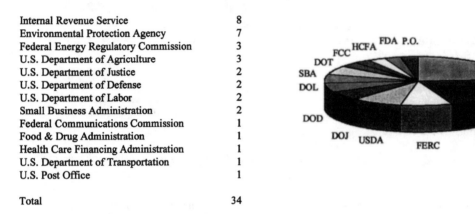

NOTE: Two federal agencies were named in one small business comment, therefore, this table shows a total of 34 small business comments.

The comments and testimony offered by small businesses show that many of the same issues with agency regulations and compliance activities are surfacing across the country and across industries. The National Ombudsman and Fairness Boards have identified four common themes in the regulatory environment that are faced by small businesses; they are:

- Agencies change their rules in the middle of the game.
- Agencies disregard the economic or other consequences of their actions on small businesses.
- Small businesses often get ensnared in conflicting regulatory requirements when two federal agencies' jurisdictions overlap.
- Small businesses fear agency retaliation.

---

[1] Of the seventeen comments which were not covered by SBREFA, eight did not involve enforcement action, four were state agency actions, one was referred to SBA's Office of Advocacy, one was referred to the IRS Taxpayer Advocate, one did not report a problem, one the client did not want to pursue and one was anonymous.

2

**Figure 3–3 (cont.)**  Summary of the Ombudsman's Report to Congress on Regulatory Fairness.

*Changing the Rules In the Middle of the Game*

Small business owners claim that agencies enforce regulations inconsistently because they change their interpretations, enforcement methods or personnel during enforcement activity. Businesses complain that there is often little or no notice given by the agency that their interpretation or methods have changed until after a fine or penalty is handed down.

*Agencies Disregard the Economic or Other Consequences of their Actions on Small Businesses*

Testimony before the regional Fairness Boards indicates that some small business owners believe federal regulatory agencies are unaware of the impact of regulations on small businesses and at times do not appreciate the effects of their actions on small businesses.

*Small Businesses get Ensnared in Conflicting Regulatory Requirements when Two Federal Agencies' Jurisdictions Overlap.*

This theme, which has surfaced in small business comments, in testimony offered at public hearings, and in the Fairness Board members' daily interactions with other small business owners, appears to be commonly experienced throughout the small business community. At times, small businesses are unaware that they need to conform their activities or certain aspects of their operations to the regulations of multiple agencies.

*Small Businesses Fear Agency Retaliation*

At the Fairness Board Hearings in Denver, Colorado and Seattle, Washington, the state Directors of the National Federation of Independent Business (NFIB) testified that many of their small business members do not want to identify themselves because they think that SBREFA and the Regulatory Fairness Boards are just a sounding board and that their business will be the subject of some further enforcement action. Concerns regarding retaliation were also expressed at two Congressional field hearings in Kansas City, Missouri and Great Falls, Montana.

The National Ombudsman and Fairness Board have addressed small business concerns about possible retaliation by drafting the Appraisal Form to assure small businesses that their identities would be confidential, unless they choose a more open disclosure. Confidentiality levels chosen by small businesses filing comments will be strictly upheld by the Fairness Boards and the National Ombudsman.

Section V of the report includes examples which illustrate these common themes using actual statements by small businesses to the RegFair Program through public testimony or Federal Agency Appraisal Forms filed under the condition of full disclosure. *Cases in this report are presented only for illustrative purposes. Most are pending agency comment and represent only the small businesses' perception of events.* They are presented as part of this report to convey to Congress some of the perceptions and experiences small businesses are reporting to the Fairness Boards and the National Ombudsman.

The cases, combined with the experience gained over the first year of operation, highlighted ten key policy recommendations to the National Ombudsman and Fairness Boards.

**Figure 3–3 (cont.)**  Summary of the Ombudsman's Report to Congress on Regulatory Fairness.

### Recommendations

The ten key policy recommendations, as identified by the Fairness Boards and the National Ombudsman, include the five following major recommendations:

- Agencies should be more aggressive in informing small businesses when they change or amend the rules, processes, or regulations that affect small businesses specifically.

- Agencies should develop an expedited review process in circumstances where their actions may have a severely negative impact or threaten small businesses' survival. Additionally, time limits should be instituted to restrict the length of time agencies may take to review the circumstances of a case and issue some kind of a response.

- Agencies should build on the Administration's policy to evaluate federal agency employees based on their efforts to ensure small businesses' compliance with federal regulations, rather than on the number of fines they collect. Also, agencies should include factors which could lead to a negative rating for employees who issue citations or penalties without careful and objective review of the actual circumstances of each case.

- Agencies must adopt and follow policies and procedures which make it clear to small businesses that they will not face retaliation for raising concerns about agency compliance and enforcement activities. While the National Ombudsman can assure small businesses that he will not reveal their identities when dealing with federal agencies, small businesses seeking resolution directly from an agency should be equally assured that no retaliation will be taken for asserting their rights.

One final, overriding recommendation for all federal agencies is the following suggestion:

- All agencies should place an executive summary on the cover of every major notice sent to small businesses to make them immediately aware of whether action is required or whether the notice is informational, the purpose of the publication, and to which businesses or industries it applies.

### Agency Assessment

SBREFA requires agencies to work with the National Ombudsman to develop a means to inform small businesses about their right to comment directly on enforcement or compliance activities (Section 222). Agency response to this language in the Act was used as a determining factor for the Boards and National Ombudsman in appraising agency progress.

Agencies can easily comply with this requirement by informing their small business customers of the Regulatory Fairness Program. However, in order to make this information meaningful to a small business owner who is focused on running a business, the information must be presented at the time of an enforcement or compliance action, as well as in general information provided by each agency.

The National Ombudsman wrote to each of 34 federal regulatory agencies identified as having regulatory authority over small businesses, and asked them to present information about the RegFair Program to their small business customers at the time of an enforcement or compliance action.

**Figure 3–3 (cont.)** Summary of the Ombudsman's Report to Congress on Regulatory Fairness.

As of December 15, 1997, 22 agencies acknowledged that request and 13 responded that they have or plan to integrate information about the Regulatory Fairness Program into materials distributed at the time of enforcement or compliance action. These agencies are clearly moving toward a more cooperative regulatory environment for their small business customers and have earned appropriate recognition of this fact.

The following agencies have agreed to integrate information about the Regulatory Fairness Program into materials distributed at the time of enforcement or compliance action.

- Commodity Futures Trading Commission
- Consumer Product Safety Commission
- U.S. Customs Service
- Federal Trade Commission
- Food & Drug Administration
- U.S. Department of Health and Human Services
- U.S. Department of Housing & Urban Development

- U.S. Department of the Interior
- Internal Revenue Service
- Securities and Exchange Commission
- Small Business Administration
- U.S. Department of State, Office of Small & Disadvantaged Business Utilization
- U.S. Department of Transportation

These agencies deserve the highest possible marks for their efforts to inform small businesses about their new rights to regulatory fairness. The IRS, in particular, deserves recognition as the first agency to agree to inform their small business customers about the process.

**Early Signals**
Because the Federal Agency Appraisal Form has been in use for only five months, the Fairness Boards and the National Ombudsman have a limited number of Appraisal Forms and agency responses. To date, a total of 50 small businesses filed completed Appraisal Forms with the RegFair Program. Of those 50, SBREFA was applicable to 33, meaning they involved enforcement or compliance activity undertaken by a federal regulatory agency with regard to a small business. Additionally, 60 small businesses initiated cases, but did not file completed Appraisal Forms.

This report provides general observations about agency activities and clarifies how information on these activities will be collected next year.

One general observation is that OSHA has positively influenced small businesses' perception of their regulatory enforcement efforts. This observation was indicated to Fairness Board members and the National Ombudsman by testimony at public hearings, small business comments and information provided by the agencies.

OSHA was praised at the public hearings for its efforts to change its approach to small businesses. One example of OSHA's responsiveness is a very positive pilot program developed for the home building industry. To date, the RegFair program has not received any negative comments that address enforcement or compliance issues with OSHA.

**Figure 3–3 (cont.)** Summary of the Ombudsman's Report to Congress on Regulatory Fairness.

**Agency Progress**

Fairness Board members believe that federal agency requirements put into place by the President through Executive Orders, policy memoranda, and by legislation, are beginning to engender positive changes in the regulatory environment for small businesses. These positive changes are apparent in the new and existing agency programs designed to help small businesses comply with federal regulations. The effectiveness of the programs that have been put into place will be one focus of next year's report.

The following three agency initiatives indicate methods by which federal agencies are beginning to address their responsibilities under SBREFA and how they are changing their approaches to working with small businesses.

OSHA    The Occupational Safety and Health Administration (OSHA) of the U.S. Department of Labor challenged its offices to be more small business friendly, and its Denver office took this challenge to heart. Working with the National Association of Homebuilders, the office published a booklet called <u>Homesafe</u> to help small business home builders better comply with the regulations that affect their industry. This pilot program uses a 67-page picture book to illustrate and simplify thousands of regulations in the <u>Code of Federal Regulations</u>. The OSHA office in Denver has agreed that home builders who follow the 10-point list shown in <u>Homesafe</u> in good faith, and who do not have a history of serious OSHA violations, will not be fined if they also agree to abate any hazardous conditions identified during an inspection within a specified time limit.

EPA    In testimony at the Seattle Fairness Board hearing, the U.S. Environmental Protection Agency described programs it has developed in compliance with SBREFA, and programs developed on its own initiative predate SBREFA. Two programs earning special recognition are EPA's Project XL and the Common Sense Initiative. Both of these programs test innovative ways to achieve better, more cost effective environmental protection by cooperatively examining and implementing objectives which meet both environmental and industry objectives. According to the EPA speaker, this represents a shift in EPA thinking: Normally, EPA regulation is via the medium: air, water, land, waste, etc. However, these initiatives look at environmental issues by the impact they have on the industry, rather than by medium.

**Figure 3–3 (cont.)** Summary of the Ombudsman's Report to Congress on Regulatory Fairness.

Commerce    The National Oceanic and Atmospheric Administration (NOAA) within the U.S. Department of Commerce has an excellent civil penalty waiver /reduction program called the Fix-It Notice, or FIN. According to the agency, under the FIN program, dozens of minor, first-time violations which are technical in nature and which do not have a direct natural resource impact receive a Fix-It Notice which allows the violation to be corrected in lieu of a penalty. Fix-It Notices can be issued by either NOAA Enforcement personnel or by U.S. Coast Guard Boarding Officers acting in their deputized capacity. According to the agency, as of April 15, 1997, 186 Notices had been issued, instead of penalties, and many were issued to small entities.

These initiatives illustrate positive changes occurring within the federal environment. Fairness Board members agree that progress has been made in creating a more friendly regulatory atmosphere for small businesses. They attribute much of this progress to the 1995 White House Conference on Small Business and its follow-up activities.

**Conclusion**

The progress and results shown by the RegFair Program over the past months of actual operation are very encouraging. The RegFair Program is receiving steadily increasing numbers of Federal Agency Appraisal Forms. Press and media coverage has been rising, especially for the regional Fairness Board public hearings. The biggest challenge for the Fairness Boards and National Ombudsman is to increase public awareness of SBREFA and the RegFair process, as most small businesses in America are not aware of their new rights.

The RegFair program has established a solid foundation with which to build the next year and future years of the program. Fairness Board members remain enthusiastic about the progress of the program, and are looking forward to accelerated activity in the second year of operation. SBREFA is materializing into a valuable new tool which will produce a less burdensome system of regulation for small business.

**Figure 3–3 (cont.)**  Summary of the Ombudsman's Report to Congress on Regulatory Fairness.

# Setting and Reaching Goals

As you can see, setting up shop is not a simple task, and neither is goal setting. Goal setting is not merely an academic formality; setting and reaching goals are two of the most important elements in setting up shop.

The independent producer has to assess real, rather than wished-for (or imagined), capabilities. How ambitious can you really expect to be, given your initiative, capitalization, equipment, location, available talent, and other resources? This is all part of discovering your limitations. Only you can determine them, and doing so takes a good deal of honesty. When you know your limitations, you can establish a system for setting realistic goals and then striving to achieve them according to a regular schedule.

In your business plan, you projected some of your goals. Included in these goals are an estimate of the amount of business you hope to do, what costs you anticipate incurring, and how much income you see as a result of the successful implementation of the plan. Each month, evaluate your status in relation to that business plan.

Let's say that you expected to have four accounts in hand by the end of the first quarter and you have only two. You obviously have a problem meeting the goal you set for yourself. Analyze the situation, and determine the reasons. Perhaps you've spent too much time on one account at the expense of the others you had in mind. Maybe you've encountered sales resistance from potential clients. Get back to them, and find out what you can do to overcome it, if anything.

How did you spend your time during the period in question? Check your records. Ask yourself how much of that time was devoted to the active pursuit of those clients. If you find that much of the time was wasted on hopeless causes, putting things off until tomorrow, or dealing with problems that could have been delegated to someone else, then you need to work on using your time more produc-

tively. There's nothing hard or mysterious about this angle of the business. All it takes is the ability to assess accurately what you should be doing and then doing it.

Make a list of personal goals aside from those stated in the business plan. It may sound silly, but writing goals on paper helps to make them concrete. Here are some sample goals other producers have set for themselves:

I want to feel good about myself and my business.

I want to be financially independent in five years.

I want one month off every year to go fishing.

I want to manage my time efficiently.

I want three days off every week by the third year of this business.

I want to learn to handle stress better.

I want enough time to enjoy my family.

I want my employees to respect and like me.

I want people to know that my word is my bond.

I want to do award-winning work.

Notice that each item begins with "I want." Once you've determined your own goals, you have a basis for implementing plans to achieve them. Don't expect them to remain the same year after year, though. Establishing goals should be an ongoing process. Writing them down regularly helps you keep sight of the real ones. It also helps you recognize those goals that become less important as you continue to grow.

There is one danger in setting and keeping goals for both yourself and your business; you risk losing your flexibility. Resist this pitfall with all your might. Keep your mind open to suggestions from your employees, friends, business associates, and family, even if they don't fit your preconceived goal statement. Many opportunities have been missed by people who got so wrapped up in achieving their goals that they couldn't see that a new one presented to them might just have been better. The function of goal setting is not to cast you or your company in cement. It is to give you a touchstone on which to affirm the major reasons why you are an independent producer and a yardstick by which to measure your progress.

# Summary

As you can see, setting up shop is not a simple task. This chapter provided a method to help simplify it for you. No one can guarantee that you will make it in business, of course, but others have blazed a trail before you, and help is available.

As you begin the process, remember that the U.S. government is really on your side. Call on the Small Business Administration for free information and advice. Finally, don't be afraid to go back to school. Many universities and community colleges offer night courses in a wide variety of business subjects. You'll find them informative, frequently fun, and a good way to meet other people who may be going through the same process as you.

Being in business for yourself will require all of your skill, organizational ability, and belief in yourself. It is frightening at the outset, but if you dare to venture forth, the rewards for having done it on your own may bring you the most satisfaction you have ever known.

# Notes

1. Small Business Tax Kit, U.S. Small Business Administration, Fort Worth, TX.

2. *Starting and Operating a Business in California*, Michael D. Jenkins, The Oasis Press®/PSI Research, Portland, OR, 1995.

3. For annual listings of video equipment suppliers and manufacturers, see *The Source Annual Buyer's Guide* (New York: Broadband Information Services).

4. J. Brett Garwood, interview with the author, January 1989.

5. Theo Mayer, interview with the author, January 1984.

6. Peter Inova, interview with the author, January 1984, January 1998.

7. Theo Mayer, interview with the author, January 1984.

8. For further information on government loan sources and requirements, request the booklet *Loan Sources in the Federal Government* (Fort Worth: U.S. Small Business Administration).

9. For assistance in preparing a financial statement, see Consumer Information Report 5, *How to Prepare a Personal Financial Statement,* available from Bank of America, Consumer Information, Box 37018, San Francisco, CA 94137.

10. For a discussion of the tax ramifications of sole proprietorship, partnership, and incorporation, see Circular E of the *Employer's Tax Guide,* available from local IRS offices.

# 4

# Promoting and Marketing Your Company

There's an important business axiom that goes like this: "There are those who advertise and those who go out of business." There are no exceptions. Although advertising and promotion will not guarantee your company's success, their absence will surely cause it to fail. The challenge is figuring out how to advertise and promote a company whose business is frequently that of advertising and promoting other companies!

Unlike consumer businesses, the independent production company must reach a very specialized clientele. You aren't selling bread or Beanie Babies—tangible products with a huge number of potential buyers. If you were running a shoe store, selling a product that virtually everyone in the country needs, then advertising your product would be very simple. You would plan an annual strategy employing a media mix that includes newspapers, throwaway shopping papers, radio, and TV. You would try to reach all of the potential shoe buyers in your market and to position yourself demographically. For example, The Rack Room appeals to teen-

agers. Holmes Shoes is for the affluent, active crowd. And The Foot Locker is for every would-be Michael Jordan, Brett Favre, and Martina Hingus. Very simple.

Homing in on the potential clients for your video production house is not as simple. Production houses, like ad agencies, remain behind the scenes. They are largely unknown to the public. There aren't any credits on TV commercials to let viewers know who created them. Very few people could tell you who created the anthropomorphic Chihuahua for the taco chain or the battling beer bottles that played their own game on Super Bowl Sunday, for example. And only rarely do we get to put credits on corporate or educational projects. That leaves us looking for ways to establish our name. Placing ads in newspapers and magazines with sufficient repetition to reach our target audience is a frightfully expensive proposition that most small producers can't afford. So what do we do?

There are some conventional advertising tactics that you can use, of course. This chapter will discuss these, as well as a variety of creative methods that will promote your company at little cost to you. You'll find also several examples of effective pro-motional techniques that have been used by other producers.

# Print Advertising

Even though video production is a business that makes moving images, print of one sort or another remains a vital part of your mix. The sort of print advertising you undertake will be dictated by two main considerations: how much money you have to spend and your target market. Advertising and promotion costs must be a part of your annual operating budget. Although there are no "standard" figures for how much to include in this category of your business plan, most conventional firms budget between 5 and 15 percent of their anticipated gross receipts for advertising. If you are starting out in a highly competitive location, you may have to spend somewhat more than this amount to position yourself in the marketplace. Set a reasonable figure that fits your specific situation.

After calculating a dollar amount to spend, the next step is to figure out where to spend it. This decision will depend on your advertising strategy. That means, very simply, getting the right message to the right buyer at the right time.

There are many trade publications and journals widely circulated in our industry. Because the readership of these publications consists mainly of video producers, most of their advertising is directed at you, the producer. The ads, for the most part, are for firms that offer services and supplies for production and postproduction. If you intend to provide these services as part of your overall game plan, then these publications are a target for some print advertising. Take a look at each one. One or two might have the type of circulation appropriate for an announcement of your existence, even if you do not offer technical service. In general, there's not much use in spending money to advertise in a trade publication that goes mostly to other people in the same trade. So, pick periodicals that reach targets who need your products or services.

For example, *Successful Farming* would be a great place to advertise your video on modern farm machinery and conservation practices. *Video Systems,* the official magazine of the ITVA (Independent Television Association), however, is aimed *at* you, not *for* you. So you probably won't advertise there.

As provocative as it sounds, you have to beware of your ego here. Some producers place ads in slick magazines and periodicals simply because some big-name, big-time companies are in them also. It makes them feel important to see their names alongside that of Universal Studios or Warner Brothers. Placing an ad in a publication directed at show-biz types, such as *Variety* or the *Hollywood Reporter,* is almost pure egomania. Your friends and family may be impressed when they see your name there, but the potential client whose eye you wish to catch won't see it. The same is true if you leap in and buy quarter-page spreads in the big, slick national publications geared to the video trade. The businessperson who needs a sales promotional or training tape won't be looking for you there.

It makes more sense for you to advertise in journals and papers that reach your target market. If, for example, you plan to make your living doing video depositions for trial lawyers, place a small, tasteful ad in the journal of your state's bar association. You can make a good living in many locations doing real estate videos. Advertise for this market in the bulletins and journals of the local and regional real estate associations. The point here is simple. Choose your target, find the publication that serves that target, and advertise there.

## Designing Effective Ads

Designing an ad for your company should be simple. You know your capabilities and your limitations. You know what your pricing structure is and how it stacks up against the competition's. You have two options in print: the simple classified or the display ad. Because a classified is rather simple to construct, concentrate on designing a display ad, which can normally be run in full-, 1/2-, 1/3-, 1/4-, and 1/16-page dimensions.

Many people gifted with the ability to produce film or video have no idea about the fundamentals of print advertising. Larger publications come to your aid by providing copy-writing and layout services when you buy an ad from them. Remember that these people are professionals in their area; don't hesitate to turn the project over to them. Smaller publications don't always offer this service. They expect you to give them a camera-ready layout. All they do is shoot it, size it if necessary, and print it.[1]

In general, remember two things about making an ad. First, know the personality of the intended reader. Second, understand that your ad is in tremendous competition for the eye of that reader. If you're trying to reach conservative businesspeople, your ad must have a different feel and texture from one designed to reach creative directors at advertising agencies. With the latter, you might want to inject some humor as an indication that you recognize their position. For example, use a picture of you and your staff doing headstands with the caption, "We'll stand on our heads to get your attention!" Things like that work with creative types. The photo would be followed, of course, by copy telling creative directors just why they should pay attention to your company. With businesspeople, you have to be much more subtle in implying that you are creative. Their concern is how reliable and businesslike you are.

In any display ad, a good-quality, high-contrast photo or computer-generated graphic is almost essential as an eye-grabber. What you choose to show depends again on whom you wish to impress. A dynamic shot of you and your crew on location in a busy factory might work to attract the eye of an industrial client. A tight shot of a stylized hamburger with a futuristic video camera behind it might be the thing for one of the agencies handling fast-food accounts.

Try not to generalize. Ads that proclaim, "We do everything for everybody," usually draw a "Who are they trying to kid?" response. Evaluate your own feelings about such specious claims. Tailor your ads for each specific market. The hotel owner will feel more comfortable believing that you specialize exclusively in hotel training aids. Make the Realtor believe that all you do is real estate, and have the burger stand owner eating out of your hand because of your specialization in food. None of this implies that you can be fraudulent. If you do a wide variety of video work, do not say anything to the contrary in your advertising. It is perfectly all right, however, to talk about only one of the areas of your work in each ad.

## Repetition Counts

Once you have selected the publications that you feel will do the job, stick with them. It takes multiple insertions to reach your reader. Each publication gives you circulation figures so you can calculate your cost per reader (this "reach" is normally calculated in cost per thousand readers). Your cost per reader will be much higher than the cost per thousand for a breakfast cereal maker, obviously, because your target audience is much smaller. The return on a successful ad, however, is a great deal more than the cost of a box of Wheaties!

To increase your chances of an ad resulting in a contact and a sale, you must be able to sustain it over a series of repetitions. It will do you no good at all to place an ad once. It must appear over and over again during the course of a year. This gives your company a solid, stable image in the field. It builds one thing only: your company name.

Remember that the main function of any kind of advertising is to place the name of the advertiser in the mind of the buyer. If you want some tomato soup, the first thing that comes to your mind is probably the name Campbell's. Other companies trying to sell tomato soup know that and have to position their soups against this industry leader. One of the reasons for the Campbell's phenomenon, aside from quality and price, is that the name has been repeated over and over again for a long time in advertising. Every single product, service, or manufacturer that pops into your mind when you think of a trade name does so because of repetitive advertising.

Bear in mind that advertising alone will not sell the products, nor will it sell your production company. What it will do is establish the name of your firm in the minds of potential clients. If and when they do decide they need video production services, you will have a much better chance of getting the call or being accepted when you make inquiries than will someone who considers advertising dollars a waste of money, simply because your name is more familiar.

In the battle analogy that many businesspeople use to describe the fight for survival, advertising your name is the offshore artillery used to soften up the beachhead you hope to establish. It's as simple as that.

# Promotional Literature

There are three primary pieces of printed promotional material that you can use: business card, company letterhead, and brochure. Each is a "first-impression" item: A potential client will draw an impression of you and your company from these things. Because of this, the concept and execution of each piece of promotional material demands your best effort. If you can't draw or have trouble with basic composition, you're well advised to outsource this job to an expert. If you have limited resources and have a good eye for design, then plunge ahead on your own.

You need to think first about the image you want to project. This, in large part, is determined by the name you choose for your company. The natural tendency for many people opening a business of their own is to put their name on it. After all, it's your money, your time, your gamble, and your statement of freedom, so why not call it Sally Smith Productions if your name happens to be Sally Smith? You certainly may use your name in your business, but it is not always the best idea. Stephen J. Cannell and Aaron Spelling call their companies Cannell and Spelling, respectively, but they were successful writers-producers before they went into business for themselves. They had track records of hit shows. Their names on the front door and the letterhead meant something to prospective clients as well as to investors.

Ron Bullock from Oshkosh, Wisconsin, did not have a name that would sell. When he went into business, he chose a company name and logo designed to convey, first, a sense of what he did and, second, an image of stability and creativity.

## Business Cards

The card designed by Bullock is simple but clever (Figure 4–1). It is a conservative card because the Fox River Valley of Wisconsin, in which he does the bulk of his business, is a traditionally low-key, conservative place. It reflects, however, a growing movement toward humor and lightness in advertising through the use of a cartoon in a TV monitor.

**Figure 4–1** Ron Bullock's business card.

The card contains the basic information with emphasis on the company name. The ink is also raised, giving the card further dimension and texture. Bullock chose the name, as he says, "because I wanted to have the word *video* in it, because the word *trend* has a positive connotation to a lot of people who want to feel like they're in on something, and because the word *associates* is used in many of the businesses, such as law firms, that I wanted to attract. That word is also pertinent to my operation because I'm essentially a one-man band and I employ creative associates on a per-project basis."[2]

Bullock's use of the job title *production manager* on the card is a deliberate ploy. Although it describes the job he does on each production, it also implies that his staff is considerably larger than it really is. He could have called himself "owner," but in choosing a less egocentric job title, he has created the impression of a larger operation without crossing the line of misrepresentation. He is the production manager. He is also the owner. He chose not to broadcast the latter.

In contrast to the essentially conservative business card of Bullock's Video Trend Associates is the flashy, silver-on-silver card designed by Metavision, located in Burbank, California (Figure 4–2). Industrial and entertainment giants in Southern California are Metavision's prime target clients; therefore, the card is used to present an image of size and high tech. With this metallic image, it is not surprising that Metavision did the incredible

Space Lounge attraction at the Las Vegas Hilton Hotel in 1998.

The simple business card is not as simple as you might think. It can be packed with persuasive power. Done poorly, with no attention to detail, it can be just another economy print job that ends up in the circular file of potential clients. It is your first and most lasting printed impression. Give its design all the care you'd give to producing any creative project. Figure 4–3 presents a sampling of cards for you to analyze.

## Letterhead

Your company letterhead, of course, follows the design of the business card.

## Brochures

A brochure serves two functions. First, it is a summary of your company's capabilities. If you leave it with the client after a sales meeting, it should reinforce what you or your sales representative has said. The second function of this document is more important. The brochure is the graphic representation of the quality and creativity that you want your company to project. It is, in short, your image on paper.

The design and execution of a brochure is an artistic endeavor in itself. Very few producers have the training in graphic arts to be able to do that job. For this most important piece of printing, consult the specialists in your area. Look at several samples of their work. Choose the style that most closely fits your own personality and the image you want your company to project. If you can't afford to hire a professional designer, study a number of brochures, pick the one you like, and try to emulate it. In Figure 4–3 you'll find a clear statement of design purpose and some samples from one of the country's leading young graphic designers, Lisa Romanowski. She owns Roman Design in Golden, Colorado (roman@ccentral.com), and has clients throughout the United States. She writes:

**Figure 4–2** Metavision's business card.

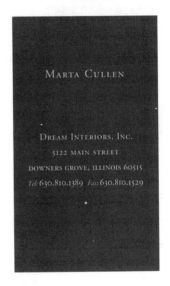

**Figure 4–3** Sample cards designed by Lisa Romanowski of Roman Design, Golden, Colorado.

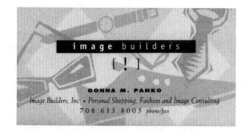

Figure 4–3 (cont.) Sample cards designed by Lisa Romanowski of Roman Design, Golden, Colorado.

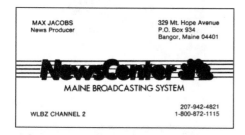

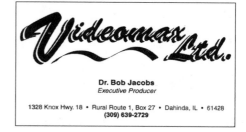

Figure 4–4 Additional business card design examples.

The impression that is conveyed through an organization's business materials, including a business card, logo, or letterhead, is often the first, and sometimes the only, visual indication of your company's image. The simple purpose of these materials is to identify. Your business card or logo becomes the spokesperson for your company, conveying your company's attitude, personality, and purpose. Be sure these materials speak of your company in an appropriate voice. They should seek to identify your company's unique personality, as well as provide the necessary information including company name, contact, address, phone, etc.

Organization of information is a key component. A balance must be found between communication and information. Too much information or decoration can overload a small space and become unreadable, yet communicating the many numbers and addresses that are so common in today's workplace is often a requirement. A two-sided or folded approach can often help this balance.

The most basic brochure is a piece of 8 1/2-by-11-inch paper. It can be folded in a variety of interesting ways. The most conventional flyers are folded once either lengthwise or crosswise to form a four-page pamphlet. They are printed on both sides of the page. One panel is left empty except for your logo and return address; in this self-mailer, there's space for a stamp and the recipient's address.

From this very simple format, brochures explode into a complex array of everything from die-cut works of paper art to small books. Costs for a promotional brochure can run from less than a hundred dollars to several thousand.

# Other Image Considerations

## Your Personal Image

Although you gain certain things by going into business for yourself, you lose a measure of freedom. If you have worked as a producer for someone else, you were probably able to shed the suit and tie at the office door—along with many responsibilities—when you went home for the day.

In some locations, especially big cities, you may still be able to retain a degree of anonymity in your personal life. In smaller areas, however, anonymity may not be possible. As an independent businessperson, you are on display at all times. The only places you will really be able to relax and let your hair down are in your own home and on vacation. In any small or medium-sized market, you never know when the couple at the next table in a restaurant or the guy behind you in line at the supermarket is either a possible client or someone who works for a business account that you'll be trying to land in the future. Just one impression of you as irresponsible or slovenly or uncivil can ruin a potential relationship. Memories of ill manners, in person or in a road rage incident, last forever.

The way you dress whenever you appear in public is just as important as the way you dress to call on a business account. Fashion modes vary from region to region in this country. What's in style for casual wear in Southern California might get clucks of disapproval in Minnesota. Use your common sense in this department.

Even though you are in a creative business and "creative types" are allowed to show off now and then, responsible businesspeople are not. As a producer in business for yourself, you are caught between both worlds. Your public impression should always mirror the more conservative side of style. A smart, toned-down suit for a man or a woman is a uniform, to be sure. But it is one that puts the wearer and those around him or her at ease. It says to clients that you are aware of social convention, that you accept the rules of good conduct, and that you are not a threat, but a solid, trustworthy player in the game of business. Leave flamboyant attire to your creative people. It is their uniform, after all, not yours.

## Your Motor Vehicles

Your appearance in person and the appearance and condition of your company vehicle are just as important as the appearance of your printed material and your office. On the road, you become a moving ad for your company wherever you go. The car or truck you drive is a mobile billboard, and it can be an asset or a detriment to the cause, depending on what you do with it.

If you can afford it, your business should have two primary vehicles—a car and a production vehicle (a truck or van). Here is some advice on choosing each. The choice of a car requires a lot of thought on your part. Just as Realtors and salespeople, stockbrokers and interior decorators know, the company car is a status symbol. It will take you to meetings at your client's place of business. It will also take you and your clients to luncheons as well as to shooting locations. Every time people see your car, they form an impression about you and your company.

America's complex and often irrational relationship with the automobile has been studied and written about ad nauseam. We don't just like cars. We don't just need them to get from place to place. We love them. And we choose them, typically, as external manifestations of our personalities. With this in mind, choose your company car to reflect the personality of your business, not yourself. This choice will depend on your location and your intended market as well as on the image you need to project. A bright yellow Mustang convertible might be a tempting ego booster for your youthful self, but a nice champagne Chrysler sedan is a much more sensible statement of purpose. Besides, modern four-door cars by any major carmaker are *not* your father's sedan! You can have style and élan and still project an image of good value.

The car should make an understated comment on your success and stability. Beware of the temptation to overstate your case with an expensive luxury car. In the first place, a Mercedes or a Jaguar may offend your clients' sensibilities. In the second place, the Internal Revenue Service is no longer allowing such extravagance as a legitimate business deduction. Check with your accountant to find out how far you can go in this department.

The truck or van you buy presents an opportunity to do some advertising. In addition to carrying all your equipment, the production vehicle should be a mobile billboard. The sides and rear gate present canvases for the brush of your artist or sign-painter. Take full advantage of this space, and let it sing for you. The type of display advertising you paint on your vehicle is an important decision. Take it seriously, and use your best creative judgment here. You can choose anything from the company logo in small gold leaf on the door to a full-blown master painting on the side of a large van. Talk it over with your local sign painter and include a healthy dose of your own sense of good taste.

Production vehicles run the gamut from simple station wagons to 18-wheel monster mobile studios. Your choice will depend entirely on the number of location shoots you anticipate and the amount and kind of equipment you will be hauling. If your firm is small and the items you will be carrying around consist of a couple of crew people, a camera/recorder pack, a tripod, and a light kit or two, then a full-size van like the Chevy Astro, any of the wonderful minivans like the perennially popular Dodge Caravan, or a four-door sport utility vehicle like the durable Ford Explorer with a fold-down rear seat and fold-up rear gate will probably do.

The biggest consideration when choosing a vehicle is the interior space. It must be big enough to carry all of the equipment and some of the technicians to the location. It must also be air-conditioned. This is not for you, but for the equipment you will be carrying. Heat is the enemy of electronic gear. It will tolerate a lot of cold but will fry in heat and humidity.

If you want to keep your key grip happy, purchase a vehicle with a cargo area big enough to stand up in (Figure 4–5). In the ideal vehicle, the inner walls are arranged with hooks on which power

**Figure 4–5** Grip truck.

cables, light stands, and other equipment can be secured. Containers for breakable items are arranged for easy storage. A workbench can even be put in place for such things as on-location cable and equipment servicing and repair. This type of configuration makes your entire operation portable. For producers with a large production volume, the pure time savings that a rig like this affords, along with the organization and protection of your expensive equipment, mean that the vehicle will pay for itself in a very short time. A more elaborate vehicle is shown in Figure 4–6.

A promotional vehicle can and will attract attention. It can make your company look larger than life and can enhance your image of strength and durability in the community. If you aren't careful with your design, however, the vehicle can be your worst nightmare if it crosses that fine line between creative and corny. Finally, since the vehicle is your company's image in motion, choose a good, careful driver, and be one yourself. If you cut off someone

trying to merge on the freeway in your personal set of wheels, that's between you and the lords of road rage to settle. If you do it in the company buggy, your firm itself takes the brunt of bad will and hostility. Remember also that courtesy is contagious.

## Your Web Site

Creating a Web site offers you the chance to do the thing you do best: produce audio/video images. Here is a place where you can show off with remarkable ease, have a great time creatively, and link your site to a host of others.

A Web site should have a commanding home page that speaks of the same quality image that went into the business card, letterhead, and brochure. The fun part is that you can animate images, link in video, and make truly superb audio presentations. A site that shows real creativity (check out Warner Brothers at www.warnerbros.com, for one) will get millions of hits and earn word-of-mouth benefits for you, your company, and your Webmaster, as well. There

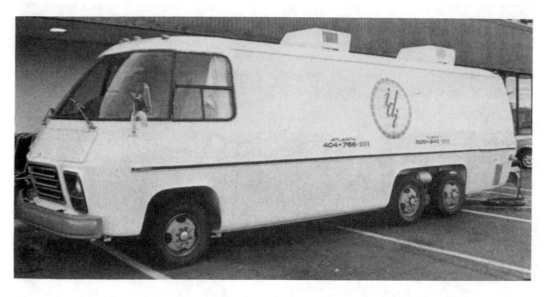

**Figure 4–6** Production vehicle for large-budget location projects. (Photo courtesy of Image Devices International, Atlanta and Miami.)

is an increasingly large number of fine Web site designers who can help you get on-line without costing you your firstborn. Colleges and universities are excellent places to cast around for creative young computer "nerds" who would be happy to show you what they can do at remarkably low costs.

There are books on the market that teach you how to become your own designer and Webmaster. One of the simplest and most fun to play with is Kim Komando's *Dummies 101: Creating Web Pages* (Chicago: IDG Books, 1997). It's a step-by-step tutorial guide that comes complete with a CD-ROM. No previous Internet experience is necessary.

## Community Service

Many independent producers donate their time to worthy causes. They feel that it is essential to become a part of the community and to return something to it. You meet many businesspeople in service groups, and it doesn't hurt that people who know one another and socialize together also tend to do business with one another. To put the lesson simply, a member of one of your service groups who wishes to invest in a video production will probably be more inclined to do business with you than with a producer he doesn't know. If you wish to give something back to the community in which you live, you can offer some of your services as a video producer. There are literally hundreds of worthy causes in this country. Here are just a few ways in which you can offer your expertise to your community.

You can make TV public service announcements (PSAs) for a local organization. Large national charities like the United Way and the Red Cross have major PSA campaigns. However, your local boy's and girl's clubs, youth hockey association, church service league, and Big Brothers and Sisters organization do not. Area television stations generally prefer to run locally originated PSAs because doing so helps them fulfill the community service function required by the Federal Communications Commission. The only investment for most PSAs is a day or so of your time. The payback in terms of the goodwill you generate is incalculable.

You can also offer a seminar in video production at your facility for one of the youth groups in your area. Let the kids develop a script and shoot a project under your supervision. You may be astounded by the creativity and visual sophistication that most young people have today. The end product can run on one of your local stations as a public affairs program presented by the organization and your company.

Try contacting your community social services administration. Various states have different names for this organization, which handles such things as residential care for the developmentally disabled, programs for the physically and mentally handicapped, public housing, and so on. Frequently, organizations of this type need such things as training aids for new personnel and progress reports for state and country funding agencies, both of which can be accomplished with video. You can provide a much-needed volunteer service and have the double benefit of helping those who can't help themselves while reducing the burden on the taxpayer for production services.

With very little research and effort, you can find many more community service projects. Volunteering in these areas will certainly enhance your standing and prestige in the community. Always project the positive image of a mover and a shaker. According to the producers from whom these examples were drawn, you can be assured of an additional benefit—you will feel very, very good about yourself.

# Making Use of the Media

Laypeople feel that video production is a profession with a built-in "glitter factor." You and I know that producing video is not glamorous; it is 95 percent sweat and drudgery and 5 percent pure joy. That 5 percent is what keeps us going. Most "outsiders," however, see producers and productions as emanating from a world of fantasy and fun. Knowing this fact enables you to turn the media to your own ends.

## On-Location Shooting

Most of us who work in the field have had the experience of being out on a city street with a crew. We know that a crew always draws a crowd of spectators. You may be doing the most pedestrian kind of shot, an exterior of a model entering a shoe store, for example. But the sight of the camera, the crew, and a couple of Colortran kickers puts you in the same league as Paramount or Twentieth Century Fox as far as passersby are concerned. This is especially true if you are in a small or medium-sized town. Since productions in these areas are not as common as they are in cities like Los Angeles, Vancouver, British Columbia, or New York, your mere presence on those city streets can be a media event. Play it as such for the impact it can have on your company name.

Many television stations use feature material, and not all hard news, on their daily newscasts. This is especially true in small and medium-sized markets, where there may not be that much hard news in a day. Therefore, local stations may welcome your on-location video production as a feature story on the evening news. If this opportunity comes your way, take advantage of the exposure, and cooperate with the station to make their story a good one.

## The Media Release

To let the news operations in your town know what you are doing, use the media release—a basic tool of public relations. Write it from the third-person point of view, and use language that reads well aloud (i.e., write it the way people speak). If your press release reads well, the local announcer or editor will not have to bother with a rewrite, and you have a better chance of having the piece aired. Don't be afraid to make the project sound a little more glittery than it seems to you. Remember that to the other folks in your town, it's really show biz!

PRESS RELEASE                    For Immediate Dissemination

Date:_____

HEADLINE:

## LOCAL PRODUCTION FIRM LANDS NATIONAL CONTRACT

An Oshkosh production company has been chosen to make a series of national television spots. The theme of the public service announcements is "Aging in America". The California-based sponsor of the series chose the Oshkosh firm after meeting here last week to review the facilities and the budget. The contract was awarded on the basis of a low bid and a high quality demonstration reel of past projects. The first two spots will feature Wisconsin aviation pioneer Steve Wittman and famous author, Ray Bradbury. Production of the series will begin here with Wittman in March.

The sponsor is The Elvirita Lewis Foundation headquartered in Soquel, California. The purpose of the Foundation is threefold, according to its Executive Director, Steven W. Brummel.

"We provide funding to programs for the elderly", he said. "We believe that older people are resources, not drains on society. We fund several projects a year where older people run the programs for themselves."

"The second part of our operation is to lobby on behalf of elder citizens in the areas of health and nutrition", he went on. "We are in touch with other foundations and government institutions worldwide on these subjects".

"Finally", he concluded, "we are trying actively to change America's attitudes about aging and the aged. That's the reason

**Figure 4–7** Press release.

for the first in our series of television spots. We want to show older people being active and productive long past the point where many younger people feel they can be".

Dr. Bob Jacobs, Executive Producer of the local production house called The Media Ranch, expressed his enthusiasm for the project.

"We took this on at essentially no profit", he said, "because we believe very strongly in the message. When I told Mr. Brummel about Steve Wittman's willingness to do a spot for us, I think it helped clinch the deal!"

Steve Wittman, for whom the Winnebago County Airport is named, still builds, flies and races airplanes. Wittman is now in his 80's.

"That's exactly the message we want to get across", Brummel verified. "People in normal good health can do just about anything they've always done no matter how old they are".

The production will start here in March and move to Los Angeles for the Ray Bradbury segment in June. Release of the spots on a national scale is slated for December. There will be minor roles for extras and background characters in Oshkosh. Interested performers should call The Media Ranch for tryouts.

**Figure 4–7 (cont.)** Press release.

The first paragraph of the media release, the lead, usually includes the "five *W*s and an *H*" of journalism: who, what, where, when, why, and how. All significant information is included in the lead because that paragraph may be the only one that is read or printed in its entirety.

In subsequent paragraphs, expand on the information. Include colorful details and quotes from those who are involved in the story. When you want to say something directly, quote yourself as if you had been interviewed by the writer. Conclude the release with a recap of the most important information.

Look at Figure 4–7, which shows a release that I used to receive media coverage for my company and to recruit some local talent for a major commercial production. Note that it states, "For Immediate Dissemination." Be sure to include this, or a similar phrase, unless you want the news held for a specific date. This sample follows basic journalistic rules. All of the essential information is contained in the first paragraph, the lead. In the second paragraph, I expand, naming the sponsor. In the paragraphs that follow, the sponsor's executive director explains the reason for the project. I put the sponsor above the name of the production company for a couple of reasons. First, it is good form to let the sponsor have top billing. Second, it is always good publicity to be connected with an altruistic foundation and project.

I blow my own horn lower in the story because I don't want to look as if I am seeking publicity. There is a perilously fine line between newsworthiness and advertising. If the news director or editor feels that you are trying to advertise, your release will be ignored.

Do not overdo this public relations tool. If you get in the habit of sending out media releases each time you do a production, your welcome at the local newspapers and television and radio stations will be short-lived. Three or four times a year, though, when you have something unique, fire up the typewriter. You may very well find friends within the media who appreciate your occasional bulletins because they fill some space for them.

## Direct Mail

Personal computers have opened the way for even the smallest business to make use of direct-mail promotion. Computers are also becoming more and more user-friendly; if you can type, you can use a word processor. Word processing makes scriptwriting—with the frequent changes required by clients—a real pleasure.

The major advantage of direct-mail promotion is that you can send a personal letter to a large number of people. Each letter will look as though it has been typed individually, provided you use a laser-quality printer with your word processor.

Figure 4–8 is an example of a promotion letter sent out by Video Trend Associates. It is an introduction to the general services VTA offers and a pitch for its new Video Real Estate Service (discussed in detail in Chapter 5). The text of the letter is one file, the address blocks for more than 100 real estate firms in the state are in another file, which then feeds the information to the printer. The name of the person or firm from the address block is programmed to print in the appropriate spot in the form letter. This simple merging device makes it look as though the letter was written specifically for this individual. The cost per letter is computed simply by adding the cost per sheet of letterhead, the printer toner used, and the time it took to write the original document and get the computer to begin the merging process.

Once you have established a mailing list of potential clients and filed them in your computer, make personalized mailings a regular part of your promotional efforts. Here are a few direct-mail ideas used by other producers:

- Send a monthly newsletter. Tell potential clients about new equipment, problems that you have solved for others, and so on. Make this newsletter chatty, and add some humor if you can. You are not making a sales pitch; you are simply making prospects feel as if you value them as part of the "family."
- Send personal holiday greetings. Include some quips about yourself, your staff, and the company in general.
- Pass on helpful hints that you have picked up from trade journals.
- Write about some new technique that you have adopted. Tell your clients why it can help in the next project you do for them.

With a little imagination, you can invent dozens of ways to use direct mail as a first-line public relations and sales tool.

**VIDEO TREND ASSOCIATES**

Century 21/Paul Schmidt Realty
325 Pearl Avenue
Oshkosh, WI 54901                                    December 3, 1985

Dear Paul Schmidt:

    We're writing to introduce ourselves and to tell you about a
new service of ours.

    Video Trend Associates began in a very small way six years
ago, believing that there existed a need for a high-quality
alternative to the production services of the three Green Bay
television stations. While much of their production is of a high
standard, their overhead costs demand an equally high price.

    We have been able to keep overhead costs low while being
more than competitive in terms of production values. Some of our
satisfied clients include The Federal Aviation Administration,
The Experimental Aircraft Association, Air Wisconsin and The
Marcus Corporation in  Milwaukee.

    We offer a complete range of services in 3/4-inch
professional video production and post-production. We can also
reproduce works in 1/2-inch Beta and VHS formats.

    Of special interest to Century 21/Paul Schmidt Realty is our
new "Video Real Estate" Service. Professional tours of your
listed properties, showing their best features, can be recorded
on video and shown to your potential clients in the comfort and
privacy of your office. This saves you both travel time and
money. It is especially effective in winter months which are
traditionally bad for your business.

    This service is already widely used on both the East and
West Coasts with great success. Video Trend Associates would like
to join Paul Schmidt in bringing video sales of real estate to
the Fox Valley of Wisconsin. We would be happy to show you how
remarkably inexpensive and very effective a video production can
be.

    For an appointment and free screening, please call us today.

Cordially,

Ronald J. Bullock
Ronald J. Bullock
Production Manager

RJB/ac

744 WISCONSIN ST. ● OSHKOSH, WI 54901 ● (414) 231-9218

**Figure 4-8** Promotion letter.

# Unconventional Tactics

Promotion can be a silly business. The limits are really only defined by your sense of propriety and an awareness of what your clients will tolerate.

Gimmicks can range from giveaways like pens and books of matches, available through a number of specialty advertising firms, to some truly outrageous stunts. One producer, for example, has gone to the extreme of staging phony shoots in close proximity to clients he hopes to land. He sets up lights, hires actors, and pretends to be involved in a major production. A few days later, he makes his sales call, and in most cases, the client recalls having seen him "at work."

Most producers avoid gimmickry. It comes close to going over the ethical demarcation line of sound business practice. On the other hand, production is a highly competitive and creative line of work. A well-controlled and harmless stunt may occasionally mean the difference between your landing a contract and someone else's getting it.

# Summary

As in any other business, video producers are in competition for a limited number of customers and a limited amount of money. This chapter discussed a number of methods of advertising and promoting your business, many of which are currently being used by other producers. The type of promotion technique you use is unimportant, but the decision to promote at all is crucial.

If you feel that you will not excel in the area of self-promotion, you can use the services of an industrial advertising or public relations agency that specializes in advertising and promoting businesses rather than products. It will probably cost less to do your own advertising and promotion; however, these are important enough to the success of your business to pay professionals if you feel you do not possess the necessary expertise.

# Notes

1. For help in designing your own advertisements, see Albert C. Book and Dennis Schick, *Fundamentals of Copy and Layout* (Chicago: Crain Books, 1984).

2. Ron Bullock, interview with the author, February 1994.

# 5

# Finding and Developing Markets

Typically, the independent producer develops one or two primary accounts that serve as the foundation for his or her business. These bread-and-butter accounts might occupy 60 to 70 percent of the producer's time.

Once you secure these types of accounts and lock them in solid, and once your major bills are being paid on time, you have two options. You can sit back, relax, and feel as if you've got it made, or you can go after a series of secondary accounts. If you're smart and want to stay in business, do the latter. Complacency leads to disaster in this game, as some of the examples that follow illustrate. In this chapter, we will discuss both the bread-and-butter accounts and the secondary accounts—how to get them, how to keep them, and what they can mean to your bank account.

## The Corporate Client

Major corporations spend billions of dollars collectively every year on audiovisual productions. Their projects include multimedia presentations for annual sales meetings, training, intracorporate communications, sales promotions, and new product research and development, as well as television spot commercials and special programs for broadcast. Some of the larger players have regularly scheduled television-style programs beamed by satellite to global affiliates; it's hard to distinguish these from broadcast news or chat shows. Caterpillar, Inc., is one of these giants. A case study of how one independent producer tapped into this lucrative account is detailed in this section. This is a fascinating time in history for corporate communication, and there are opportunities for your company to participate in it with outsourced production.

Many large companies have in-house production units that handle their day-to-day needs. Some of these, however, employ outside freelance help from time to time on a per-project basis. A larger number of corporations have no audiovisual production capability in-house and instead contract exclusively with outside agencies for their production work. Write letters of inquiry to those companies with which you would like to work. Ask if—and to what extent—they subcontract for production work and how you can get on the bid list. The world of corporate audiovisual production offers a multitude of possibilities. For each giant that relies solely on its own production capability, there are dozens of smaller firms that hold interesting and potentially profitable opportunities for the independent producer. Landing one of these as your primary account can put your business on a sound, relatively stable base.

## The Game Plan

To land a major corporate account, you must develop a game plan and follow it. Although no one can tell you exactly how to go about doing this, you'll find techniques and tips throughout this book that can be used to land almost any type of account. In addition, the four case studies at the end of this chapter should prove helpful.

When meeting with potential corporate clients, remember that you are dealing with people who probably have had previous experience with productions. Treat them accordingly. Don't try to dazzle these clients with false glitter. They won't buy it. Just relax and be yourself. While you are selling your idea, be certain that you are also being an effective listener, concentrating not only on what is being said, but on what is being implied. By listening carefully, you can often pick up on problems that the prospect has had in the past, or you could learn of one or two issues that might lend themselves to a video solution. Make a note of these, and ask direct questions relating to what you've been told.

Remember that corporations are not impersonal, calculating entities; they are made up of human beings. Approach them with that in mind at all times. Often, corporate people need services like yours. Approach them in a businesslike manner with a solid proposition at a fair price. Deliver it on time and on budget, and make your word your bond. If you run into

a brick wall, if the corporate person you're trying to sell to just won't make a decision, then move on to another prospect. If you follow these few guidelines, you have a good chance of enjoying a long and profitable relationship with the corporation of your choice.

## The Proposal

You will have to submit a written proposal to a corporation for your production. This will follow one or two meetings with the client, who has agreed that there is a problem in the corporation and that a video solution is needed, as long as you explain just how that video project will solve the client's problem. Be aware that there are standards of practice for you to follow here. Remember that your time is valuable; do not give away too much of it for free. The informational meetings that you conduct and the research that you do into the nature of the problem are your investments of time. The written proposal is the final investment you should be expected to make without remuneration.

In the proposal, recap the problem that your client has revealed in your penetrating research phase. Simply stated, tell your clients what they told you. They will agree with you. Then tell them that a video solution will solve the problem. They will agree again. Then tell them that you have a script idea in mind and that you would be happy to work on it with them. Then give them a rough estimate of the cost, telling them that you cannot give them a detailed production budget until the script has been written. Then tell them how much you will charge to write the script.

Many producers have found themselves so eager to land an account that they do the script on spec, believing that this will impress potential clients. Keep in mind that you are a professional and that your time and talent have value. Corporations understand this and play the game accordingly. If your proposal is not strong enough to sell the prospect and to land a contract that will pay for the rest of the stages, move on to another prospect. (See the case studies at the end of this chapter for more information.)

In Appendix C, the proposal that I used to land an account with Mercury Marine is reproduced. You can see each of the steps outlined above in this proposal. The goal was a single recruiting production for the product engineering department. In the proposal, the preliminary research with the prospect is detailed. The problem is discussed, and a solution is proposed. The estimated budget is outlined, along with the terms of the production contract. Feel free to use this example as a format for your own proposals. (But don't pitch it to Mercury Marine!)

## The Caterpillar Connection

Caterpillar is the largest employer in Peoria, Illinois. They have a large, skilled, professional in-house video production unit. Normally, this unit does all of the work for the hundreds of CAT® operating groups. In a reorganization during the early nineties, CAT® management declared that each unit in the company would be a "profit center" and would have autonomous control over its budget. That meant that the engine division, the crawler tractor division, and so forth, could elect to go outside the company for video production services. Likewise, certain of those divisions had to advertise within the corporation for internal clients.

The Advanced Materials Technology (AMT) Group at the Mossville, Illinois, Tech Center had an unusual problem. Research scientists who explore new materials and techniques at the far leading edge of the sci-tech envelope, these people needed to reach potential users in the worldwide CAT® organization to encourage design engineers to make use of their innovations and materials discoveries. With surging globalization, many of these 8,000 to 9,000 target engineers and technicians worldwide spoke English as a second language and came from a wide variety of ethnic and cultural backgrounds.

The manager of AMT became convinced that the in-house production specialists were not in tune with his need to communicate his message nonverbally and to convey a multicultural message. Having seen an Emmy-nominated musical program produced by Videomax, Ltd., one that relied heavily on nonverbal visual elements and music, the manager asked if we could help by making something like that for him. The challenge was daunting. The result was a fascinating experiment.

We had to convey the excitement of the research being done. The result of these efforts by the scientists at CAT® will virtually revolutionize transportation in the near future. That's an exhilarating concept. But the visual elements were mostly of people typing at computers or pouring liquids into beakers and watching the results bubble. It was about as exciting as watching grass grow.

As the proposal reproduced in this chapter shows (see Figure 5–1), our first vision was to do an adequate but pretty conventional treatment of the industrial video. We felt that it would be lively and colorful enough and that the hook would be the workers themselves telling the story. As we began shooting interviews, something emerged from the faces of the subjects. There was immense energy suffusing their eyes, a passion for the work that simply did not match the visual references of them sitting at computer terminals in their labs. What they said was good, but how they said it was better. And that "how" is what we needed to capture.

It became clear that we had to find a metaphor to match what we were seeing reflected in these wonderful faces. We needed a bridge to make the real connection that we talked about in the proposal, something that was not verbal. It came one day while taping a woman working in a plasma-coating lab. Here, in the spinning wheel of flame that applies a thermal coating to valve parts, we saw the connection suddenly. She and the machine were engaged in an incredible ballet of flame and movement. It was the language of dance.

So we chose dance as a universal symbol of experimentation and the stretching

Connections

Proposal for a video project

presented to
Manager/Advanced Materials Technology
Caterpillar, Inc.
Technical Center, Building E
Peoria, Illinois 61656-1875

by

Bob Jacobs
Videomax, Ltd.

**Figure 5–1** Video project proposal for Caterpillar.

1.

## INTRODUCTION

You have expressed a need for a video production that will tell the story of the scientific and technical activities and projects conducted in your center to other constituencies within the Caterpillar organization. It is fair to assume that such a video program might also be used as an intercorporate promotional tool. To that end, you need a piece that will sparkle with professional quality, capture the attention of a variety of viewers, and transmit the exciting essence of the work being carried on by your staff, rather than merely documenting the rather prosaic surface vision of that work.

The facts are that the activities going on in a large number of your laboratories seem disjointed and unrelated to the casual passerby in the hallway. A visitor is hard-pressed to synthesize the astonishing variety of chemical, electrical, mechanical, and theoretical work into a meaningful whole. One might question just what all of this seemingly random experimentation has to do with the present and future operation of the world's largest and greatest "tractor company." You are looking for a way, stated at its simplest, to say, "See—*this* is what we do, and *this* is why it's important."

You have come to regard the medium of video as the best way to state your message, primarily because creative video can enhance that message. It can take what seems superficially to be dry and boring and make it seem colorful and intriguing. You have seen several samples of the type of video work that we produce, and you sense in that style the same elements you would like to see in your program. This includes our use of colorful lighting, close-up imagery, musical underscoring, stimulating editing pace, and personalization of concepts by having the story told by the people who do the work.

We have toured your facility and discussed the project in some depth. This is our response.

**Figure 5–1 (cont.)**   Video project proposal for Caterpillar.

2.

## THE ANALYSIS

The outcome of the future for Caterpillar is dependent on a number of factors. Some of these are uncontrollable, such as possible natural calamities, like being struck by an asteroid and seeing humanity suffer the fate of the dinosaurs. There's not much we can do about such eventualities.

Others are *quite* predictable and in our hands to control. With surety we must prepare for change, for change is the only inevitable consequence of existence. We know that

- Materials and usable resources on Planet Earth are finite.
- We are interconnected with the rest of the world.
- The need for constant, controlled growth of the economy is quite real.
- Those businesses that do not progress, fail.
- Progress is one imperative goal of your corporation.
- Research enables progress.
- Research therefore leads your corporate interests into the future.

As we walked around your facility, a striking pattern emerged. In each lab, there were technical experiments going on: testing paint for durability and tone, testing metal parts for stress, concocting chemical cocktails that turn from green goo to high-density ceramic tiles, transforming complex mathematical formulas into exhilarating animated, three-dimensional models on the computer screen, altering the basic structure of fuel to run diesel engines on mixtures of pure imagination! And each of these sorcerer's workshops contained trinkets and toys that could be lit and photographed to make them seem as ethereal as any science-fiction gadget in a Hollywood space opera.

But that wasn't the real story.

**Figure 5–1 (cont.)**  Video project proposal for Caterpillar.

The real story was in the faces and excitement of the sorcerer's apprentices who spoke in mysterious tongues about fusing this with that, making these from those, brewing fire from ice, envisioning the invisible, diving into the mystery and intrigue of the molecule, and squeezing pristine motive power from the most abundant resource on this water world of ours.

The future was in their eyes!

The real story is in the connection between them and the commonplace daily miracles that the people who use CAT® machines produce without having to think about what went into their manufacture.

- For instance, a small breakthrough in chemistry leads to a superior insulating ceramic . . .

- . . . which connects with a new mating process in metallurgy and the result is . . .

- . . . a new cylinder head assembly that can absorb and dissipate the extreme temperatures . . .

- . . . that a fuels researcher finds necessary to burn a mixture of half carbonaceous fuel and water . . .

- . . . which connects to an economical exhaust scrubber that works without precious metals . . .

- . . . and the future unfolds with profitable improvements to Caterpillar products built to make work easier and life better for all of us.

**Figure 5–1 (cont.)**  Video project proposal for Caterpillar.

3.

## THE PROPOSAL

We will produce one fast-paced, informative video illustrating the connection between your Tech Center and the rest of the Caterpillar mission. We will feature the scientists and technicians themselves to personalize the connection. All of us are intrigued and interested far more by the stories of people than we are of things. We identify with the struggles and the dramatic conflicts that people overcome on the way to solving problems, developing new technological devices, and triumphing over obstacles. A project that might seem mundane to one of your researchers can seem earthshaking when revealed to someone who hasn't ever thought of it before.

To illustrate a broad concept, such as the mission of your center, we need to encapsulate it in a single story line. By doing so, we get the viewer to identify with the subject through the individuals involved in the work.

You will select a sample project that we can follow through from initial idea to application. We will interview the researchers who worked on that project, in depth and in detail. From these interviews, we will draw the story line, letting the researchers themselves tell their own story.

That story will be illustrated with "flashback" scenes shot in the laboratories, on the manufacturing line, and finally in the field application, counterpointed and underscored as needed by music and voice-over narration.

The connection will be made. We will show what it is that we do here and why it is important.

You have samples of our series called "Postcards from the Heart," and it is that format that will form the basis for your program. The running time is to be between 8 and 14 minutes. This would be a single program as a pilot project between us, introducing your center. We would suggest discussing other possible programs after completing and evaluating this one.

**Figure 5–1 (cont.)** Video project proposal for Caterpillar.

We propose to begin the project immediately after an initial conference with you and your selected participants. After determining the featured players and the project that we will dramatize, we can develop a shooting schedule and begin taping interviews and planning the script. Shooting the illustrative scenes will follow. The postproduction phase follows shooting, with a completed program to be delivered by an agreed-upon date. We anticipate that the entire project will be completed within 10 working weeks from the outset.

4.

## THE BUDGET

To write, produce, direct, and deliver one finished Betacam SP edited master, between 8 and 14 minutes in length, with music, narration, graphics, live action, and on-camera interviews:

| | |
|---|---|
| 1. Above the line | $15,000 |
| 2. Production staff | $5,500 |
| 3. Equipment and facilities rental | $8,000 |
| 4. Materials and supplies | $2,000 |
| TOTAL | $30,500* |

* These are not the actual budget figures for this project. The client retains a proprietary right of confidentiality over the real cost. These are typical figures for such a production, and are included here only as a rule of thumb.

## TERMS

One-third to begin, one-third on completion of principal photography, and one-third on delivery of the final print.

**Figure 5–1 (cont.)**   Video project proposal for Caterpillar.

of physical limits. Anyone who has ever watched Fred Astaire or Mikhail Baryshnikov will understand the metaphor. Using a montage of ethnic music and images from around the world, including the machineries manipulated by the AMT folks, we created a 14-minute music video, with minimal words, consisting of a select few of the most animated sound bites from our interviewees. The fusion of music and image was unique in industrial video production. One media critic called the piece "a triumph of the will for Caterpillar!" This happy outcome was the result of flexible corporate management and a producer who was flexible enough to reach beyond the ordinary and make an artistic course correction rather than just going for the money. Postproduction took us a lot longer than the original estimate accounted for, but the resulting piece was a lovely statement that opened more doors for the future. Figure 5–1 is the very simple proposal that sold the project.

## The Advertising Agency

In recent years, a rash of advertising agencies has been springing up in small and medium-sized towns and cities across the country. Licensing practices for these agencies vary so widely from state to state that there is now some disagreement about just what constitutes an advertising agency.

Sometimes, what bills itself as an agency is a one-person shop with two or three clients for whom the owner does everything—from writing and laying out newspaper ads to appearing in local television spots as a spokesperson. Radio and television stations frequently reject taking business from such operations because the station will not pay the commission for such small peanuts that real agencies charge. You'll want to exercise great caution in dealing with outfits like this because many are shaky at best and have reputations for not paying their bills. If you're the one doing production work for these fly-by-nighters, you can get stuck with a very bad debt. This is not to imply that you should avoid all small agencies, but use care and good judgment when evaluating them. To be as safe as possible, do business with agencies that are members of the American Association of Advertising Agencies, Inc. (AAAA or Four A).[1] When you deal with a Four A agency, you can be sure that it has been around long enough to prove that it can study the advertiser's business and products, analyze the market, form sound judgments, give constructive advice, and render an adequate quantity and quality of service. These places are all blue-chip investments with earned reputations to protect.

There are some legitimate agencies that fall between the local scam artist and TWDA/Chiat-Day. Some perfectly reputable agencies may have been in business too short a time to qualify for Four A membership. Some may have no need to join the association because they work with a select client list. Before striking a business deal with any agency, consider the following: A respectable agency should be happy to provide you with a client list. It is more likely to operate out of an office than out of a private home. It will probably have more than one employee; at the very least, a marketing research person, a graphics specialist, and a media production person should be on board. Before approaching an agency you know little about, check with the local television stations, as many small agencies use these types of production facilities. Ask some straightforward questions regarding the agency's credit history. Check also with the local Better Business Bureau to find out if it has any complaints on file, and ask the local Chamber of Commerce about the agency. Most respectable businesses (like yours, for example) are members of the chamber and have agreed to abide by its code of ethics and standards of practice.

Beyond this, let your instincts be your guide. If the agency representative seems slippery or avoids answering several questions, back away . . . fast.

Once you're satisfied that the agency is solid, follow essentially the procedure that was outlined in Chapter 1 Some elements of selling an idea and landing a contract are the same regardless of the potential client; other techniques must be tailored to a specific prospect. Following are some characteristics of a typical advertising agency; they are very different from those of a typical corporation. It is essential to keep individual industry characteristics in mind when trying to land a contract. First, the agency is on your side of the fence. Its employees know all about production and already have the client. Consider the agency as an intermediary. You don't have to sell agencies on the benefits of video; they already know the facts about media power. Therefore, your job is much easier.

Your most likely contact will be with either the creative director or one of the in-house media producers at the agency. These people often have years of experience in or around production. They are creative people, much like yourself. Because of this similarity, it should be easier to establish a rapport with them than it is to get on the same wavelength with corporate presidents. It also means, however, that you can't put anything over on them, so don't try! You can't bluff your way around these folks. Either you've got the "chops" or you don't.

## Costs

Be prepared to demonstrate that you can do superior work. Assemble a high-quality reel showcasing your best pieces. Remember that the demo reel is the main, and frequently only, tool you get to use to prove yourself to an agency. Because most agencies are already doing business with other producers, you may have to offer a lower production cost and be able to prove this on paper in order to take a share of this business for yourself. Point out your lower overhead, for instance. Because agencies almost always operate on a percentage of their clients' media buys, they are inter-

ested in getting the most out of their production dollars without sacrificing quality. In some cases, the client is assessed a production charge. It makes the agency look better if the figure comes in lower than planned, and that may be your only advantage.

Production budgets for television spot commercials vary according to the size of the agency, the size of the client, and the nature of the spot. In small and medium-sized markets, a typical production cost for a 30-second video commercial for a small business runs from $500 to $3,000. Fees for film-to-tape commercials run from $5,000 to $10,000, depending on film stock, processing, telecine costs, and effects.

From these minimum fees, the costs can go up to the astronomical. (One spot by a major brewery for Super Bowl XXXII had a production budget of $1.5 million.) Factors that determine costs include talent (AFTRA and SAG talent is very expensive), special visual effects, length of the spot, and whether you are doing a series or a one-shot spot. The agency will give you this information when they call for bids.

## Other Factors

In addition to cost, a typical medium-sized agency will look at the following when deciding which producers to place on its bid list:

- *Creativity:* It wants to know that you're capable of pulling off a range of productions, from the humorous to the heart-tugging. Your demo reel needs to really sizzle. (The demo reel is covered in detail in Chapter 1.)
- *Technical competence:* It pays close attention to lighting, audio, editing, acting, and any special effects.
- *Past credits:* Nothing impresses more than past success. Even if you have to work for free at first, develop some high-impact spots for your reel.
- *Time allotment:* Will you be able to put in full-time or overtime hours and whatever else is necessary to deliver the project on time? Agencies love to beat

up on production and postproduction people, to work them for days on end, 15 to 20 hours a day without a break. Don't ask why. It's just the nature of the beast. If that sounds like too much work for you, put down this book and go into another field immediately!

- *Staffing:* Be prepared to introduce the agency to your videographer, editor, artist, and other staff members. It is difficult for one person alone to hook into a real agency account.

# Alternative Markets

The corporate account and the advertising agency are traditional markets for the independent producer. For the energetic entrepreneur, there are also secondary markets that offer profit potential. Here are some of them for you to consider.

## News Stringing

Every broadcast news operation—from the networks to your local TV station—is a potential client for the producer who keeps an ear tuned to an emergency-band radio scanner. The scanner picks up the police, sheriff, fire department, and other emergency or official frequencies of the radio band. If you hear what sounds like a major breaking news story, you or your videographer can grab the camera and VTR and go to the scene of the story. Although all news operations use the scanner, stories are often over before news teams can get there to cover them. If you have the only coverage, you can sell it to one or more stations. In major disasters, there is good money to be made in this odd adjunct to your real business, especially if you hit on something of national interest.

Almost anyone with broadcast-quality gear can become an official stringer. This means that a news service or station has given you a press card, which affords you the same rights and privileges as a full-time photographer covering the news. Get in touch with your local stations and the networks if you want to become a stringer. Bear in mind that members of the press are often denied access to hazardous situations. The card, however, does distinguish you from the curious onlooker.

In hot situations, you will have to fight for your right to shoot. The members of the press are a scrappy bunch of people. Don't be surprised if you find yourself in shouting and shoving matches when trying to get your camera to the front line of a major event. And don't take it personally. It's just the nature of the game. You can be polite, wait your turn, and possibly miss the action, or you can assert yourself and get the shot. There is no in-between.

News stringing requires you to keep the batteries charged on your camera and VTR at all times, and good stringers always have their gear packed in the trunk of the car. These people often get big breaks because they are prepared.

Fred Schuh, an international freelancer who now travels the world at network expense shooting the news, got his big break this way. He was driving to dinner over a causeway in Tampa Bay when a huge freighter rammed the bridge, knocking out an entire section of it. Fred was not only the first one on the scene, he was the only one on the scene with a camera and a VTR. Schuh's coverage of this major accident was sold to all three networks and helped establish him firmly as a top freelancer.

## National Program Stringing

Not only is it possible to string for local and regional news operations, but you will find good-paying opportunities to work with the growing number of reality-based entertainment programs. In addition, the History Channel, the Military Channel, E! Entertainment, and others use freelance producers, directors, and photographers frequently. I have been hired a number of times to produce, direct, and shoot material in the Chicago area for production companies on the West Coast. My credits have included Field Producer and Second Unit Director.

A simple way to tap this market is to read the credits at the end of shows that interest you. The production company is always in the end credits. Once you find that, get a copy of either *The Hollywood Reporter Studio Blu-book* or *LA 411*. (These and other helpful publications are listed in Appendix A and the bibliography.) You'll find the address, phone number, and fax number of most large production companies in these annual publications (along with *lots* more information). Contact the company, send a reel, and don't be surprised if you find yourself getting a credit on a national production. Day rates for this kind of work run from $500 to $1,500.

## Light News Features

News operations in small to medium-sized markets are generally strapped for help. Their requirements to provide programming continue to rise as the audience is sapped away from broadcast television by cable and Internet alternatives. In most parts of the country, the local staff that used to do a 6:00 and 11:00 newscast (6:00 and 10:00 in the Midwest) now strains to do a morning show, a noon show, and a live-at-five show in addition to the two others. At the same time, there is a growing market for light feature material and series. This is where you enter the picture.

Sell one of your local stations on a warm-and-fuzzy series, to run once a week or even biweekly. We do such a series called *Postcards from Home* for WEEK-TV, the NBC affiliate in Peoria, Illinois. Here's the pitch that accompanied our demo reel and was used to sell the idea to station management:

## Postcards from Home— A Modest Proposal

This is a composite of three programs in a continuing series called *Postcards from Home*. Their purpose is to illuminate positive aspects of life in our part of the world and to show ordinary folks doing extraordinary things. Our premise is that too much of what we see on the news is depressing, defeatist, demeaning, and demoralizing. The heart of America still resonates with life-affirming, decent people, living out their American dreams, no matter how small those may be. We think that seeing examples of success and enchantment in the face of so much aridity and disenchantment gives our viewers reason to hope—to feel good about life, their neighbors, and themselves. In the case of the three selections submitted for your consideration in this composite, we make a point of heralding adults who do good things for children. One runs a camp for troubled teens. A second story in Peoria introduces a single woman who attacks street violence by teaching self-respect in the form of martial arts to urban youth. Finally, two women in a town so small it almost doesn't qualify as one round out the trio with an amazing library—all for kids and all for fun. Too many of us talk about what's wrong with young people these days. Here is a touching look at a few good folks who are doing something about it. Our program shows that the heart of America is still beating strong.

The subjects of these short stories, as Charles Kuralt proved so well, are everywhere one looks. All you have to do is be mildly curious about your neighborhood to find dozens of stories waiting to be told.

We get paid enough to cover costs, the station gets a high-quality local feature that looks like a network production, and the evidence of our quality work in video brings in unsolicited business. "Oh, yes! I saw you on television. I like your work,"—this is a very good icebreaker coming from someone you just meet on a cold call! This kind of thing will not be a big profit maker in itself. But as a promotional tool, it's hard to beat.

## Music Videos

There are at least 200,000 bands in this country. They range from preadolescents with a three-chord guitar ability and a five-tune repertoire to top-40 recording artists with major label contracts. Thanks to the phenomenal success of MTV as an alternative to radio, all of these bands are potential music video clients.

Providing a music video is really quite simple. The band records a song. The song is lip-synched in playback, and you shoot visuals of the band members (and any of a stunning variety of other characters and images) to go with the song. Then you edit all of this visual material into a series of flashy pieces cut to the beat of the music. A typical 2- or 3-minute pop video will have more than 100 separate cuts in it. With any good nonlinear editing system, such as Avid or Media 100, which delivers digital audio and multiple tracks of digital video, you can make some truly amazing visual effects that will thrill your clients and make them feel just like MTV performers. It is also more fun than you've ever had!

Finding clients is a fairly simple matter. Between the preadolescents in the garage down the street and Barbra Streisand lie the serious professional or semiprofessional bands. These young musicians play in nightclubs and on college campuses, and they finance their own recordings hoping to attract the attention of a major label. They have money to invest in their careers. And a virtual necessity for any serious band trying to land a recording deal with a major label is a high-quality video. A nearby audio recording studio or serious music store is a good place to find these musicians and to advertise your services.[2]

Check, too, with local colleges and universities. Most have booking services for music and other entertainment. They can put you in touch with the national publications distributed to the groups that play the college circuit. Finally, look in your newspaper's entertainment section. Find out where the live music is happening in your town, and go see the groups in person. Present a brief, colorful flyer advertising your music video service. Word of mouth will spread among the musicians if you provide a good product at a fair price.

A minimum figure charged by most producers for a music video is $3,000. From there, the price goes up according to the resources of the musicians and the level of technical difficulty and flashy special effects they desire.

## Weddings

Luckily for video producers, there is hardly a bride- or groom-to-be in the country for whom the wedding video is not as mandatory as flowers, photos, and cake! This lovely turn of events opens up another market for you, if you can stand it. For some producers, the wedding season from June through August has become a primary source of income. Getting the business, should you elect to do so, is fairly simple.

Advertise your services at the local bridal shop. A brochure describing just what you will do makes a good handout. You can also place ads in bridal magazines if you want to attract business from a larger region. This is one area where you can benefit from some television spot advertising, too. Local stations frequently have very low spot rates on late-night programming in nonmetropolitan areas. Your sales pitch should be that you will deliver a "living, moving reminder of this most important of days."

Most wedding videos are very simple in concept, although exhausting to do in fact. The shoot lasts all day in most cases, from before the ceremony, through the wedding, and then to the reception. It's a full day's work. You'll have to follow the wedding party from arrival at the house of worship or civil venue, through the ceremony, and into the reception. Remember the standard wedding photos: the bride and groom in front of the altar, kissing, and cutting the cake; the dance with the father of the bride and the mother of the groom; and all that stuff. Get plenty of shots of the guests, including all the in-laws, the toast by the best man, the tossing of the bouquet, and dozens of happy faces for the couple to remember after the reality of marriage sinks in. Choose a piece of music long enough to cover 10 to 15 minutes. Lay it down on the audio track of a blank tape. Then simply insert video edits in time to the music, using fades and dissolves to enhance the romantic feeling. Be sure to include natural sound and bites from significant guests at appropriate moments. Then hope you got everybody whom the happy couple regards as crucial to the affair!

Be aware that most music is copyrighted. Many favorite wedding songs require a license to reproduce. If you want to use a copyrighted song, obtain a license from the publisher. The licensing fees for noncommercial, nonbroadcast use are usually very modest. Contact the American Society of Composers, Authors, and Publishers (ASCAP) or Broadcast Music, Inc. (BMI). Stock music sources are listed in most of the trade publications to which you will subscribe. If you do music videos, you can cut deals with your local composer-musicians to do some original tunes in appropriate moods in exchange for breaks on their production costs. Don't be afraid to barter. It's an old and honorable method of exchange.

## Real Estate

The real estate video market is growing at a rapid pace, especially in the Midwest and northern parts of the United States. When the weather is inclement and valuable properties are buried in snow, you can help local Realtors make sales in the warm comfort of their offices.

The process is very simple. You make video tours of homes that the Realtor has listed. The Realtor can do commentary as you go, pointing out the features and highlights of the property. These tapes are so simple that often little or no editing is required. It's very similar to shooting news; include a B-roll of fine details that you might wish to edit in later.

The Realtor advertises this video tour of homes as a nifty service for both sellers and buyers. The tapes give homes added exposure with less intrusion on the life of the seller, and they save potential buyers the trouble of traveling to see houses that they would never be interested in.

You update the reel biweekly or monthly as properties are sold and new

ones are added. Fees for video real estate services can be negotiated on the basis of a flat fee or a monthly retainer. An average of $1,000 to $2,500 a month is customary for the latter. When you point out the savings to the Realtor in terms of expensive color photographs, brochures, wasted house visits, and so on, you have a fine selling tool. For those offices that do not have a VCR, many producers offer a package that includes the VCR and maintenance. Many times, Realtors will buy airtime on a local station, usually on Sunday morning, and run your program or a version of it. Make a separate contract for this use of your material.

## Other Possible Markets

The number of potential secondary markets for the creative independent video producer is almost infinite. Keep your mind open to new ideas. A few innovative suggestions follow.

### Direct Marketing

Do you have a hobby or a passionate interest in something? Most people do, and they tend to seek others like themselves. Hundreds of magazines and periodicals are dedicated to niche markets of fans of one thing or another. Take, for example, pets. Americans spend close to $8 billion a year on their dogs and cats alone. That's *billion* with a *b*. There are specialty publications for dog owners, cat owners, horse owners, bird lovers, fish and insect collectors.

In the advertising pages of these magazines and newsletters is space for you to promote a video of interest to the readers of those periodicals. Consider a video on buying and training a horse, for instance. Get a local horse expert in your area involved and advertise your video in *Western Horseman* magazine at a price of $19.95. How about getting the best dog trainer in your area to do another in the long line of obedience videos? Advertise it in *Dog World,* and see what happens. Insurance companies recommend that holders of homeowner's policies take a careful inventory of all valuable possessions. They also advise that photographs of these belongings be kept for identification purposes. The entrepreneurial independent producer should be able to see how these facts can mean increased business.

Explore the notion of video yearbooks with your local high schools. Producing a yearbook on tape can be time-consuming, as you will have to be involved throughout the school year, covering major events, homecoming, student leaders, and the graduating class. The music score might be the high school alma mater, the fight song, and so forth. On one day, just as the printed yearbook does photos, you do short spots of each senior making a comment on life at good old Washington High. The video yearbook has caught on in many areas of the country, especially with the more affluent school districts. Many offices—including those of dentists, doctors, and others—are turning to mood tapes to keep patients, clients, and employees relaxed. The types of visual images included in these tapes depend on the mood that your client wishes to create.

Make a sample reel of the sorts of things you'd like to watch and hear at the dentist's office, for example, and try to sell it. You might even package the tape with a playback system that you rent to the client as part of your monthly service charge. Production costs for mood tapes are usually fairly low, and the return comes in monthly for a long time. Be sure that you use stock music, music in the public domain, or original tunes for this type of service. The Music Cops will be very litigious if they catch you using copyrighted material without written permission. You might examine some of the relatively inexpensive stock libraries for this kind of thing. Soothing subjects might be wind, surf, sea—or extreme adventures like base jumping or hang gliding. If that's your

bent, then McGillivray-Freeman in Laguna Beach, California, would be the stock library to go to. There are lots more. They advertise in many of the trade publications.

### Cablecasting

If you come up with an idea for an innovative show with regional appeal, it is possible to market the thing to the large number of UHF or low-power stations in small markets. You can become your own syndicator, as Video Trend Associates in Oshkosh, Wisconsin, did. Through a mutual friend, owner Ronald Bullock met the wife of Green Bay Packer football legend Reggie White. Mrs. White loved to cook and did so for Reggie and his teammates. Bullock came up with the idea of a celebrity athlete cooking show, took it around, and got expressions of interest from a station in the Green Bay metro market. With a commitment to air a trial run, he solicited and got sponsorship from local, regional, and even national companies. The show was deliberately cornball in concept and featured more horseplay and bad jokes than actual cooking. It proved to be such a smash hit that Bullock syndicated it to a large number of stations throughout Wisconsin. It became the central profit center for his company.

Don't think that you can't make the big time with a small idea. Just consider producer Vin di Bono and *America's Funniest Home Videos*. Who in their right mind would ever have thought that such a silly, low-quality concept would become a national network success and lead to copycats ad nauseum?

I could go on here, listing possibilities for the creative producer. Use this list as a starting point. Don't get locked in on two or three potential markets and ignore all else. The world is an electronic playground. Go out and have a good time with it.

# Case Studies

The following case studies reveal how four independent producers tried to land and keep major corporate accounts. Two were successful, and two failed entirely and

went bankrupt. The case studies are all true, although names and places have been changed for the usual reasons.

# The One-Account Jump

Spec Video, Inc., was a medium-sized Midwestern production house. It began in the late seventies as the graphics arm of a small ad agency. Its director at the time, Bill Miller, did a small amount of 16mm film work for a few clients but specialized in technical drawings and illustrations for the ad agency's mostly print-oriented accounts. One of these accounts was Garden Corporation.

Garden Corp. manufactured a line of power garden tools, riding lawn mowers, and snow throwers. Garden was comfortably positioned as the leader in its field. Its prices were high, but so was the quality of its products. The company was controlled by members of the founder's family, all of whom were very conservative. Spec Video's main job was to produce the annual catalog and equipment brochures; they also produced an occasional video to demonstrate the new line of equipment to dealers each year. The ad agency lost the account after a number of years. At the same time, Miller decided to buy out the production wing of the agency. He took on Garden as his main account, and Spec Video was born as an independent production house.

Soon after, the competition heated up for Garden as other manufacturers got into the rapidly growing garden tool market. Large firms like John Deere, Toro, and even Honda launched major television campaigns in an attempt to steal the position once dominated by Garden. The company hired a larger ad agency in Ohio but retained Spec Video as its production house. Though it had started primarily as a graphics producer, Miller's company found itself doing large-scale television spot commercial production for the full line of Garden products. The staff swelled to eight full-time employees and a host of freelancers as demand grew for a variety of services ranging from technical illustrations and brochures to film-to-tape video productions and multimedia presentations.

And it all hinged on one major account. Up to this point, Miller had been very fortunate. He had landed a lucrative corporate account and had understood that to keep it, he had to try to provide a full range of services. He could not just stick with producing film and video. He established a personal relationship with the people at Garden and enjoyed their corporate loyalty to him for a long time. Corporate loyalty, however, can be fickle. When Garden's new management saw a spot commercial featuring stop-frame animation, they decided that the company needed to change its prosaic image. Garden suddenly dropped Spec Video as the producer of its spot commercials and went with a Chicago outfit whose specialty was animation. The cost of the new spots was very much more than the fees that Spec Video had been charging, and that stung Miller's sensibilities. The cost to him of losing the video production for the Garden account was nearly fatal. And that really stung.

Although it continued to do much of the graphics and multimedia work for Garden, Spec Video reeled under the impact of having placed all its eggs in one basket and then having lost most of them. After enjoying nearly two decades of sustained growth and prosperity primarily from this one corporate account, the producer had to shift gears and make a concerted effort to go after other accounts to pump up the business's deflated bankbook. Soon after this turning point, Miller sold the company. Subsequently, unable to change the image of the place, the new owner was forced into bankruptcy, and the doors to Spec Video closed forever.

The lesson to be learned here should not be forgotten. Never rest on one account, no matter how solid the foundation seems to be. Diversity is the essential stuff of long life.

# A Case in Point

Jack and Bill were young producers who had just left the U.S. Air Force, where they had worked for five years as officers in television and film production. They had saved their money and, with a small boost from the Veterans Administration, opened a production company north of Los Angeles and close to major industry in Southern California.

They were complementary partners; Jack was strong in production, Bill in graphics and sales. Each had established good contacts with industry while he was still in the service. Their town had some modest industrial firms whose needs they could fill at a lower cost than any producer in Los Angeles.

The partners decided to go after a major account, a nationwide chain of fast-food restaurants called Joe's Café. Jack and Bill knew that the fast-food business had a high turnover rate in wait staff. They had done some research and found that Joe's Café was spending a relatively high percentage of its income on training. With this knowledge, they devised a proposal to provide video training to Joe's wait staff. Their package would include programming and video playback units supplied on a rotational basis to the restaurants around the country. They spent a month in preparation (time that included making up charts and graphs and designing a tasteful brochure), and then Bill made an appointment with the president of the restaurant chain.

The presentation went well. Joe, the president of the chain, told Bill that it was very timely because he and his management team had just been considering the subject of training. He wondered if Bill and Jack would be interested in putting together an entire package that would include a handbook and other materials for trainees. Bill was ecstatic.

At Joe's request, Bill left the entire presentation package, including storyboards for the training video that he had completed in an effort to show just how ready he and Jack were to roll on this project. Then he went back to the office to prepare a sample of the training manual at Joe's request.

Several meetings between Joe, Bill, and Jack ensued. At each one, Joe expressed his delight with the work that the two producers were submitting. By the eighth meeting in as many weeks, Bill and Jack had presented the complete outline for the

manual, the script for the training video, several pieces of finished artwork, a shooting schedule, the final storyboard, and even some sketches for new menu art that Bill had done in his enthusiasm. All work on trying to land other accounts had stopped, as the promise of landing this one seemed to be the pot of gold at rainbow's end.

Joe was absolutely thrilled with Bill and Jack. He told them this many times. He also told them that the contract between them was "being worked on" and that they could expect the go-ahead and a check for a substantial down payment on the production budget at the next meeting.

The next meeting never came. First Joe was "called out of town." When he came back, he was "unavailable" to answer telephone calls from Jack and Bill. Rumors began to spread that Joe's Café was in trouble of some sort. Needless to say, Jack and Bill's production company was in terrible trouble also by this time.

The two men, believing with absolute certainty that Joe's was going to be their bread and butter, had eaten deeply into their marginal capitalization. The one or two other clients for whom they had done some small jobs had turned to other producers. Unable to get back in touch with Joe or anyone else in the organization, Jack and Bill folded their dreams along with their tent, paid their creditors with the last of their money, closed up shop, and went to work for another company in Los Angeles. Both were ultimately successful, but their partnership was never recovered.

The final salt in their wounds came when they found that their script and storyboard had indeed been used by Joe's Café, which had never been in trouble at all. The two producers had literally been robbed, conned by a gifted artist who had inherited the huge food chain from his father. Poetically enough, five years after conning Jack and Bill, Joe himself lost the whole chain; it folded, the victim of corrupt management and till pilfering.

Jack and Bill made some very big errors. First, they assumed that a corporation would be honest. They were, in short, suckered. Second, they presented work, time after time, without asking for payment and without having a written contract. Because the meetings were always with Joe, they had no way of proving after the fact that the training video that another company produced for Joe's Café was actually theirs. They had not copyrighted work on it, and in court, it would have been their word against Joe's. Finally, they had lost sight of their primary goal, which was to produce a training tape. Writing manuals and doing cover art for menus obscured their vision of what they had set out to do in the first place. And this loss of vision proved fatal to their company.

## The Front Desk

Don worked for several years as a musician and a freelance cinematographer. He had a good financial cushion and a growing interest in video. One day, he replaced the movie camera with a video package, including a modest editing setup. He became hooked, and the next logical step for him was to go into business. We will call his company Bootstrap Productions.

His local university had a good program in radio-TV-film. The campus also had a fine college of business. Don enrolled in a series of courses that he tailored to fit his needs. Concurrently, he managed to develop a growing list of small clients. Thanks to his on-the-job training approach, he soon paid off his equipment and added more sophisticated gear. By the time he was finished with his courses at the university, his company was almost paying for itself.

Don recognized that to get his company on a sound footing, he had to get a large corporate account. Because he disliked selling, he also wanted to find a salesperson. He learned of a young woman named Janet who was in the graduate program at the college. She had enough technical knowledge of the field to speak with authority, and she enjoyed sales and marketing. Janet became his associate pro-

ducer and chief salesperson. Janet had been working part-time at a hotel that was part of a large chain. She knew that they needed help in training the staff and suggested approaching the corporate headquarters, even though they already had an outside production company. Because of Bootstrap's low overhead, Janet felt that they could undercut the competition. She and Don prepared a modest proposal for a training video, which included a demo reel of Don's work.

The president of the corporation was very impressed with the presentation and agreed to let Don and Janet take a crack at a short training tape for the hotel's housekeeping staff. The go-ahead was based in large part on Bootstrap's low cost estimate. The budget had been whittled down to no more than a break-even deal if Don and Janet could stick to the three-day shooting schedule. Even one extra day would put them in the red.

They took the risk of a relatively small financial loss to get their feet in the door. And taking this chance paid off. The shoot went smoothly, the tape was finished, and the client was as happy as a clam about it.

A couple of months later, Don and Janet were invited to bid on a new contract for the corporation. The president called them in to discuss his need for a similar training tape for his front desk personnel. This time, he also wanted a written training manual thrown in.

Having literally given away the first project, Bootstrap was now in a serious situation. Neither Don nor Janet was competent at technical writing—certainly not competent enough to do a complex training manual from scratch. The corporation was putting on a squeeze play as well. Although the president knew that the first production had been a nonprofit trial, he made it clear that he expected Bootstrap's new bid to come in substantially lower than any others he had been offered. Don and Janet knew that the price they quoted for the video production would be accepted if they could figure out a way to come through with the manual.

Don and Janet agreed to try to find someone who could do the manual. The president, knowing that he was, in fact, getting a good deal on the video, agreed to let Bootstrap have a few days to put together a separate proposal for the manual. Don knew a woman who was a good technical writer, and he subcontracted with her to do the writing. He then added a 50 percent markup on the writing as a profit for his company. The figure he presented to the corporation was lower by several percentage points than the next bid, even including Bootstrap's markup.

The manual was completed on time, the training tape based on the manual was finished on budget, and Bootstrap Productions landed its first ongoing major corporate account as a result. Today, the company has grown solid and stable under the same ownership. It produces, among other things, a wildly successful cooking show for regional syndication.

It is clear that no matter how badly you want or need a corporate account, you have to stick to your game plan. In this case, the manual did not fit into the plan. It would have been wrong, as Jack and Bill discovered, to agree to it. Don and Janet understood two things: their limitations and their financial needs. Although both of them were tempted to capitulate and give the corporation something for nothing, they understood the first rule of good business. You can't stay in it if you don't make a profit. By standing their ground on the amount of their bid, they won the respect of the corporate president. By delivering what they agreed to deliver for the price quoted, they won his continued business.

## The Community Chest

Scott Nichols was as independent as a hog on ice. He enjoyed his freedom doing a variety of freelance projects. When he decided to settle into a pristine part of the country and open a production company, Wooden Nichols, he brought with him a demo reel of high-quality national work that impressed clients and won contracts. Scott hired Denise Peters as an assistant to run the office, and they enjoyed a couple of years of quiet growth, doing corporate and educational pieces for the most part. They even sold a project to *Encyclopaedia Britannica* that put them in international educational distribution. Scott made enough to buy a small farm and provide a nice living wage for Denise.

The company needed to find some way to grow at a more rapid pace if it was not to be outstripped by inflation. As a newcomer to an insular community, Scott was not making headway toward moving up to the large manufacturer that dominated the town and paid big money for productions.

Denise came up with the idea that would help Wooden Nichols turn the corner into real profit and growth. She was taking night classes at the local college. One day, she told Scott that her professor had remarked that the city had called him about doing an informational video about the newly installed 911 emergency system. The professor did not do outside production because of regulations prohibiting the state from competing for business with for-profit companies. Several states have such laws to protect entrepreneurs from unfair competition.

Scott called on the city's director of public safety the next day. Her name was Dorothy, and she told him that they had a small budget of $10,000 and wanted a video produced to tell the public about how to use 911. She said that it would be about half an hour long and that other production companies had refused to touch it for that much. All she wanted was a few talking heads and some footage of the communications room. Scott realized why other producers had turned down the job. First, $10,000 was not enough to turn a profit on a half hour program, and second, it would be the most boring thing since making peanut butter. He thought there might be a benefit in doing it if he could talk the safety director into letting him show off a little. When he made his pitch, Dorothy beamed and gave him the green light.

Realizing that the 911 system was fraught with drama, as proved by a highly successful reality-based network show, Scott set out to produce his own version for the local community. He recruited free actors from the drama department at Denise's school, solicited the willing cooperation of the police, sheriff's, and fire departments, the ambulance company, and even the highly visual Life Flight helicopter team. Over the next month, he orchestrated a production that had the look of Hollywood, playing it for all the publicity he could muster. When it was finished, the local ABC affiliate station played the half-hour program with a blaze of pre-show promotion that Wooden Nichols could never have paid for.

Scott and Denise didn't make a penny of profit on this community service, but soon thereafter they were making regular productions for the large manufacturer. Today, they make a tradition out of doing at least one community service, nonprofit project a year as payback for their success. As a sidebar, their 911 emergency program won a national award from the Broadcast Education Association and an international diploma of merit from a competition in Badajoz, Spain.

## Summary

This chapter discussed some of the nuts and bolts of getting your accounts receivable column moving toward the black. All of the case studies came from the actual experiences of independent producers. Your circumstances may not be similar to theirs. From their stories, however, you should be able to glean information that will help you avoid the snares and traps that they have gone through and stimulate your mind into productive channels for current and future profits.

## Notes

1. For an annual listing of Four A members, write to AAAA, 666 Third Avenue, New York, NY 10017. The *Roster and Organization* directory is available free of charge.

2. For a list of many U.S. audio production houses, see *The National Register,* which is available from the National Register Publishing Co., 5201 Old Orchard Road, Skokie, IL 60077.

# 6

# Procedures and Practicalities

Previous chapters covered the business of business in detail. Management is management in any kind of enterprise involving people and materials. In this section, we'll look at several standardized practices that relate specifically to independent video production. This is where we specialize.

## Establishing a Rate Card

In the retail business, pricing a shovel or a pair of slippers is easy. Merchants figure their cost for the product, factor in their overhead, compute a figure for losses due to theft and damage (which they call "shrinkage"), and add on a profit margin. It's just that easy.

In some ways, the independent producer does the same thing. You know at the outset of a project, with some certainty, what equipment, tape, talent, crew, and postproduction costs are going to be. What you may not have a firm handle on is the cost of your most valuable assets: your own training, skill, and time. These are the same intangibles for which people willingly pay doctors, lawyers, and psychiatrists. Lawyers charge $200 to $500 an hour for their training and time, and no one shouts in outrage about it. A physician crams people into a crowded waiting room and runs through 20 or 30 patients in an hour, charging $50 to $200 dollars a head for services rendered. People smile and say, "Well, that's the way it goes." Yet many of those same people fail to recognize what costs so much in a video production, and they give professional video specialists no respect at all for the years and years of education and training that separate us from Uncle Fred and his Sears special camcorder at the Fourth of July picnic. The fact is that the talent and training of the professional video producer is a commodity, just like that of the doctor, the lawyer, and the psychiatrist. It has worth. And in the final analysis, it is what we have to sell.

Because we are not horse traders, car dealers, or Persian rug sellers in the Casbah, we don't want to haggle or negotiate the price every time we make a deal. That way of life is demeaning and unpleasant. Therefore, our profession uses the rate

### Remote Location Rate

**EFP:**

**$150.00** per hour- 1 hour minimum

**$    .35** per mile

**$1000.00**  day rate- 10 hour day

### Electronic Still or 35mm Slides:

**$ 75.00** per hour- 1 hour minimum

**$    .35** per mile

**$  5.00** per slide mounted

### Videotape Editing Rate

**BetacamSP Cuts-only Suite:**

**$100.00** per hour

**$250.00** per hour

**Avid Non-linear offline:**

**$400.00** per hour- 1 hour minimum

### DUBBING:

**$  5.00** per running minute plus tape
1/2 BetacamSP to BetacamSX
1/2 BetacamSP to VHS
1/2 VHS to BetacamSP or
BetacamSX

10 minute minimum

### Videotape Purchase
Prices vary
### Videocassette Dubs:

**BetacamSP**

| | |
|---|---|
| 10 minute | - $25.00 |
| 20 minute | - $ 35.00 |
| 30 minute | - $ 55.00 |

**1/2 Prosumer**

| | |
|---|---|
| T 30-120 | - $35.00 |
| Digital | - $55.00 |

### Legal Video Services

**Depositions:**

**$ 500.00** plus **$0.35** per mile

TERMS OF BUSINESS: Net 10 days.
Accounts past due 30 days or more
shall have a 3% per month service
charge applied to outstanding balances.

NOTE:   Short notice, unscheduled, or
weekend hours may be subject to
overtime rates which are 1.5 times those
posted.

**Figure 6-1** Rate card for an independent video production company.

card. Without one, you can be lost at sea. A rate card serves two major functions: It is a menu of the services you offer, and it lists the standardized hourly, daily, or weekly rate you charge for those services. An example is shown in Figure 6-1.

Here's how you make one. First, decide what standard services you can offer. The more you provide on a continuing basis, the better your chances of getting a fairly steady flow of business—and income.

If you have an older postproduction room with at least two tape decks, a controller, and a system for enhancing and transferring audio, you may want to rent out that facility for off-line editing, dubbing, and so on. Although editing is done mostly on nonlinear systems, many smaller projects can be completed on that old analog system that you have sitting in the corner. Advertise it and turn that white elephant into a goose laying golden eggs by tapping the rapidly expanding home and semiprofessional market. Family histories, weddings, bar and bas mitzvahs, and so on don't need $500-an-hour Avid bays. This rental arm of your facility can bring in a steady flow of cash in many areas of the country. Don't do it, however, if you anticipate doing a great deal of your own production in analog or can't afford the increase in equipment maintenance costs that will result from extra use. Factor upkeep into your hourly rate for this service.

Many producers started out as writers. If you are one of them, offer writing as one of your services. Many writer-producers make nearly as much money doing everything from technical manuals to newsletters, speeches, and corporate reports as they do from producing videos.[1] There are many other services that you can provide. The only limit is the number of your talents.

## Compare Yourself

Once you've decided what services to offer, put a price tag on each of them. To be competitive in your marketplace, get rate cards from other producers and from your local television stations, and see what they charge. Merchants who advertise on TV often employ local stations to do their productions. Advertising agencies with no in-house production capabilities also use TV stations. You want to take away some of that business, which means that you will be less than popular with the station management. Use some tact, therefore, in getting your hands on station rate cards.

Once you have an assortment of these cards from stations and other independent producers, compare their prices with what you had hoped to charge for your services. Two types of businesses charge the lowest rates: the large outfit that does enough volume to allow for reduced unit prices and the one-person operation trying to under-

sell everybody else. The latter is usually the lowest quality in town, too, and will probably disappear from the scene shortly. You will find a comfortable position somewhere between the highest and the lowest figures quoted.

After calculating your real overhead costs (the very minimum you have to make to break even), add on a reasonable charge for your time and profit for the company. Never forget that the company is a separate entity from you and any employees you have. It must have its share of each project to stay alive.

There are no standards for profit margin and owner's salary. Some producers work regularly with 100 percent markups, and others squeak by on 15 to 20 percent, relying on high volume. A more typical profit margin runs between 40 to 50 percent of the budget. You should calculate a minimum profit for your company by considering the real expenses of day-to-day operation (what it costs to keep your doors open), what your salary is going to be, and what financial cushion you need to continue operating between productions.

## Remember to Pay the Business

Use before-tax profits to sustain the business, to purchase and maintain equipment, to provide for expansion, and so forth. Put after-tax profits to work in interest-bearing savings accounts or other investments for which you should consult a financial adviser. A good rule-of-thumb is that businesses must grow at least 10 percent per year to survive inflation.

Determining your own salary is a matter of conscience. Many producers just starting out take no salary beyond the necessities of food, rent, transportation, and so on. Stephen J. Cannell, one the most successful Hollywood producers, took no salary at all for himself in the early days of his company, at a time when he was producing one hit show after another. He sold shows like *The A Team* to the network at less than the production cost, hanging on to the rights and waiting for syndication and foreign release to return good profits. He paid his staff well and earned their loyalty and talent. He was able to support himself from other income, and his gamble paid off in spades. This is an example of pumping all of the income back into the business. If you can afford this kind of gamble, you're better off than most of us. In fact, this practice is neither fair, wise, nor necessary. Suffering for the cause can lead to anger, frustration, employee resentment, and other traumas for producers who are less noble than Cannell, so think about the consequences seriously.

Pay yourself a fair salary in relation to the business and its employees. Remember that you will need a vacation and that your family, if you have one, should not have to suffer unduly because you have gone into business for yourself. As the business grows, remember too that you are entitled to a large share of the salary schedule because you have taken all the risks and, without you, there would be no company. That's not greed—it's the American dream!

## Fair Play

Although it's tempting to try to undercut the competition as a method of taking away some of their business, use extreme caution if you decide to go this way. Remember that a number of factors go into the decision of a corporate executive or small business owner to contract for a service—the cost of that service is sometimes one of the last considerations.

Businesspeople know that quality costs money. They are, for the most part (as you should be), very suspicious of anyone who promises high quality at an exceptionally low price. The terms are antipodal. As with Gucci shoes and Rolex watches, you get what you pay for. The $50 Rolex offered on the street corner looks really good until your wrist turns green and the thing falls apart. Practice high-quality production techniques, and charge what they're worth.

In fact, here's a note of caution. Some states have laws to prohibit unfair competition and impose a minimum profit margin on businesses. In Wisconsin, the minimum is 6 percent. Check with your state to find out if this law applies to you. Remember, too, that if you are cast in the role of Cheap Sam, you may never be able to raise your rates. Aside from that, when negotiations with a client hinge on cost, it is always to your advantage to be able to come down a percentage point or two to clinch the deal. It is almost never possible to hike your price when you reach this stage of negotiations.

When you have decided on an appropriate rate structure—one that is fair and in line with your competition—have it typeset and printed. Include your logo and a brief promotional pitch if you choose. The card will become a fixed part of your presentation package. It can be adjusted annually to account for inflation, market fluctuations, and so forth. Exercise due care when making it up, for it will become the basis for your tenure in this business.

Do not include pricing in your promotional materials, such as your Web site or brochure. Leave cost for your face-to-face meeting with prospective clients, and leave it until the end of the discussion whenever possible. Avoid getting trapped into answering the "how much" question until you've had a chance to present all of the other factors that go into your product. If you're having a house built, the first part of the plan is deciding what features you want, in what neighborhood it will be, and how many square feet you'd like. The builder can tell you then how much your dream home will cost.

# Billing and Collecting

It seems like a simple matter to charge somebody for your services, send them a bill, and collect your money. For some reason—in the production business especially—it frequently isn't this easy at all. The product that we sell is much more intangible than a car or a refrigerator. Once it's completed, it runs for a brief moment on a screen. Then, as far as clients are concerned, it's gone. Perhaps that is why it is sometimes difficult to wrestle payment from clients and why the single biggest complaint of small and medium-sized independent producers is slow-to-no collection of bills.

At the outset of a production, clients are usually excited, cooperative, and enthusiastic. At this stage, they are quite friendly with the producer. It's a honeymoon in every sense of the word, and in the best of all possible worlds, this beginning stage is the best time to collect the full budget. Unfortunately, as in most other business transactions, the bill is not rendered until the product or service has been delivered. By that point, the client is often disinterested, disenchanted, disappointed, and sometimes suffering the postproduction blues, which are common to many producers, as well. This odd syndrome is comparable to the postpartum blues experienced by some new mothers. The anticipation, exhilaration, and camaraderie of the production disappear suddenly with the birth of the finished product. Life seems mundane again. And minor troubles or slights are magnified out of all proportion.

Producers who have other productions in the offing can cure these blues by getting back to work. Clients have no such diversion. They may vent their frustration by inventing reasons not to pay for the production. Their blues may be further aggravated because they have no immediate feedback on the success of the project. They may begin to doubt the validity of their initial decision to spend a great deal of money on something so ephemeral as a video production. This is a frustrating time for the producer, who has done nothing wrong, has delivered the product as promised and on time, and cannot understand the sudden chill.

Before a project begins, there is no sure way of determining whether clients will pay their bills on time or at all. However,

the following sections offer independent producers some guidelines for correct, businesslike billing procedures. They also discuss the actions you can take when you're confronted with clients who will not pay.

## Collecting the Down Payment

Most independent producers collect a substantial down payment in advance of each production. Usually, the payment schedule is designed so that each of the three major phases of a project is paid for along the way. Once you have a complete budget approved by clients, tell them that payment would be appreciated as follows: one-third on script approval, one-third on completion of principal photography, and one-third on delivery of the completed tape.

Some producers divide the budget four ways, calling for one-fourth on approval of the proposal to develop the script, one-fourth on script approval, and so on. With either method, the idea is to refrain from dipping into your own pocket during a project. The final payment on delivery of the tape is normally the profit for the job. If, for some reason, you are not paid this final installment, then you should at least break even on the deal.

## Keeping the Client Involved

During production and postproduction, make clients feel as though they are part of the team. Although you can't and shouldn't tolerate unnecessary interference from clients, you do want to cultivate a feeling of mutual respect. Put the dazzle of "making television" to your advantage. While the cameras are rolling and everything is in full swing, be sure to escort clients onto the set (but keep them out of the way of your director). Watching the fun of shooting gives clients a break from the daily routine of normal business, and even though it's old hat to you, production is exciting to them. People pay lots and lots of money, for instance, to go to Universal Studios and the MGM sets at Disney World to pretend they're watching movies being shot. Let your client play a little at this stage of the game. If you have a wrap party at the end, as most producers do, be sure that the client is there and that compliments and thanks for letting you have the job are passed around. Little things really do mean a lot.

In postproduction, when you have the off-line ready to go on-line, invite the client in to see some of the final stages of the process. You don't want clients breathing down your neck during the hard work and tough decision making. You don't want them seeing all the blown takes and goofing off that frequently show up in off-line. But letting them in at the finish builds good rapport. And although it's a pain in the neck, let the clients have some input on the editing. Letting them make a few suggestions makes the project theirs. And with nonlinear editing, it's not a big deal to make the changes; just be sure that you duplicate your original cut beforehand so you can go back to it if necessary.

## Billing and Collecting

Establish a standardized procedure for billing as part of your general accounting practices. Send itemized statements on a regular basis. Develop a form of your own, or adapt one from the numerous printed forms available from office supply firms or with computerized office programs.

A professional billing statement is the hallmark of sound business. It should have a printed logo and include at least the following:

> Description of the service rendered
> Date of completion of this service
> Contract reference number
> Total amount of the initial budget
> Amount already paid on account
> Balance due now
> Statement of terms of contract
> Statement of interest or service charges
> for unpaid balance (This is normally 1
> percent per month after 30 days. Some
> states have usury laws that put limits
> on the amount of interest you may

charge. Check the law in your state before adding interest charges.)

Here are some sound tips on helping your company maintain a positive cash flow.

- Bill your clients. Do it as soon as the work is done. Many firms have 30- or 60-day payment schedules, meaning that the sooner you bill, the better because you will wait 30 to 60 days after the receipt of your bill before you get paid.
- Put your payments into interest-bearing accounts as soon as you get them. Many businesses deposit cash receipts into money market funds on which they can write drafts instead of checks. The interest on these accounts is generally higher than a business banker can offer. Investigate such possibilities. Benjamin Franklin said, "A penny saved is a penny earned." It's still true.
- Send past due notices as soon as the 30- or 60-day period expires. And charge interest on past due accounts.
- Do not pay your own bills before they are due. Keep your money earning interest for as long as possible.
- Check out the possibility of leasing equipment, rather than buying it. Unless you have a really favorable depreciation schedule, you might find it cheaper in the long run to lease.
- Be certain that you don't overpay your estimated quarterly taxes.

## Handling Collection Problems

If your clients have not paid their bill after a reasonable period of time, attempt to work with them personally. Even offer to meet and discuss the situation in person. If they are having trouble with cash flow, offer to work out a monthly payment schedule. We all have problems from time to time. Try to stay cordial, nonthreatening, and compassionate. Always present yourself as a rational, good-natured problem solver. Most people respond well to an honest attempt to communicate. Threats and temper explosions never work. Some of what follows does. Note: Seek legal counsel before proceeding with anything described here: I am not a lawyer, and this is not legal advice. It is merely a composite of case histories from other businesses and what passes for common sense.

If you still encounter resistance after about 90 days of trying to resolve the problem, you need to move ahead. Basically, there are two alternatives: You can go to court, or you can hire a collection agency. Neither is pleasant, and neither guarantees that you will ever get your money. But if you don't put forth any effort, it's a given that you won't collect. Weigh the potential costs of collection against the amount owed, and proceed as the circumstances dictate. If the amount is a few hundred bucks, write it off. The loss is usually deductible, and trying to collect it will cost more that the original debt. If the amount is substantial, hit 'em with your best shot. That does not mean sending in a gorilla with a violin case under his arm. It means taking legal action.

## Going to Court

You will, of course, want to consult an attorney before deciding whether litigation is a viable solution. For the most part, lawsuits for unpaid bills are tricky. Courts insist that you have proof of the contract. Under almost all circumstances, this means that you must have something signed on paper between you and your debtor. In legal terms, this is called a "writing." This can be a letter of agreement or a contract. For very small amounts, a "writing" may not be required. In any case, you're on much more solid legal turf if you have a signed contract. In spite of what you've heard about verbal contracts, in most cases they aren't worth the breath it takes to make them. In court, it will come down to your word against the client's word. Usually, that is not enough for you to win. Another tenuous aspect of a lawsuit is that you will no doubt have to prove that through no fault of your own, a breach of contract has taken place. We'll discuss this in the next section on contracts.

If you do go to court, you have two options: You can either go to small claims court, or you can file a more complex civil suit. The maximum awards for small claims court vary from state to state but normally range between $500 and $2,500. You do not need to hire an attorney in small claims, although both you and the defendant may do so. You can file the papers for the lawsuit at the Clerk of Courts office for a modest fee. If the defendant does not appear at the hearing or otherwise raises an objection, it is possible for you to win the suit by default. If the defendant does show up, you will have to prove to the satisfaction of the court that the defendant owes you the amount claimed. If you prove this, you will be awarded a judgment for the whole amount or for whatever portion the judge rules is proper.

Bear in mind that the defendant may file a countersuit against you for damages that could be in excess of what you sued for in the first place. The court will weigh both sides of the issue and make a determination. The appeals process for small claims courts varies widely. In some states, the decision of the judge is final. In other states, you or the defendant may appeal to a higher court within a specified amount of time. The best advice is to know your state laws and consult a licensed attorney before you enter into any action.

For dollar amounts in excess of the maximum for small claims, you must bring a more complex civil suit. Most courts in America have tremendous backlogs of pending cases. Filing a civil suit and waiting for the case to appear before a judge and jury can be an incredibly time-consuming process. In many states, it can take from one to five years before your case is ever heard. You will also have to hire an attorney, whose fee can exceed the amount of money for which you are suing. If you win the case, it is sometimes possible for you to get a judgment for attorney's fees in addition to the amount of the suit. This is not guaranteed in any case.

Nor does winning the suit mean that you can rely on getting any money in the end. Receiving a judgment does not guarantee that the defendant will ever pay you. It simply means that the court agrees that you are owed the money. Collecting the money involves another set of legal maneuvers that may end up costing you more than the amount of the judgment. Among these recourses are garnishment of wages if your debtor works for a company and the seizure of certain assets. Neither is easy to accomplish, but sometimes they work.

Once you have filed a suit and your clients realize that you are serious about being paid, it may be best to negotiate with them out of court and settle for a sum lower than the amount actually owed. Defendants will often settle out of court rather than risk a judgment in the full amount or incur the expense of hiring an attorney and defending the suit. Attorneys are never inexpensive, and once a lawsuit is looming, chances are good that clients will simply pay the amount agreed upon. You have to give them the solid impression that you will go all the way to the wall if that's the way they want it. As with all legal matters, if you have any doubts or questions about proceeding, check with an attorney in your state.

## Hiring a Collection Agency

When all other avenues have failed to get a debtor to pay up and you've decided that a lawsuit is too much bother to be worth it, you have a second set of options. One is to give up and write the episode—and the loss—off to experience. The other is to turn the bill over to a collection agency.

These outfits generally work for a percentage of the total bill, and you pay them only if they collect. Laws regulating collection agencies vary in each state, and there are restrictions on just how far an agency can go in its badgering of debtors. Usually, credit agencies can send notices to the party threatening in vague terms some kind of "action" if the debt isn't paid. They can report bad debts to various credit agencies, which may influence the person's credit rating. If your client is concerned about such things, the collection agency just might be paid.

In general, though, the collection agency is the last resort. Do not count on it for much more than a final blast at the villain in your life, who has more than likely gotten away with not paying you. Move on quickly to more productive pursuits, and cut your emotional losses by trying to forget about it.

# Making a Contract

The contract is the most important document you will use in business. In the "good old days," people made contracts with a handshake, and reputations were based on keeping your word. Those days are as dead as Hopalong Cassidy and Roy Rogers. Put every deal in writing now.

Not only is the contract your principal device for holding a client to the payment of your bills, but it is the foundation for all business you conduct with freelancers and suppliers. Producers frequently contract with technicians (such as editors and DPs), who are not regular employees of their companies. This is beneficial to the small producer, who does not need to withhold

taxes, pay for worker's compensation or health and unemployment insurance, and so forth, for such contracted work. Independent producers usually contract for rental equipment and supplies, too. Finally, if working in broadcast, you will also be dealing with distribution contracts for anything you sell to television, either network or syndicated.

Though there are elements common to all contracts, be advised that no contract is "standard." If anyone hands you a "standard contract" for some service, run, don't walk, to your favorite lawyer before signing! Contract law is complex, and you should always have an attorney draw up your contracts and interpret all but the most routine agreements presented to you by other parties.

## What Constitutes a Contract

In essence, a contract is simply the written form of an agreement between two or more parties before entering a project. The three basic elements of a contract are offer, acceptance, and consideration. These three items are the heart and soul, the legally binding cement, of any contract. Breaching, or not abiding by, just one of these can invalidate the contract and may open the breaching party to damaging civil action.

## The Offer

When drawing up a contract between your business and a client in which you offer to produce a videotape, you must specify exactly what will go into this project. (Figure 6–2 is an example of a contract that could be used for the Jones Hotels project.) In your contract, specify the subject of the videotape, and state that you will consult with the client; that you will write, or have written, a script for the client to approve; and that you will make a videotape from this script to the best of your ability. You must also state that the videotape will be of a certain length and format in its final delivered form, that it will take a certain amount of time to produce it, and that it will cost a certain amount of money. The money will be paid to you in a certain manner according to the formula that you specify here in the contract.

In making the offer, be as specific as possible. Include such items as the kind of music (either prerecorded or original), whether the tape will be sync-sound or narrated voice-over, what actors will be in it, and so on. Remember that you will be held to providing everything you include in your offer, so be careful what you promise here.

Be very specific as to what the clients will be expected to provide. These are the conditions of the offer. Always provide for some sort of approval (e.g., if the script is approved and the project is an accurate reproduction on tape of the elements of the script, then the clients must accept the videotape). If you aren't careful in this area, you may encounter clients who refuse to pay because they don't like the product.

## The Acceptance

After you make your offer, it is imperative that the other party accept it with all of the conditions that have been set forth. Typically, the acceptance appears at the end of the contract form with a statement that reads something like this:

I have read, understood, and agreed to abide by all of the provisions of this contract on this _____ day of _____ , _____ , in the City
*(day)* *(month)* *(year)*

of _____ , State of _____ .

Both parties to the contract sign in spaces provided beneath this acceptance. A witness to the signatures (preferably a notary public) is highly advisable. At least two copies of the contract must be signed in ink. One copy is for you; the other is given to the client. It is a good idea to make an extra copy to give to your attorney.

## Consideration

Consideration is the aspect of a contract that is most open to dispute, interpretation, and misunderstanding. Think of consideration as the inducement for both parties to enter into the contract. For a production contract, producers will get an agreed-upon sum of money for their work, and clients will get a completed videotape—quid pro quo. Most contracts contain wording like this: "For X number of dollars and other valuable consideration, the parties hereto agree . . ."

MY OWN PRODUCTION COMPANY
123 First Street
Anytown, USA 01234

PRODUCTION CONTRACT

1. The purpose of this document is to establish a contract between My Own Production Company, hereinafter referred to as PRODUCER, and _____, hereinafter referred to as CLIENT, for the production of a videotape program, hereinafter referred to as the PROJECT.

2. PRODUCER offers to produce the PROJECT for CLIENT in exchange for valuable consideration, as specified in Paragraph 9 below.

3. DESCRIPTION OF THE PROJECT: The PROJECT is to be a ___- minute, color, sound videotape about the procedures used by the housekeeping staff of the CLIENT in the operation of CLIENT'S hotel/motel business. The purpose of the PROJECT is to provide CLIENT with an audiovisual training device for use in indoctrinating present and future housekeeping staff in their duties as housekeepers. No other use of the PROJECT is anticipated, nor have terms of consideration been agreed to for any but the use specified herein.

4. PRODUCER shall provide CLIENT a written script in a format standard to the video production industry prior to the principal photography of production. CLIENT shall have the right to approve said script for production or to stipulate changes thereto in order to make said script suitable for approval by CLIENT. Said approval shall be in writing with a signature block for CLIENT on the front page of the final script, to wit: THIS SCRIPT IS APPROVED FOR PRODUCTION.

**Figure 6–2** Production contract for a video project.

5. PRODUCER shall, subsequent to script approval, exercise sole discretion in the hiring and firing of cast, crew, and other production staff, exercising his best professional judgment in this selection to ensure the highest possible standards of production for the specified budget.

6. CLIENT shall approve the written production budget submitted in advance by the PRODUCER. PRODUCER warrants that the production shall cost no more than the grand total listed on said budget without prior written consent of the CLIENT.

7. PRODUCER shall submit a shooting schedule to CLIENT for approval. Once said shooting schedule is approved in writing, any deviation or delay therefrom caused by CLIENT shall be considered unreasonable, and any costs for said delay shall be charged to the production budget over and above the original grand total of said budget.

8. PRODUCER shall provide a finished version of the PROJECT to CLIENT no later than the ____day of _____, _____, at the CLIENT'S place of business, which is

_____.

*(address, city, state, and zip code)*

9. The grand total of the production budget for PROJECT approved by CLIENT is $_____. This total is payable as follows:

(a) 25 percent at contract signing, receipt of which is hereby acknowledged by PRODUCER.

(b) 25 percent upon written script approval.

(c) 25 percent upon completion of principal photography.

(d) 25 percent upon delivery to CLIENT of the finished videotape.

**Figure 6–2 (cont.)** Production contract for a video project.

10. There are no other agreements or codicils relative to this PROJECT between either of the parties hereto, either verbally or in writing, and this document constitutes the entirety of the contract.

I have read, understood, and agreed to each and every provision of this contract and with my signature hereby certify and avow that I accept and agree to abide by them and that I am competent and legally qualified to enter into such a contract.

Executed this _____day of _____, _____, in the

                 *(day)*               *(month)*           *(year)*

city of _____, county of_____ ,

state of_____ by:

_____       _____

CLIENT                       PRODUCER

_____

WITNESS

**Figure 6–2 (cont.)** Production contract for a video project.

The legal jargon phrase "other valuable consideration" may mean merely the privilege of doing business with a client with a big name, the opportunity to prove oneself worthy of further work, the enjoyment of associating with a celebrity, and so on. Consideration is what each party gets from the performance of the contract.

Note again that nothing in the preceding section has been written or offered as legal advice. This section has been informational in nature only. For assistance with any contractual needs, consult a licensed attorney in your state.

# Bartering

Another standard practice in this unstandardized business is called "trade-out," and it involves the ancient concept of bartering your services. Here are a couple of examples of bartering:

- You might get a car dealer or manufacturer to lend you a car for a shoot, provided that the vehicle is prominently featured and the supplier is acknowledged in the credits.
- You might trade the production of a TV spot in exchange for services. For example, you shoot a commercial for Joe's Garage, and Joe services and repairs your car. You could also trade a screen credit line to a local café in exchange for free meals for the cast and crew during production. You might even shoot a scene at the café, making sure that the name of the place appears.

In trading out, let your imagination be your guide. It never hurts to ask; the worst that can happen is that the prospect will say no.

# Summary

As Prospero remarked in Shakespeare's *Tempest,* "Our revels now are ended." There is little left to tell about the art and science of independent production. My purpose throughout this book, in part, has been to present you with an overview of information based on the practical, real-life experiences of dozens of independent video producers. A great amount of research has also gone into providing you with methods for keeping a continuous flow of information about this business coming your way. Remember that information is power. Stuff yourself with it in every possible way. Gobble books and poetry, music and magazines, theater and art and movies. Set aside an hour a day to do nothing but surf the Net to see what the world is doing today and what it will be doing tomorrow.

Another purpose of this book, stated at the outset, has been to give you a comprehensive vision of what a producer is, what

a producer does, and how a producer sets up a business and runs it.

What may not be apparent in all of this is the love. Most producers will confide, quite frankly, that going into independent production is a nutty thing to do. The purely rational mind would recognize at the outset that it makes more sense to work at a job where the checks are regular, the health plan is paid for, the phones work, and somebody else has all the headaches. The desire to be an independent producer is not rational. Just think about it.

In the end, the producer is an unsung hero. Remember this: If you are the producer and the project fails, it will be all your fault. If it succeeds, it will have 100 mothers and fathers—none of whom will be you. Everyone associated with it, including the person who serves the sandwiches at lunch, will take the credit.

Accolades will be heaped on the actors, the director, and the DP—all of whom deserve them, of course. But none are likely to come your way. Your director will ignore your contribution. The editor will claim it was due to all that great Avid stuff. The client will claim the whole piece, leaving you out altogether. This odd truth of our business is something you will have to learn to live with. So draw whatever satisfaction you can from the awareness of your own accomplishments as the prime mover in the piece, since that is all you'll get. Approve of yourself because producing is, by and large, a thankless job. Even the grips think they know better than you. As does any Team-ster! And that's where the love comes in. You have to love doing it.

Of all the producers who contributed their time and combined wisdom to this book, of all the producers who ever dreamed up and then sweated a project through to the end, most often misunderstood and unappreciated, not a single one can think of anything else they would rather be doing with their lives. This is as good as it gets. If you understand that, then you are one of us. Good luck, welcome aboard, and remember those words of Rudyard Kipling's! You'll need them.

# Note

1. For an annual listing of freelance markets for writers, see *Writer's Market* (Cincinnati: Writer's Digest Books, annual).

# Appendix A

# Directory of Guilds and Unions

The locations, addresses, and phone numbers of regional and East Coast offices of the following guilds and unions are available by inquiring at the offices listed here.

## Actors and Artists

American Federation of Television and
  Radio Artists (AFTRA)
1717 North Highland Avenue
Los Angeles, CA 90028
(213) 461-8111

Screen Actors Guild (SAG)
7065 Hollywood Boulevard
Los Angeles, CA 90028
(213) 856-6849

## Directors

Directors Guild of America (DGA)
7920 Sunset Boulevard
Los Angeles, CA 90046
(213) 289-2000

## Sound

Broadcast TV Recording Engineers
International Brotherhood of Electrical
  Workers (IBEW)
3518 Cahuenga Boulevard West,
  Suite 307
Los Angeles, CA 90068
(213) 851-5515

International Sound Technicians, Cinetechnicians, and TV Engineers Local 695
International Alliance of Theatrical Stage
  Employees
11331 Ventura Boulevard, Suite 201
Studio City, CA 91604
(818) 985-9204

# Talent Agents

For this and other "insider" information covering agents, production companies, postproduction services, support services, location services and equipment, sets and stages, crew and union rules, camera and sound equipment, props, and wardrobe on the West Coast, invest in a copy of a fine directory called *LA411*. It is available from:

LA411 Publishing Company
P.O. Box 480495
Los Angeles, CA 90048
(213) 460-6304

Also recommended is the annual *Hollywood Reporter Studio Blu-Book Directory*, available from:

The *Hollywood Reporter*
6715 Sunset Boulevard
Los Angeles, CA 90028
(213) 464-7411

# Technicians

International Alliance of Theatrical Stage
  Employees (IATSE and M.P.M.O.)
13949 Ventura Boulevard, Suite 300
Sherman Oaks, CA 91423
(818) 905-8999

National Association of Broadcast Employees and Technicians (NABET)
333 North Glenoaks Boulevard, Suite 640
Burbank, CA 91502
(818) 846-0490

# Transportation

Studio Transportation Drivers Local 399
International Brotherhood of Teamsters
4747 Vineland Avenue, Suite E
North Hollywood, CA 91602
(818) 985-7374

# Writers

Writers Guild of America (WGA), West
8955 Beverly Boulevard
Los Angeles, CA 90048
(213) 550-1000

# Appendix B

# A View from the Top: Interview with Ralph Kendall Berge

In this book, I have presented case histories from small to medium-sized projects. Although most of us will spend our lives producing this type of project, it might prove useful to examine a slice of life from the top of the heap in our profession.

The following edited interview will take you through the process of making a major, made-for-television movie from the standpoint of the line producer. Ralph Kendall Berge, vice president of production—long form at Paramount Pictures Television in Hollywood, discusses his production of a picture for Turner Network Television (TNT). The movie, *Honor and Glory*, was based on the first successful assault on the North Pole; it premiered on TNT in 1998. The most interesting aspect of this monumental journey was that it included the first black man (Matthew Henson) as well as the first white man (Robert Peary) to reach the Pole.

How the picture came to be is itself a fascinating story about the inner workings of major network operations. It is also noteworthy because, in the end, the producer of this major production had essentially the same concerns and tasks as the producer of a training video for Caterpillar or the Jones Hotel. The primary differ-

Ralph Kendall Berge

ence between the two is that much more money and many more people are involved in the production of a feature, and of course, the end product is seen by a much larger audience. The lesson in this interview is that a producer is a producer is a producer. And the lesson is taught here in a producer's own words.

# The Interview

*Jacobs*: Tell me about the process of producing a picture like *Honor and Glory*. Start at the top, and tell me how you produced it.

*Berge*: I'll split it into two: before I got involved and after I was involved. Before, ideas and projects come from anywhere. Someone comes up with the story and script, some sort of a thing. In this case, the idea came from a *National Geographic* photojournalist named Robert Caputo, who travels the world taking photographs. He was digging around in the archives of *National Geographic* at the time and possibly the Explorers Club in New York, I think, and he came across the volumes of research that Peary had done in the Arctic, which involved a lot of Eskimos. He found a virtual chorus line of half-naked Eskimo women in this research. I'm not sure if that's what first piqued his interest in it, but beyond that, what really triggered it was the packs of letters from Henson to Peary. Matthew Henson, before and after [the first expedition that failed], and all of the letters from the wives and all that stuff.

*Jacobs*: What triggered these letters?

*Berge*: The [Arctic] explorers would take these journeys for up to two years at a minimum. Henson and Peary met on a trip to Nicaragua—first on a trip there.

*Jacobs*: How did a white man meet a black man in the elevated atmosphere of adventurer-explorers? How did they meet? Because back in those days it wasn't common, certainly.

*Berge*: I believe it was that Henson had done some extensive traveling, a lot of ship work on his own, you know as a ship's mate, that sort of thing, and was working and came across Peary. And Peary, much to his credit, saw the potential or the value in someone who knew what they were doing and so took him as a valet. You know, the guy was way overqualified, but in order to go on the adventure he signed on as a valet. Actually, he was a fine carpenter and a ship's mate.

*Jacobs:* But in those days, blacks weren't ship's mates and carpenters; they were valets and cooks.

*Berge:* Yup. Especially in the States. So Henson signed on with that and went on the ship, and the letters were prompted by either Peary's orders to Henson in terms of "Make sure you get 38 bundles of coal" and that sort of thing—instructions to him. Often the wives, when Peary's didn't go with him. There were letters from Henson's wife to Peary saying, "I've not heard from my husband in a year and a half. Have you seen him?" Which prompted me to think there was a whole other reason these guys went to the Arctic. Maybe they wanted to get away from their wives! [Laughter.]

*Jacobs:* So this cosmic connection of the first black man in history going to the North Pole started as a guy thing to get away from the womenfolk? That's not going to be a popular angle these days.

*Berge:* That's what makes history interesting, isn't it? It was a different time, a different place. So, anyway . . .

*Jacobs:* Yeah. Back on track producing a movie. It started . . .

*Berge:* So it really started with Caputo finding that stuff, and then he wrote up, not knowing any better, wrote up something like a 40-page treatment, instead of one page. Robert Caputo . . . was basically a journalist. I mean, he drops in, gets the mule; 200 miles into the jungle he meets the people who have never seen white guys before, looks at them, writes the article, and goes out. So his work's in that story, what's a good story and what's not. So he wrote it up as a 40-page treatment. It went to, uh, I have to check on the exact chain here, but maybe it's not consequential anyway.

*Jacobs:* You mean, who he gave it to?

*Berge:* I believe it went to Bruce Gilbert after that—who is a producer—or maybe it went to Meryl Streep. Anyway, somehow it got to Bruce Gilbert . . .

*Jacobs:* . . . who is a producer.

*Berge:* Yes. *Coming Home* was his first one.

*Jacobs:* Jane Fonda.

*Berge: On Golden Pond.* Major credits. . . . So he got it at a meeting at Turner. You know, when you're in development, you bring in a project that they can't think of any reason to say no to because you've got that many good elements in it.

*Jacobs:* Say that again. That's an important concept here.

*Berge:* You've got to bring in a project that they can't possibly think of any reason to say no to, so they will go to development.

*Jacobs:* The producer . . .

*Berge:* Bruce Gilbert . . .

*Jacobs:* . . . now has this treatment. He goes, "Wow! Here's the story . . ."

*Berge:* Yes.

*Jacobs:* "I could make this into a movie." He then goes out at this point with the treatment—and does what? Does he do anything with it?

*Berge:* Well, he may ask the writer to address the treatment. He may say something else. Some people may get a writer to write the script; that doesn't happen very often. There aren't that many people that would put up their own money to have a writer write a script. There aren't that many writers that will write a script without . . .

*Jacobs:* We're talking about this specific case. With *Honor and Glory,* he's got a 40-page treatment from Robert Caputo.

*Berge:* Yes.

*Jacobs:* It comes to his attention somehow, and he says, "Whoa, here's the movie." What did he do with it then?

*Berge:* What did he do? I believe he came to TNT.

*Jacobs:* And said?

*Berge:* "Look at this. Wouldn't this be wonderful?"

*Jacobs:* Did he get any actors beforehand, or did he just come in with the idea and say, "Hey, what do you think of this as an idea?"

*Berge:* Just came in with his idea.

*Jacobs:* Now why would he go to Turner with this idea? Why not ABC or Home Box Office or NBC-movie-of-the-week or miniseries?

*Berge:* I believe it would be because they're into historical dramas. They do them well. It's a larger project, a more expensive project. You know, they spend more money. They matched up better than anyone else. This one was designed, not quite a feature, it wouldn't sell well enough theatrically. So all those reasons led him to Turner.

*Jacobs:* Why wouldn't it sell as a feature?

*Berge:* It might be a small feature. But to try to get someone to put up feature money . . . If you wanted to do it as a feature, you would have to do it in a manner that would be, you know, "We're going to do this for $5 million or $3 million, and it's going to be this *little* piece."

*Jacobs:* We're going to have it at Sundance, maybe?

*Berge:* Yeah, we're going to have it at Sundance. And you may see your money back. And to take this to the next level, which would be having it in any studio, it would suddenly cost them $30 million or $40 million to make. Well, we can make it for nine. And if it's going to cost them $40 million, then they've got to have a $20 million star in it so they've got a chance of somebody seeing it. It's that sort of mentality.

*Jacobs:* So that's how we get from feature to movie-of-the-week for TNT.

*Berge:* Yeah.

*Jacobs:* Plus Turner has a reputation for doing historical dramas. True-to-life.

*Berge:* Yeah. Funny thing is that while we were in the wilds of Canada shooting this, we were in the hotel for lunch one day, and I looked up and went, "What's Lily Calvert doing here?" [She's] one of the top production designers in the business now. And Bruce looks over and goes, "Well, that's so-and-so, from Columbia. And there's Wolfgang Peterson's producer, and there's that location manager we know." This is a town of 3,000 people in the Arctic. We're in a little hotel and we run into other people from Hollywood and they're up there scouting for *Shackelton,* which Mel Gibson was attached to star in. So, how would it be a feature? Mel Gibson makes it a feature. That sort of a thing.

*Jacobs:* Okay. So Bruce Gilbert now comes to Turner, and who does he talk to at TNT?

*Berge:* Being Bruce, with his record—*Coming Home, On Golden Pond,* a long relationship with Jane off the record—he would go to Alan Sabinson.

*Jacobs:* And Alan is . . . ?

*Berge:* Alan was . . . executive vice president for original programming at TNT.

*Jacobs:* The Man?

*Berge:* Yeah, the head guy.

*Jacobs:* Now he goes into Sabinson and says what?

*Berge:* "Here. Great story." You know, whatever song and dance you do. You pitch it on the basis of the strength of the concept and the treatment and your track record of what you've done and who you are and what kind of a deal you can put together.

*Jacobs:* Indicating that at this level, you have to have some background. Somebody in Waupakaneeta who's just started up a little company is not going to do this kind of thing right off the bat, probably.

*Berge:* Right. They may be able to put together a good enough treatment like Caputo has . . .

*Jacobs:* To get a producer interested . . .

*Berge:* . . . in the idea. And then you get some very nominal fee of a couple of thousand dollars for your story and your credit.

*Jacobs:* And you get credit for the picture, and the picture gets done.

*Berge:* And you go away.

*Jacobs:* As Caputo did.

*Berge:* Yeah. He got Associate Producer credit, which he got . . . mainly based on the strength of the treatment he had written. And as an added bonus, should it get produced, you get this title. We'll give you this much for the treatment, a couple thousand dollars and a credit based on his actually being in the business and being a photojournalist for that long and having a good reputation throughout the world.

*Jacobs:* And then, as a fledgling producer, as somebody who might want to be a producer himself, he now has an Associate Producer credit that could parlay into . . .

*Berge:* Yes. And develop that relationship with the producer.

*Jacobs:* And Turner.

*Berge:* With Bruce. There are stories everywhere and we're always looking for stories, and here's a guy, Robert Caputo, who's out there around fantastic stories all the time, and he's into doing this research and that sort of thing. So we're always looking for people like that, too, who have a different perspective from a different locale. People who have a different take on things. They see things differently. So we're always looking for that. So Caputo was able to take that and parlay that into an Associate Producer credit on a major television film.

*Jacobs:* OK. So now the producer has hold of it, and he's taken his statement and he makes his pitch. His pitch is "I've got a great story here that's never been told. It's based on true life. We've got the documentation, we've got the records, we've got an exclusive. We've got a story here that nobody knows we've got." Is that part of the pitch?

*Berge:* Yes. It hasn't been done before; it's something different. It's a true story, which always helps. For some reason, it has always worked; it always helps out. It lends credibility to the marketing, to the sales somehow. So you get him hooked on it. And then if it's hot, somebody agrees, "Yes, this would work for our network. This could be right up our alley. We're interested in it." Then once you're interested in it, Business Affairs gets involved, and they make the deal end of it.

*Jacobs:* Business Affairs is the business part of Turner Network Television—the business guys. They come out and say, "OK, here's what we'll pay you. Here's what the budget will be for the film." Is that where that happens?

*Berge:* Yes. . . . It's the whole thing: "Here's what you're getting paid, here's what your credit is, here's what your exposure is, here's the turnaround."

*Jacobs:* "Exposure" meaning your liability?

*Berge:* Yes. Everything down to net profit, participation, definition.

*Jacobs:* Are these lawyers?

*Berge:* Yes. Yes, they're lawyers. Now [at] Business Affairs, you have two levels: One guy . . . will make the deal, basically typewriting a deal memo. Then it goes to the lawyers, the legal department, and so on.

*Jacobs:* Typewriting a deal memo? Now explain that.

*Berge:* They basically take a memo. They sit down, they go through the deal, you hammer it out, you've got your points or whatever—although they often don't release those. So as soon as someone has a deal memo, you'll never get the contract completed. So they'll send a letter saying, "Here's essentially what we've agreed to. The long form will be coming to your attorney shortly." It goes to the attorneys. They do the 45-page document, which includes . . .

*Jacobs:* Just about anything anyone can possibly think of.

*Berge:* Yes. And clauses for anything you don't think of.

*Jacobs:* Basically, as the independent producer here, you're told, "You are going to take all the responsibility and suffer all the exposure, and you're going to produce the thing, and then we'll look at it."

*Berge:* No, not like that. They had switched to in-house productions. So basically what it says at this stage is, "These are your responsibilities as a producer. Here's your fee. Here's what you agree to do for it." A portion of your fee may be reduced by a quarter portion if the picture goes over budget. So there's a limited exposure you incur.

*Jacobs:* So this is a TNT picture now, and they're hiring Bruce Gilbert to produce it?

*Berge:* Yes, essentially. On paper. They will own the project; they'll be the copyright holder, you know.

*Jacobs:* The independent producer gets paid a fee to do his job, and if he brings it under budget, he gets his fee and he gets a share of what he brings it in under?

*Berge:* No. Not in these studios nowadays. For the most part, those deals are pretty rare.

*Jacobs:* But if he goes over budget, it comes out of his pocket.

*Berge:* Yeah, yeah. You don't get to keep it.

*Jacobs:* If it goes over, you pay.

*Berge:* Yeah, out of profits. So, you make a producer deal, then they look at a list of writers.

*Jacobs:* "They" being . . .

*Berge:* The network and the producer.

*Jacobs:* OK, now the producer's part of the team.

*Berge:* Yes.

*Jacobs:* He's working with the television team now to do all the estimates?

*Berge:* Yes.

*Jacobs:* But functionally he's the producer. The guy who's putting it all together.

*Berge:* Since the network is paying all the bills at this point, which is no money to the producer at this point. [The bills to pay preproduction expenses are paid out of TNT coffers. The producer gets a salary at this point of the deal.]

*Jacobs:* This is in development, he gets nothing?

*Berge:* Nothing. And then they get together, that being the network, whoever may be the head—Sabinson—and one or two other people. They look at a list of writers and say, "Who would be good for this project?"

*Jacobs:* Based on . . . ?

*Berge:* A lot of it is based on who you've worked with before and how did they perform.

*Jacobs:* You mean, who the producer worked with before? Who Turner's worked with before? This is a mutual investigation?

*Berge:* Yeah, absolutely. And they come down to that person.

*Jacobs:* Because everybody on this team now has the goal of producing the best product for the least money?

*Berge:* Yes.

*Jacobs:* So you want a good writer, not just some hack or some newcomer.

*Berge:* Yes.

*Jacobs:* You're looking through the files of decent writers with track records.

*Berge:* You're looking for who matches up nicely for this, who can capture the essence of what this project is and put it on paper.

*Jacobs:* Is getting along with the producer part of the criteria here?

*Berge:* For a writer?

*Jacobs:* Mm-hmm.

*Berge:* The second time. The first time isn't always.

*Jacobs:* We won't know that until after this project is over.

*Berge:* Right, right. And even then it depends on your definition of getting along and not getting along. There's all sorts of arguments, discussions, enthusiastic debate we have on the way just to get to the point where you have something that all parties can live with. It's often the case where you get a script and it's not what it needs to be and the writer doesn't see it any other way. You end up with differing opinions, and you part company with the writer and move on to someone else who you think can take it to that next step or get it ready for production—those sorts of things. And unfortunately, that's fairly common. Assuming that it's a matter of time, too, you've got writers on a project, you sit for six months, he's on something else, you get a star and you need to bring someone in to do the polish, to do the next rewrite, the next two rewrites. And in the case of this one, you started with a writer who did three versions of it, [and when we] were very close to production, we brought in someone else who Turner had worked with [on] a number of scripts, a very fine writer who started out on *China Beach.*

*Jacobs:* By the name of . . . ?

*Berge:* By the name of Susan Rhinehart, and she did a fantastic job in no time . . . [The first writer] got to a point and had a different take on it than . . .

*Jacobs:* Than the producer?

*Berge:* Yeah, the producer. And so now all of this is on an accelerated schedule, and you have to move.

*Jacobs:* This case, I'm assuming, is not a case of someone who's absolutely right and somebody's absolutely wrong. It's a matter of a difference of opinion, difference of artistic taste.

*Berge:* Absolutely.

*Jacobs:* The writer says, "Gee, it'll work better this way." The producer says, "No, I think it'll work better this way." And the writer goes, "I just can't do it that way." "Well, I'm sorry, you're out the door. I'll have to get somebody who sees it my way."

*Berge:* Yeah. It's happened to a lot of people we know who are very good writers, in fact. You've created things, we all have, and you get, "There it is!" And you can't possibly see it a third shorter. Where does it come from? You get a long script, and in this case, we're in an accelerated . . .

*Jacobs:* Where could I possibly cut anything out of this?

*Berge:* Yeah. You say, "All right, we want to make it this year, not next." By the time you've got a director attached, suddenly you're 12 weeks out from shooting.

*Jacobs:* And a big script.

*Berge:* And eight weeks out you start heavy prep, and you don't have the script ready yet. So you're racing now, and we've pushed back a week on the start of production. Actually, pushed it back two weeks; you could never get the script going. And I'm close to running out of snow in the Arctic. I'm in the dangerous period where the snow can melt up there. Still, it'd snow in the bay, but . . .

*Jacobs:* There goes the movie.

*Berge:* Yes. And then it's, "Look at all the dark ground here in the Arctic." It just wouldn't be, "Jeez, we're lost in the snowstorm, and don't stumble over that rock." You run into that, and it gets really frightening. So that accelerated schedule is moving along, and you're trying to get that done. You lose patience trying [to] deal with different points of view that aren't propelling the project.

*Jacobs:* As a producer.

*Berge:* Yes.

*Jacobs:* You simply say, "We've got to move."

*Berge:* Yes. And that's going to happen with anyone. You're either moving in the right direction, or it's not happening. So given time, the first person may have gotten it there. But sometimes you don't have time. You've got to go to someone you know can do it and maybe isn't carrying the yoke that the first writer did.

*Jacobs:* Because especially after three drafts and you're still not there . . .

*Berge:* Yeah. And it's not anything against the original writers, you know, because you read it and you go, "Wow! I think this is really amazing. I like this. We can't *make* this, but I like it." That's what it comes down to. And even once we had the second writer on, it ended up being a 134-page-long script for a 90-minute movie. So, you end up still having to cut 40 pages out. You know, better to do it ahead of time, before you start shooting the movie, than afterwards when you're trying to fix the holes because you shoot all the stuff and then you lose it all because you cut 40 minutes of movie away.

*Jacobs:* And you spent a lot of money to make that 40 minutes.

*Berge:* Not only do you spend a lot of money making 40 minutes, but there's going to be a lot of holes and it's going to be noticeable. It's going to look hacked up because that's what it is. Rarely can you get through a movie and cut that much out of it and still make it work well. Or, what's almost worse is, sometimes it's so long, you cut so much off, that it's a different movie, but it works. When you don't have that much material, where you have like four story lines and you cut away one or two completely and it works, what happens in these lengths, you end up cutting away half the story line. Because you've got to hold scenes that contain part of a story line, so things start and never go anywhere. Or things pick up and they never go anywhere. And it's really obvious.

*Jacobs:* As we've all seen in those movies where you say, "Where'd that guy go?" or "I don't remember their having a fight earlier in the movie. How come they're suddenly mad at each other?"

*Berge:* And it's hard to fix all of that stuff afterwards. . . . Three weeks before we started shooting, [the writer] sat three days with all of us. Somewhere in that time period, all of us—the director, myself, the producer and the writer, and an executive from the network, the creative executive—came out, and we all sat in a hotel room, much like this, for three days, page by page by page by page, and argued, "What can we cut out? Can we do this? What else can we do?"—all those things—and it really worked out for the best. We got there. And even with that scenario, we left certain scenes to be written. So she ended up coming up to the Arctic, spending time in the hotel. A week in the Arctic, we had her in the hotel for all but about 15 minutes. We just kept her strapped to the typewriter the whole time.

*Jacobs:* It was frozen . . .

*Berge:* Yeah, all because they said, "Well, we want to make this movie," and if we didn't make it that year, it wasn't going to get made for a whole other year, at which point it could easily go away. The project can easily die, never to be seen again. So you've got this sort of thing between "Can we get it ready and make it well" or "Do I walk away and wait until next year?" There's a better chance that won't ever happen. If they're ready to make it, you want to make it.

*Jacobs:* "They" meaning the company with the money?

*Berge:* Yeah. Somebody's ready to pay for it. You want to make it when they're ready to pay for it. Unless you've got the power to say, "I want to make it in nine months. Let's do it." Then they go, "OK." But even those guys at times will go, "That doesn't fit into our plan." And so I don't have the money. I don't have the job anymore. "I'd love to green-light it, but I got fired."

*Jacobs:* But I'm guessing that Mel Gibson can probably say, "I'll do it in nine months" or "I'll do it next year."

*Berge:* I would say yes, he most likely could.

*Jacobs:* Right now.

*Berge:* Those kind of guys could, but when you start also looking at that sort of a project, which would be the large feature version of what we did, they've got to be looking at $100 million, $120 million, that type of thing. I could see them going, "Well, we were interested last year. Would it fit into our release schedule and all that? It fit last fall, but it won't fit next year the way things are now." It's . . . it's . . .

*Jacobs:* . . . a story about a guy who finds a mailbag. [The reference is to *The Postman*, which was one of the larger flops in movie history.]

*Berge:* Something like that.

*Jacobs:* Kevin Costner: "I found a bag of mail. I'm going to deliver it!"

*Berge:* It's a slacker mentality.

*Jacobs:* We may be digressing now because we've jumped ahead. Let's go back to part 1 now, back before you come on board. OK, we've got a producer, we've got a writer. We've developed three scripts, but now that writer's gone and we've got a second writer on board now, and now we've got the project moving, things are going. When do we talk about talent? When do we get the talent—above-the-line, below-the-line, that sort of thing?

*Berge:* It's always above-the-line first.

*Jacobs:* So we fill in all the rest of above-the-line.

*Berge:* Yeah, these type of projects are cast driven, and no one's going to jump into something thinking we're going to get somebody. So, I'd say Bruce was on board, we had the script, we had Bruce Gilbert, and we were looking for a lead for Henson. It was really Henson's story.

*Jacobs:* A black actor with some stature?

*Berge:* Yes, and they found a very fine actor by the name of Delroy Lindo, who has been in *Ransom* and *Get Shorty.*

*Jacobs:* OK, you've got an actor now, and you have the window where the money is available. The company, the network, says, "OK, we've got money this time period, and we're going to let you spend it." Then inside that window you have to put the window for the availability of a director, the availability of an actor, the availability of other cast members, the availability of crew. All that stuff goes into separate windows. If we imagine a series of windows intersecting, that's what we're talking about for the producer to visualize. So now you have an actor, and now you have to get a director.

*Berge:* Now we have the actor; now we need to find a director. In this case, we were talking to a director. He came in, had the meeting with the producer, the director, and the network. At this point, the guy who originally brought the project to the network is gone; someone else is in charge. The network tells him what they expect of the movie.

*Jacobs:* Davidson is gone now?

*Berge:* He's gone now.

*Jacobs:* Someone else is now here.

*Berge:* Yeah. The director gives his take on the film, what he expects of it, the budget parameters—sort of where you're thinking what you're going to spend so he has an idea of what he's working with. That meeting happened. Everyone felt comfortable. Three weeks go by, time ticking away. You're still trying to get this thing started, and you still have script work to do. You know you've got budgeting work to do. You've got all sorts of deals to make because you're planning to go [to] the Arctic. It'll take a lot to get up there. A couple of weeks go by, and his series takes off and his series gets picked up, so he's off to do the previous commitment.

*Jacobs:* Good-bye director . . . window . . . the end.

*Berge:* Yeah, yeah, yeah.

*Jacobs:* You start off with a window, and from the moment you start the project, it begins to close on you. The opening begins to get smaller and smaller.

*Berge:* It does. And then every time you put something in or don't put something in it, that's what changes the shape of the window. That's a bad analogy. . . . The panes get knocked out on you.

*Jacobs:* Something changes to affect the opening, the amount of window you have left to get through.

*Berge:* . . . and the more stuff you have through on the other side, the better. Then just by luck, right about that time Kevin Hooks was then available. Kevin had directed *Passenger 57*; he had done *Heat Wave* for TNT previously, won him an Ace Award. . . . [And he had] directed a lot of *St. Elsewhere,* a lot of dramatic TV, a very good director. When he came on, then it was really full speed ahead, let's go. He's committed to the project, let's make it happen. That's about the time I got involved. My involvement starts with . . . all right, here's the script, we've got the star. So you read the script.

*Jacobs:* You've got the script, you've got the star, you've got the director, so you have all the cast now? One? You've got one star, one director . . .

*Berge:* . . . and you need two . . .

*Jacobs:* . . . and one script? The script is done, or pretty much done, and now they say, "Hello, Ralph . . ."

*Berge:* The script is not done. The script is in progress. In this case, it was in progress way too long!

*Jacobs:* The script is in progress all through the production, until the last day of shooting when the script is finally over.

*Berge:* Yes. And now you've got your basic team: producer, director, line producer, and your star who you keep in contact with—whatever input they have, on script and the story and their character and what they'd like to do with it. Then the nuts and the bolts begin, which, first off, is you schedule the script. You have to break it down into boards, how much work you have to do every day, how many days it's going to take to do it, when you have to move things around, when you have to go to the Arctic, when you have to come back, what you're going to do, set up on a stage, do the interior when it's cold, all that usual stuff. You also do a budget immediately, which at this point is nothing more than a good guess. You've done some research. From experience you know what things cost. You lay that out on a budget form. The next step is a scout. Between the scout and budget, you pick up a production designer because one of your biggest costs is what do you have to construct, what do you have to build, what do you have to design. So you get the production designer on board, which we did with Michael Nevotney. Great guy, did *The Arrival,* has done a number of things really. You talk about picking the right guy for a project. Here's a shipbuilder who loves to build ships. He can walk out there, he loves the cold. He just worked on *True Lies,* knows [Steve] Quale [the second unit director on James Cameron's *Titanic*]. So the four of us finally scout to Montreal and Baffin Island.

*Jacobs:* "Scout" meaning you're looking for a place to shoot the picture. . . . The script says it's set in the North, the Arctic, so what you have to do is find a place in the Arctic where you can shoot but you are still close enough to civilization that you can get support.

*Berge:* Yes, exactly, exactly. You're looking for that. Then also, one of the primary things I'm always concerned about is where's my base? Am I going to location? I'm going to the Arctic, I'm putting crews up in a hotel, and then I'm going to location. Do I then have to go to location again by sending everybody out another two hours every day and back two hours, or can I find a place to put the crew in a hotel and work within 45 minutes of where the hotel is? Now within that 45 minutes you try to find Greenland, Elsemere Island, and the North Pole, which is almost impossible. But you do the best you can. You look further out, to find second unit spots, maybe places you can't travel to. So we arrange the scout.

*Jacobs:* You physically go to Montreal? You take pictures and stuff?

*Berge:* Physically we go to Montreal. Because it's a distant location, and unknown territory, we pick up a local production manager who knows that area and the areas we're going to.

*Jacobs:* Plus, if you're shooting in Canada, isn't there a requirement that you pick up other Canadians as crew?

*Berge:* Yes, somewhat. It being Quebec, the rules are different than the rest of Canada. They are very proud and see things differently than the rest of Canada. So we pick up the UPM [unit production manager] there. So it's the UPM, the production designer, the director, the safety producer, and myself, the producer.

*Jacobs:* Who's the executive producer here?

*Berge:* Bruce Gilbert.

*Jacobs:* He's the exec? OK. And you're the line producer—you're the one doing the work.

*Berge:* The nuts and the bolts, as we call it. We fly into Montreal. We go out. We've all got to buy the snow boots and the clothes and the survival jacket and the seven layers of everything. You get up to the Arctic, and the first thing you know is it's 53 below. The first day we actually went out at three o'clock for an hour . . . sunset. The executive producer got frostbite. We all got in sleds and snowmobiles, covered in caribou skin, and went out. And it was so cold that your glasses and stuff would freeze up . . . frost up. And the directors there couldn't see anything. They're shouting, "I can't see anything! I can't see anything!"

*Jacobs:* Do you say to yourself at this point, "We can't shoot a movie up here. This is insane. Are the cameras going to freeze?"

*Berge:* Well, it was much colder than it was going to be when we were coming up. We were coming up at the end of winter, the end of April. It'll be up around freezing instead of 53 below. But yeah, the first day up there everyone goes into shock. I can't see it's so cold, we can't do anything, we can't look. You know, there's a feeling of panic, and I'm thinking, "Boy, everyone's got to settle down." Everyone is just whining, "I can't see !@#$," and I'm like, "Oh, my God, if this is the way it is going to be, then this is not the team to do it!"

*Jacobs:* This isn't going to work, huh?

*Berge:* We are up there for four days, and by the end of the third day everyone's getting more macho, more attuned to the mystique of the north. "Ah, it's the Arctic! You've got to take what it gives you. That's the way it is, you know."

*Jacobs:* OK, we are tough survivors. We can do it!

*Berge:* Yes, yes. Everyone slid into that attitude very quickly and really dealt with it nicely. The glasses were a big trouble. You try and put this stuff on your glasses. You get the special glasses made like the aviator things that aren't supposed to ice up. But everything is so cold it really sucks! In your heart, you're miserable.

*Jacobs:* Nothing works.

*Berge:* No, and you get cold inside all that snow goose down and everything. The only thing that actually kept you really warm was caribou-skin jackets.

*Jacobs:* Which stink.

*Berge:* Oh, yeah! Big-time smell bad. You don't finish them out completely. It's a rough finish on the inside. If you actually finish it smooth like regular leather like we're used to, the heat factor is not there. Yeah, it really worked wonderfully, in fact. So we scout, we see some stuff that can work, and now we are behind in the schedule slightly and are fighting the start date.

*Jacobs:* Window?

*Berge:* Yeah. So rather than having me go up there myself or someone else first and look all around and do a preliminary survey, we are all kind of going up there together—not the best way to do things. You want someone to preliminary survey, check everything out first, then say here's the best spot. Then we were kind of going through that ourselves, which gets frustrating because your time is better spent as a director, producer, executive producer doing something else and leaving this to a location manager.

*Jacobs:* Rather than as a committee walking around looking at stuff.

*Berge:* Yeah, yeah, and open discussions about "What could we use this hill for?" You know, that sort of thing, but that sort of thing is part of the window where you're moving things along as fast as you can. We scout back to Montreal, we scout some there, head back to L.A., continue working on the script.

*Jacobs:* Now, by scouting are you looking out? Now that you've figured out how many scenes you have to shoot, do you have that sort of thing in mind at this point?

*Berge:* Yes, you know how many scenes you have to shoot by now.

*Jacobs:* You have to shoot a thing that takes place in a tent, you have to shoot a scene that takes place in Bath, in Ireland, one for somewhere else. You're looking for places that will represent those different locales up there in the snow.

*Berge:* Yeah. You know, in this case we had like three major looks for the Arctic portion. You had Greenland, you had Elsmere Island, and essentially the North Pole.

*Jacobs:* How does Montreal fit in?

*Berge:* Montreal fit in for Washington. The old Montreal fit in for the hotel scenes, the ballroom scenes, the old Washington Street. It's supposed to be New York. After a time, it became clear that it didn't matter where they came back to. They came back to the States, to a U.S. city, then they leave again for the Arctic. And it was more important to know that they were progressing through the Arctic more than that they moved up and down the East Coast, whether they were in New York or Philadelphia or Washington. It didn't make much of a difference.

*Jacobs:* So there's city stuff and the Arctic. City and snow.

*Berge:* Yeah, so the city stuff you can dress up and change the size and that sort of thing. It's easier to differentiate that than it is the Arctic. You can't have a sign that says, "North Pole here." It doesn't work.

*Jacobs:* You can't stick a striped pole in the ground and go, "Look, there it is."

*Berge:* Lord, we wanted to! You really look for that difference where you go, "Here is a steep hilly area that can be Greenland," and you rarely find the perfect spot. You try to get the feel of it.So we scouted. We scout, you get a feeling, you kind of look at it, and you say, "It'll work for this. It won't work for that." You take all the photographs you can, you come back, and you work some more. You have to come back to L.A. because you're trying to find the rest of your crew, which, at this point, was mainly a director of photography. We knew we had a few people in the States that we wanted to see and that we had worked with before, to pull from the group here. So you're trying to get the major part of your crew here and continue casting, take care of whatever business you have to in L.A., and get, as soon as you can, up to Montreal, where you're going to hire the bulk of your crew.

*Jacobs:* Because of the Canadian . . .

*Berge:* Well, it's . . . it's . . .

*Jacobs:* Cheaper?

*Berge:* Yeah. Those are all factors, the exchange rate and other costs. Although in this case, the decision to film in Canada was really driven by the Arctic. And where we were shooting, descendants of Peary and Henson still live in those areas today.

*Jacobs:* Is that right?

*Berge:* Yes. That's a special feeling.

*Jacobs:* Peary and Henson were, uh, sexually active?

*Berge:* Quite prolific.

*Jacobs:* I guess so, if they left behind descendants.

*Berge:* Yes, indeed. Lots of them. So we wanted to go there, to the real place, and so it's driven by location, part of why we're going to Canada.

*Jacobs:* Because you could have done this in Wisconsin; you could have done it in Minnesota. There are icy places where you could go and make it look like the North Pole.

*Berge:* It's really tough to get 360-degree views around that really kind of help sell it.

*Jacobs:* Alaska? You could have gone to an American place?

*Berge:* Yes, but there aren't that many people to crew there. I mean, Montreal has a good base of people who are used to working in the cold and have done it a number of times, have the gear for it, and are ready to go. Everywhere else I looked, it was really sort of a, "Boy, where does this guy come from?" You've got to pull people from all over the place. At least in Montreal, we're shooting in Baffin Island, where we wanted to go because that's where the story happened. And it was the Arctic, and so was Alaska, but we had a decent base to work out of in Iqaluit, and I could bring the crew from Montreal.

*Jacobs:* Iqaluit is where?

*Berge:* Baffin Island, which is 500,000 square miles. It is the largest city on Baffin Island, with 3,000 people and 18 miles of roads that don't lead out of town. There's just nowhere to go.

*Jacobs:* So you can't drive out of Iqaluit. You can drive around it, but you can't drive out of it to anywhere else?

*Berge:* Yep.

*Jacobs:* You can dogsled or snowmobile out of it or fly out of it?

*Berge:* Yeah. So I needed the Arctic, New York, I needed ballrooms, I needed like the Explorers Club—something to play for that, and that means either going to Alaska or coming down to some other city.

*Jacobs:* Vancouver perhaps.

*Berge:* Yeah, where I've got to house everyone. Vancouver has one old street that won't quite work. Montreal has Old Montreal: cobblestone streets, the camera can look down half a mile, three-quarters of a mile down the street, and you're safe with the old buildings. So I've got Baffin Island, where I've got to put the crew up for two weeks for the shoot. So everyone's got to go up there. And then I go back to Montreal, which has everything else I need. The crew is local, stays there, so I only have to pay housing and per diem for half the show. If I go anywhere else, it looks like I'm paying housing and per diem the whole time. It becomes a full location show. By going to Montreal, it's actually a local show for most of the crew and a lot of the cast. We end up getting the cast from L.A., Toronto, New York—it usually works that way. So you come back to L.A. You continue working, putting your team together with a director of photography. We find a director of photography, and we like him, make the deal for him.

*Jacobs:* He knows it's going to be cold.

*Berge:* Oh yeah, and you continue casting from there; take whatever other meetings in town that we can, and we all get back to Iqaluit as soon as possible. Back to Montreal.

*Jacobs:* When it comes to casting, who's primarily responsible for the casting? The director? Or is it a team decision? Does the director consult with the producer, or does the director sort of hold casting calls? Or do you have a casting director who suggests, "Here, I've got some people I think who could do this."

*Berge:* Within the network system there is what is called the head of talent or senior vice president in charge of talent.

*Jacobs:* At TNT?

*Berge:* Yes, that sort of thing, and they are the ones that help make the deal for the star. They also help the top five or six roles wherever you are putting your money. They are the ones who talked to Delroy and got him convinced before the director was on board. That is very common in these films, and casting will try to find someone who is interested in the script, a star, because in these types of movies, a star helps sell the movie so much, especially for TV. A bit of a name will take you a long way, with a recognizable face. There is a casting director on the show. Sometimes they get involved in the top three people, but most likely not. So the top people are set usually by the studio, often with the help of the director—if the director is on yet. If the director wants somebody and the studio thinks that this person would be good, it's all a discussion over it. It happens all the time. You go, "I think this person would be good," but the studio says, "Yes, she's good, but we need a name to help sell it. Look at this person." And you go back and forth. In this case, it happened with an actress by the name of Kim Staunton, a New York stage actress brought to our attention by Delroy Lindo. She's fantastic, amazing! She has a great quality about her, and had she been coming through some other casting agent, we probably would have never come across her. We would have never found her.

*Jacobs:* But Lindo says, "Here, I've got a friend you ought to have a look at"?

*Berge:* Yeah, yeah. He went, "Hey, she is worth flying in. Let's do it. She's the best." So you've got the casting director and the director that make those decisions together. The head of talent and the director.

*Jacobs:* The producer is not terribly involved here?

*Berge:* Yes, yes. The producer is very involved because that is part of what's going to make it work or not work, make it sell or not sell. It's that package of who you've got up on screen; and not just who they are or the name, but are they right for the role? So they are all involved in that, and they all have their lists. "Who would be at the top of your list? Who do you want to see? Who can you get? Who do you have a relationship with?"

*Jacobs:* "Can we get Meryl Streep?" is always the question, huh?

*Berge:* Exactly. Yes, yes. "I know her well, but I am not going to call her for this one." Those sorts of things are the upper-level casting. Then you've got the lower-level casting, which is handled by the casting director, whose work is specifically for the show, not the network and the director. You know, you go through this thing where you tell the casting agency, casting director, "Here are the roles. You do the breakdown. I want to see the top 15 people you have for each of these roles." And you sit down and go through this, and they come and they read their lines. Sometimes you put them on videotape—actually, we always put them all on videotape now. Put them on videotape, and they come in, they read, they go out. Director and producer sit down afterwards and look through the videotapes and go, "Yeah, I like that person. I don't like that person," and you start to get down to it. More often than not, that takes up a lot of time just trying to find the right person, especially when you are location casting because you don't have the benefit of having as much depth as you would in L.A. You've got a much larger group of actors here; a lot of the Canadian actors live here. They'll fly back there to do their role, but they live here in L.A. You just have a broader base. So that is how that casting goes. You go through the game; you try to find everybody. In this case, we hired someone separately for Inuit casting, someone who knew the Inuit actors well—where they were and how to contact them.

*Jacobs:* Who are the Inuit actors? Are they doing little theater up there? How are they found?

*Berge:* By people who have gone up over the years to do shows up there. They've hired these guys to be on camera . . .

*Jacobs:* And they turned out to be able to act.

*Berge:* Yes, and there are a few roles in our thing where you want the difference in looks. Our characters are supposed to be coming up here to see people they haven't seen before.

*Jacobs:* So you want them to look like natives to the region.

*Berge:* Yeah. And they meet a black man who they think is their cousin, their long-lost cousin. You are going for the look, that sort of thing, and the Inuit certainly have it, and they have a certain way about them in terms of specific casting, which an actor could pick up, of course, and do it, but you try and find a look. You've got all the extras, and if your actors don't look like the extras, it doesn't look like a community.

*Jacobs:* OK, so now you've got actors . . .

*Berge:* Now we've got the actors.

*Jacobs:* You're beginning. You've assembled everything you need to make a movie.

*Berge:* We've got most of the actors at this point. Let's say that there are a few we don't have yet, which is part of the window. So we got that. We are moving along.

*Jacobs:* Your shooting schedule has been set: We have to start shooting here; we have to end shooting here.

*Berge:* We have to start shooting no later than April 21, and I am not comfortable with that. We should start April 1. That's not happening, and April 21 is the latest we can push back, only now it keeps sliding back.

*Jacobs:* And if we are not shooting by April 21, we're doomed. The project is over; we are not even going to start?

*Berge:* It's over. The end of the beginning. Yes. Well, it's going to be too late at this point because now you've made all the commitments, and it's going to cost you $2 million to walk away from it.

*Jacobs:* To walk away from it?

*Berge:* Yeah. If not more.

*Jacobs:* So now the pressure is up.

*Berge:* Yeah. So you're moving in that period between 12 weeks out and 2 weeks out. You're casting, you're working on the script, you're working on the production design and racing that schedule to where they have to start building things. And how much can you allow them to use money to spend on construction, which is everything else that is not in line yet? Trying to get your bids in on special effects, visual effects, the eye shots, matte shots that you're not quite sure you're going to do because you don't have the script finished. So you try to make all these decisions along the way and trigger construction so you can be ready when you get up there to shoot. You get them, then try to guess what the other stuff is going to cost. So you're triggering the process, getting things rolling, trying to get a number on a script that's not finished, and trying to hold it all together. And guesswork, patching together the quilt pattern that you're trying to get together, and you hope that you have a whole instead of being one corner short, which has happened enough times. Yeah, you see, you try to move along and do that.

In triggering construction, once you set that process in motion, there's not a whole lot you can do about it. You've committed that much money to it. You've got costumes you have to start way ahead. You have to get the costumes, you have to search the States for what you need. In London, that stuff is all happening at the same time. You've got to pull the trigger on the process so that it all gets there in time.

*Jacobs:* There's special props that have to be exact. They can't just be a hatchet; they have to be a period hatchet.

*Berge:* Yes. There're guys who have to build the sleds. You've got to find the dogs and get the dogs up there, have someone there scouting for the dogs. You're still trying to nail down locations while you're doing this, and you're out visiting other spots that will work and still be within your parameter of 45 minutes out from the hotel or somewhere close to there. Or, you know, if you need to go an hour out for two

days, you want a couple of other days when you're 15 minutes out. You try to offset it. So all that's going on. You're trying to trigger all those things and still trying to get the script ready.

*Jacobs:* It's always the script.

*Berge:* Right. You need to get the script, you get the schedule out, the schedule shows 48 days, and we can't do that. I've got 30 days. You know, you've got a 134-page script. So at three pages a day, you take off 10 pages in three days. And then you start coming down a little more, coming down, holding down, you know, you rethink some scenes—the way the scene was written and the way you want to do it. So it takes us three days to do that scene. Well, what if we could do it in two days, so you pull the schedule back, all the while the budget is attached to it. And as you plan things out, you know, you've done as much research as you can, but as you find things out, the schedule fits here, and you realize that if you do this this way, this set won't be ready in time, and then you've got to pull that one. If you try to save by doing one set and then switching over, it means you've got to carry that actor another 10 days. You might as well build the two damn sets. So you're assembling all the elements, and you look at it and say, "I can save $30,000 in construction if I can turn this house I'm building into two houses." Except then you've got to carry someone else for 10 days to do that. That actor, to carry that actor is going to cost you more than to build the two houses. So, you build the two houses. You're moving along.

*Jacobs:* So it's a juggling act?

*Berge:* Completely. Meanwhile, you're trying to find the ship. "Can I get the ship in?" You know, you can only get a real sailing ship, any ship that's available that can get there on time. You're only going to have [it] for a period of four days. Of course, it's not enough time to do two ships. And at the price to get the ship there, it's not worth it to do it. Might as well build the damn ship on a stage where we can actually shoot it.

*Jacobs:* So you've got total control.

*Berge:* Exactly. You build the decks on the stage, you build the interiors on the stage.

*Jacobs:* You rely on some long shots of the real ship somewhere to . . .

*Berge:* Yes. And you still try to work some other way to get the ship there to get the exterior shots, and then you find out that no matter where you put it, you're going to see city in the background. That's going to end up being a shot of a ship against a dock. Anyway, the production value isn't going to be there for the hundreds of thousands of dollars you're going to spend to get it there because you can't get it anywhere that's going to look correct and be a loading dock with an open view because it's two hours out of where your location is. So you end up scrapping some things. You make some other things work.

That's all moving along, all those things are moving along, and you're trying to find the right person to play the other lead. And you've got all these people cued up to be cast, and you don't want to cast anybody until you have the second lead cast. We've got a fantastic actor for Henson, you're looking for someone to play Peary, and you just finally, finally get that deal made. We ended up with Henry Chierney. Now you can suddenly put the other people in place. Costumes has been screaming for weeks.

*Jacobs:* "Give me the size of the people!"

*Berge:* Yeah. She's Italian. You know, we were cursed, and our legs were going to be broken. Everytime something came up, we got to the point where, "You go tell her. I don't want to tell her." And day after day you wouldn't have people. You'd have them there, and she knew some of these people. She would call and get their sizes, assuming they were going to get the part, so you start going on, "Thank God they got the part! It all works." So you finally get Peary. You can cast Peary's wife. You get going down that road, and you can start building her costumes. The script still isn't in yet, so you don't know—do we need this

costume for this scene? Is she going to be in the Arctic? Is she going to the exterior camp, or are we going to see her interior only? That means I don't need a room for her in the Arctic unless she's in it. If she's outside, then I need to bring her up here and I need an all new wardrobe. So all that is happening.

*Jacobs:* Practical wardrobe and film wardrobe, because you've got to keep them warm while they're not in the film.

*Berge:* Yes. Both, and that sort of thing. And also in the construction plans of the sets you're building, which are, since you're trying to see the 360-degree view, you want that, you know. If you're going to go to a location, show it. You're spending that much money to get there, you're in the Arctic, might as well show it. So the sets were always built over a hill, and you try to build or design something in the set—and Nevotney did a fantastic job of this, where you could put a heater on the back side. You build a fake wall of crates, and you put crew in there and stuff and keep them warm because the tent that you've got to set up is out of sight, so it's got to be over the hill, which is another mile or half mile from where the set is. So your base camp is not walking distance from your set. It's got to be that far away. So all of that goes into the planning. And of course, most of the stuff had to be sent up there. At the same time, I've got a guy up there seeing if he can wrangle 50 to 80 snowmobiles from the local population so we can use them to get our equipment back and forth. We've got guys building sleds. You've got all this going along . . .

*Jacobs:* Craft services?

*Berge:* Yes.

*Jacobs:* There's bodily functions to consider, of course.

*Berge:* Everything. You're trying to get a tent, you've got to get a tent, get the heaters, just for feeding lunch, which was, you know, like we were doing an episode of *M\*A\*S\*H* every day at lunch. Everybody would walk into the tent and go, "Oh, here's . . ." Walk through the catered food, which was brought up from a restaurant in town, which was very good food, and native diet, which is raw caribou, raw frozen caribou, whale, and seal. Just take a little piece of it, dip it in soy sauce, like sushi, and eat it. It was actually quite good. So you're trying to get all of these things together while you're rushing to make that April 21 date. Then script isn't coming, casting isn't actually getting done, you slip to April 29.

*Jacobs:* You're past your date?

*Berge:* You're past your date. You've passed the date when you said, "We'll not make the movie if we can't get it."

*Jacobs:* The cutoff?

*Berge:* You're only a couple weeks from your April 21 date. You don't have the movie cast. How soon is art going to be ready? You spent this much money . . .

*Jacobs:* Millions of dollars have been spent.

*Berge:* Yes. A lot of money has been committed. It's going to cost a lot to walk away.

*Jacobs:* Right.

*Berge:* Just to close things up. And the studio will say, the network will say, "Slide it. Slide the date." "No, you don't understand. We slide the date, there's a chance of no snow." "We're not going to give up now. Just slide the date." It's such a dollars-and-cents issue for them at that point.

*Jacobs:* It's simple for them to say, back in L.A., "Well, slide it."

*Berge:* Yes.

*Jacobs:* They don't have to throw away $2 million.

*Berge:* And if you actually step back yourself and go, "Do I walk away now, or do I take the chance that I'll have snow in two weeks?" . . .

*Jacobs:* You take the chance . . .

*Berge:* That you'll have snow in two weeks.

*Jacobs:* Do you hedge the snow then?

*Berge:* We brought hundreds of tons of potato flakes to the Arctic. Potato flake snow. You bet we did! . . . So you push the date and everything just keeps moving along. And you're getting it ready. You've got to rent a plane. The 737 that you've chartered to fill with equipment to take up there, that's waiting. And you pay for it for that day; if you don't use it that day, you pay for it anyway. Yeah, so all those things are stacking up. You do some more scouting, this time you take your director, who's been going along scouting all along. You take your director, right before you shoot, take the director, your DP, the producers, and your keys: key grip, key electric, script supervisor. All those people go out, and you go to every location. "Here's this location. We're going to do this." You impart as much information as you can to everyone so they know what's going on, and they will be going, "Oh, OK, so we're going to need the 12-K here, we need this, we need . . ." Everyone knows each location, what's especially needed there. The UPM and the unit manager are also on those.

*Jacobs:* And the concern to them is their lists. "We need this, we need this . . ."

*Berge:* Yes, and reassuring that the plan is in place. After you scout there, you have a few rehearsals, the stars are off taking their dogsled driving lessons the weekend before we start shooting in order to put a nice team together for the actors. You send them all out and have them spend the night five or eight miles out of town. They go out, drive the dogs. They go out, dogs only, and build an igloo, shoot a test or two, have dinner that night, and they all come back the next day loving it, you know, just completely. They had a little camp-out experience.

*Jacobs:* Now their team is ready to go. They're the "in" crowd now.

*Berge:* Right. Sleep in the igloo overnight, find out who snores, all that sort of stuff. Wonderful bunch of guys. They come back Monday, ready to start shooting.

*Jacobs:* OK, now we commence principal photography.

*Berge:* Yes.

*Jacobs:* And the producer's role in it is . . . ?

*Berge:* Is everything that was happening before this moment and is still happening.

*Jacobs:* Now this is the kick of the shoot: There still isn't a finished script. You've got a script that you've started to shoot, but it isn't the real script.

*Berge:* Right. The executive producer is working on the script.

*Jacobs:* Back in L.A., or he's there too? Everybody's up there sweating the freeze and trying to get this thing done.

*Berge:* Right. He's working on the script, still overseeing all the nuts and bolts. Things are still being built, construction's happening. The Arctic is now commencing and continuing in Montreal. Customs are still being built there. Everything that was happening in prep is still happening because you've got locations up there. You set up locations you find in Montreal, you've still got costumes to build for Montreal. You've got, practically, two whole teams. You've managed to lock down the stages, but you've still got to lay out the pattern of what's going where and that sort of a thing. So that's still all going on. The first day of the shoot, you're there. You just want to make sure things get going, make sure things move smoothly, people get through makeup on time, they get out there, their transportation is there, the transportation gets them to the set, all the equipment gets out to the set. Things are ready to go, all 80 snowmobiles and dogsleds.

*Jacobs:* First day is running the set and things are working.

*Berge:* Yep, everything gets there. Things start to happen. You get your shots, the director is comfortable with his team, things are going. At that point, you want to make sure you're making your day, which is getting all your scenes completed, all the shots you needed for those scenes.

*Jacobs:* You shot three pages a day?

*Berge:* Let's see . . . roughly three pages a day. Some days less. Some days a lot more. It all depended on what you were working with and so on. We were really lucky with Kevin. When you don't have a script finished, you end up with a lot of discussions about the script on the set. People are just seeing things. There're new things; nobody has it. So they're not exactly sure what's happening. The discussions happen, and you lose time spent discussing the script. In a perfect world, it's all done beforehand.

*Jacobs:* Hooks walks in, he's done his prep, Lindo's got his lines, and we're focused on shooting this thing and off we go.

*Berge:* Yeah. And no one is surprised. And they hand new pages to him, and he says, "But wait a minute. I like the lines I had yesterday. What happened? Now I've got to say this. I studied the other stuff." All this stuff is very real and very . . .

*Jacobs:* Important to actors.

*Berge:* They're important, and not just to actors. I think it's important. I'm upset if I prepare for something and then it changes the moment before. That sort of thing. So that happens. And Kevin, thank God, would push through, and we made our days. We did well despite everything that was thrown at us. Schedule-wise, we did fantastic and just kept things moving along. So the first day, you want to make sure it works. Every day of production you want to make sure things are working. There's a snake somewhere, you find out why and fix it. If it normally takes half an hour to get through makeup, why did it take an hour and a half today? Someone was on the phone in between, someone wasn't ready, something wasn't scheduled correctly so that everyone could get through. You know, "Where's the logjam happening?" That's a very common thing you've got to watch. That's all laid out.

*Jacobs:* So your job at that point is really as a facilitator. You're trying to facilitate things?

*Berge:* Yes.

*Jacobs:* What do we need to make this happen?

*Berge:* That's the majority of the job, really. I'm up there to deliver all the toys we've agreed upon at the right time so everyone out there can play. I've got to get all the toys in the sandbox, all the equipment, everything to the set that they need when it has to happen.

*Jacobs:* When it's not there, it's your fault. You did a bad job. You messed up.

*Berge:* Absolutely. And when things go well, it's wonderful. At times, you have nothing to do. You still have plenty to do, but it almost feels like nothing because things normally don't go smoothly. There're so many things. There're 300 or 400 people working by now. The communication can screw up. Anything can happen: a flat tire, throwing a snowmobile's clutch out, a sled gets overloaded and it gets split partway. You have to send somebody else back, you can't start, you've got most of the camera equipment but the lens, so you've got to wait for the snowmobile to go back. And so really you do facilitate all of that.

Once that's working, once you have a flow, then it's nice. Then you're also concerned with what's happening in front of the camera. What's the picture going to look like, are we there at the right time of day? Are we giving the DP [director of photography] everything we can, the best we can, the light at the right time of day? Are we going for a night shot, are we forcing him into some sort of situation, are we going to run long on this day, are we going to lose the light? Then he's going to have to spend time lighting to make it up, which won't make anyone happy, but we do it. Are the tents OK for the actors because they have to stay warm? Where's the food? Is all that happening?

You worry about all those sorts of things. But back to in front of the camera, you really want to sit there and go, "OK, it looks like we're getting our shots." The edi-

tor looks at the masters and says, "OK, we have a close-up here. Looks like we've got the interesting shots. The director's moving things along, motion seems to be correct, the actors seem to be doing a good job, and oh! look at this! Look at the sun." And there's all that, and you stand there and think it's going to work.

*Jacobs:* When everybody's working and the Port-A-Pots are working, then you're happy.

*Berge:* Yes, yes, that's very true. We had people getting very ill, and it happens often when I go to location. You switch over, and within five to six days, people start getting sick from just a change of water. And even from city to city you'll notice it. If you're in L.A., maybe in New York, it can happen.

*Jacobs:* So you bring your Pepto-Bismol for the first week.

*Berge:* Yeah, there are just different microbes in the water and different food and everything. So that almost always happens. And you just want to make sure that no one's dropping out. We had the flu run through the crew. You just pray that people can get there every day and that no one gets hurt. You know you have to make sure that the medical facilities are nearby and all that stuff. You want to make sure you are getting your day, and then you know with the script not being done . . . You got your day, and now you're heading back to the hotel after being in the snow and being bundled up, and you've been like that for 12 hours, your legs can't move, and you're famished because it takes so much energy to stay warm out there. "OK, guys, eat something. Now get to work on the script." And that's 10 o'clock and we have to leave at 5 A.M., but you've got to work on the script.

*Jacobs:* To start shooting again in the morning.

*Berge:* Oh, not even just tomorrow, even down the road, because day 3 and 4 you're going to need some work on this or that.

*Jacobs:* I don't understand. What's the problem with the script here? Why can't you get somebody to finish the script?

*Berge:* Because it goes back to how quickly can you go through and fix something? How can you take a very long script that's actually wonderful from one end to the other, and you've got to cut it down and pare it down? Take the network's notes, the director's notes, and the producer's notes, and you're already backed up. You know, you get the script, 12 weeks out, and you've got another two weeks to finish something else. So suddenly, by the time you get a version to us, we're eight weeks, say six to eight weeks, out. You finish it, you send it out, we take two days to look at it, everyone looks at it and discusses it. You go, "OK, you've got to do this, this, this, and this and to make it fit that," and you're five weeks out of production by the time it comes back to you. And you sit and go, "How in the world am I going to fix this? How do I make this work?"

*Jacobs:* The amazing thing to me here is that anybody would set out to make a $9 million movie without the script done. It doesn't make any sense to me. Not from my perspective.

*Berge:* Well, it happens all the time.

*Jacobs:* All the time?

*Berge:* Yeah, because of the window.

*Jacobs:* You just sort of say, "The window's open. Let's see if we can finish"?

*Berge:* You like the script, but it's 40 pages too long, and it's way too heavy for what you want to do, and now it's never going to end up on TV because it's way too long. But the company wants to make it, so you go.

*Jacobs:* In your estimation, does this account for why there seem to be so many bad movies?

*Berge:* Yes, absolutely—scripts that aren't finished. And there are some people who are very good at going through and reworking a script as it goes through the mill. There are directors who do that, too.

They should page you three times a day so you get through the core scheme of the script. You know, you've got 36 changes on the cover. Yeah, that'll happen with a bad script. It took so much attention away from making the movie. But it makes it difficult when you don't have that place. But sometimes it changes along the way, which is wonderful and fine, but when you spend so much energy trying to get the script ready for what you want to shoot, it takes away from what you're doing every day. It takes so much energy along the way that it really, really creates a problem in paying attention to other details on the show.

*Jacobs:* So principal photography is on, and you finally get your script done. Principal is now done—thank God we got through that. What's next? What does the producer do next? After principal, we go back, everybody goes home, we're now back in Los Angeles with a bunch of negatives?

*Berge:* Yep. You and the assistant editor set up the rooms, the editing equipment, all that, the week you start shooting. Sometimes the week before. A few days before, so you have time to set up.

*Jacobs:* Are you back here with the editor from day 1?

*Berge:* Yes, the editor gets fronted from day 1. They go through and start their assembly. They start putting things together if they can. Within a few days of being back in town, at the end of shooting, they have an assembly ready for the director to see. The director sees that and starts making his cut. He's got all these DGA [Directors Guild of America] rules here for 20 days. Yeah, up to 20 days to make his cut. They often get less. Depends on the schedule, sometimes you have to have a shorter schedule to have a director for 10 days. And you know, they can either do it or they can't. Or they either will do it or they won't.

*Jacobs:* At this point, regarding the director's cut, the editor goes in without the producer, without the company. Just Hooks and the editor who has made the first cut. Hooks says, "This is what I want you to do. Change this, change that, put this in," and so on. Then he presents his cut to the company and says, "This is the way I would have the film work."

*Berge:* Yes.

*Jacobs:* And then what happens?

*Berge:* He does his cut, and he shows it to the producer. The producer says, "Love it, it's great, but I've got a few changes. Can you do this? Can you do that?" and sometimes it's just as another eye seeing something new. When you're sitting there doing it for two weeks, three weeks, four, you lose perspective. And you know, you sit down and look at it, and your reactions run from, "Hey, we've got to move it" to "Hey, we've got a movie in there somewhere. You've just got to continue to get to it. I know it's there; it's just a matter of going through it." This one was more of the case of, "Hey, we've got a movie. It's there." And we had a few changes, not a whole bunch, actually, and they spent a day or two trying those changes and seeing if they worked. It's pretty easy to work in Avid.

*Jacobs:* So, you run it through—that's pretty simple to do—you try to change it, you don't like it, you put it right back.

*Berge:* Yeah, it's not like cutting the film and all that trouble we used to go through. But then you will do a temp dub, which this film was greatly in need of, before you show it to the network. We had fans running the whole time during production for the wind effects, and smoke machines for certain effects, and then things blowing, potato flake snow.

*Jacobs:* And ADR [automated dialogue replacement, or "looping"] at this point?

*Berge:* On the set, every time we got done with a take, we'd stop, shut everything down, do the sound only, and record everyone doing their lines . . . just for a rough track to use. Some of the generator noise was so loud you couldn't hear the actors and they were shouting at each other back and forth, with the wind in their face and the cold, and it was a nice effect. I think it works well. But it really just beats the hell out of the sound. So we would do that: record the sound after the shot for safety. The editor cut that into this cut because it's better to hear than not hear at all or to have that cutting in and out. That's so distracting.

*Jacobs:* You wouldn't bring the actors in at this point and go to the expense of ADR at this point for a temp dub?

*Berge:* We did on this one. I have in the past. Yeah, we actually did. We did bring the two lead actors in.

*Jacobs:* To have them do their lines for audio only.

*Berge:* Normally, you wouldn't, but this much work needing to be done, we had them lay some stuff in, which we knew would have to be transferred over to the final. So it wasn't a duplication of effort completely. We did some ADR, on the cut you're going to present to the network, some ADR. You fix some of the voices, and we laid in some wind effects and a few things. On the Avid you do dissolves, those sorts of a thing, and you lay in music.

*Jacobs:* Is this the final music that you put in?

*Berge:* No, just some generic music.

*Jacobs:* This isn't the score that's going to . . .

*Berge:* Something by John Barry, John Williams . . .

*Jacobs:* You find some music and lay it in there?

*Berge:* Yeah, something that matches well. You go, "That's going to work nicely there."

*Jacobs:* Something *like* that would work . . .

*Berge:* Yeah, and you lay it in. It really helps move things along, especially looking at landscapes, with this type of a film. A lot of landscapes, a lot of guys, little dots going across the snow. And a film without music is something completely different than when you put music to it. It becomes magic. You go, "Wow, look at that."

*Jacobs:* Take *Chariots of Fire*, for example.

*Berge:* Yeah, and that sort of thing. You'll try to match that mood with the actual score later. So you get that ready, and you take it in and try to sell the network. And you wait, and you freakin' wait! And you sit there, and you go batty until finally the executive producer calls, "Did they call you!?" "They didn't call me. I'm going to call over there in a minute or two." You finally call over there, and either you get the "Yeah, we really liked it" or you get the—like we did on this one—"Yes, Ralph, we love it, Ralph. Everyone's really excited about it." And I'm like, "Really? . . . *Really?*" Then they're like, "Listen, Ralph, yes, really!" I cried—OK, I cried. It was gross, and the head of talent gave me the five-hankie award.

*Jacobs:* Terrific! Good for you!

*Berge:* So you know, so you go "Wow!" And then they say, "Can you make a few changes? [Laughter.] We want to make these little changes in here. Can we do that?" and that sort of thing. So you make some of the changes, and some of the changes don't quite get made. . . . You know, you argue over what should be in, what shouldn't, and those sorts of things. And then after that, after you get the director's cut and the producer's version, then the producers give their notes to the director. They come up with a cut. You do all that; you present it to the network. They make a few changes, you show it to them again, then you lock the picture. From that point on, it's pretty well locked up. You schedule, you start making your print, you start doing . . .

*Jacobs:* You get your original score done?

*Berge:* Yes. You start doing your effects, your CG [computer-generated] shots and stuff. We had a number of those. And we made that deal out of Toronto, so you kind of set it up, you ship it off. You ship the elements off to Toronto, they do what they do, they ship it back, you look at it, you say no, you send it back there, you're scheduling ADR, calling the other actors. We've got ADR in L.A.; we've got ADR in New York, in Toronto, and ADR in Montreal, to get ADR on all these actors. Then you have the sound mixing. You've got the music recording. This is the only time I've ever seen musicians run from on the stage, inside the booth to listen to the playback. It was our composer, *Bruce Broughton* . . . big films.

*Jacobs:* Like?

*Berge:* Some of the Disney stuff. He gets his credit. He does big films. His normal fee we couldn't afford. But he likes the film. You tell him about it, and he goes, "Oh, hey?" You show him the film, and he says, "Oh, I like this. OK, let's make a deal," because he wants to work on the project as opposed to what he's used to getting. And it's a wonderful job because he's fallen in love with something. He does the score. This is really good. It could stand alone as a CD. So he does the score, you've got the ADR happening, we're waiting for the effects. You've got a delivery date; maybe you've got an airdate, maybe you don't. We didn't have one until March, so we were fine. And then you get a call from the effects house that they themselves have rejected 8 of your 16 shots because it's not up to their standards. They don't even want to show it to us. You go, "OK."

*Jacobs:* You mean something's off? Something doesn't work?

*Berge:* They had subleased, hired, an inputting company to input the frame-by-frame effects. They send in the film, they digitize it, they send it back. They weren't happy with the quality of that. They didn't give them enough to work with, so they fired that company and, at great expense to themselves, started over. What I love about these folks is that they care about their quality. But now I'm another six weeks behind, just like that. And what do you do? Then I've got audio mix dates that I can't slide because I can't get back in the studio. Even with that six-week push, I'm not getting back in because it's not available. I can't lose my dates. So you slug the shots and you go in and you mix with black holes in the picture, and you try to time the movie. You start to get your prints out, and you've got so many dissolves—480 dissolves in this film, in terms of in points and out points, something like that—then we mixed over the effects shots. At that point, I can't even finish the job, you know? I've got the effect shots, which are tied to opticals. And I can't finish the opticals. I can't cut the negative until I finish that shot to make sure it's OK. So, all this stuff is waiting. I'm seeing my film timed, but only half of it. The other half of the film is slugs. And you're mixing to a videotape; you'd rather mix to a tape that's from the cut negative to make sure it's in sync. So it goes along, and you follow that process. You want to make sure the music is right, that it's getting laid in there, that they record it and when they're mixing it, laying it in, they're not laying the cues in too heavily or too late for your optimum space for that kind of thing . . . that, you know, your dog barks are getting in, all the sounds are correct. We make sure it's looking good. You should have the map that you're having made look correct here. You are negotiating for stock footage. Trying to clear out those things. You are trying to get the licenses, trying to clear up the production things yet that keep creeping up. So you're watching the film. It takes so much time in the beginning, but you make sure it gets completed properly. You know, with the director right there, too, in the midst of everything. So you follow that whole process until you get a print. You get one that looks good, and then you also want to see the title-setting process when we transfer to video. Make sure that looks good. And deliver it to the network. You've got to prepare the paperwork, the same list that goes to the network, the music cue sheets, all the paper requirements, legal requirements, actors' contracts . . .

*Jacobs:* How many guilds are you working with here? You're dealing with SAG [Screen Actors Guild] . . .

*Berge:* SAG, DGA.

*Jacobs:* IATSE [International Alliance of Theatrical Stage Employees]?

*Berge:* Not on this one because it was done mostly out of the country.

*Jacobs:* No IA, no nothing?

*Berge:* SCTVQ [Société Canadienne Télévision Quebec]. . . . DGC . . . Directors Guild of Canada. I think that's it. You have to compile all the paperwork, close the show, and put it away. Then, at last, the show is done.

*Jacobs:* You now have a film in a can.

*Berge:* You've delivered a box of paperwork and film in a can. You've got $9 million worth of physical tapes and film, and all that goes to a postproduction person who receives it.

*Jacobs:* At TNT?

*Berge:* Yes. They OK it. It all gets quality-checked to see that it's within the parameters. Not only that it looks OK to the eye, but that it's within the parameters of the meters and . . .

*Jacobs:* FCC [Federal Communications Commission]?

*Berge:* All those things, too. . . . So they're happy and it goes into the vault, so they've got it. The paperwork goes some to them, some to legal. They check these in, they look at things, you give them things, they call you two weeks later and say, "I never got this." So you look in box 3, "Oh, yeah, here it is." You've got all that sort of stuff. That's done, that's put away. Then you've got, "Who's handling your marketing? Who's handling your PR? What shows are the stars getting on? Are they going on Larry King? *Good Morning America?* Letterman? Leno?"

*Jacobs:* This is your responsibility, not TNT's?

*Berge:* It's their responsibility. They do it, but you're asking the questions.

*Jacobs:* I see.

*Berge:* You never leave it up to them. You're always calling, "What are you doing? What are you doing for me? Did you send those guys a present? You're sure you've got a car picking him up to get him to the interview?" You just want to make sure it's happening. It's your baby, you can't let it go, so you want to make those calls and make sure it's happening. Now this is more out of the line producer more than the executive producer or producer.

It's like Sunday morning. I'm taking two framed title cards to the critics to work for Henry and Delroy to make sure they get their present *before* the show.

*Jacobs:* So they'll feel good.

*Berge:* Yes. We do appreciate them on top of this, but you want to treat them that way—and most people along the way, too. You try to do this. So you're following that through. You find one person at premiere, one's at airing, and you're questioning, "Why are you airing it then? Is that a good time?" They were originally going to air it in the summer. The way the schedule worked out, they went, "Eh, this one won't go in the summer. March is much better. The picture fits better there. We'll see how it does." And you need to ask, "Where's the screening being held? . . . Are we having a large screening, or are we delegated to some small theater in town?" Meaning, they don't think the picture deserves a large screen. Then you're concerned, are we being stuck in some screening room on some lot that holds 150 people? That means they don't care about the film; they don't want to stick any money into it. Are they putting us up at the DGA or the WGA [Writers Guild of America], or the academy that seats 1,200? That means they're behind the film; they like it. All those things play into how the film is then presented to the community in town and to the public and to the publicity that gets out there.

*Jacobs:* Now, once it's on the air, it's over.

*Berge:* Once it's on the air, you're through with it.

*Jacobs:* And you move on to . . .

*Berge:* Yeah, until it starts all over again.

*Jacobs:* And how long does this take? How long were you on this?

*Berge:* I was on this one 14 months.

*Jacobs:* And Bruce was on it . . . ?

*Berge:* Bruce was on it, I would say, three years.

*Jacobs:* From the first time Caputo says, "Look at this," three to four years later the movie's out?

*Berge:* Yeah, three to four years later, he gets a paycheck.

*Jacobs:* And he doesn't get a paycheck until it's out?

*Berge:* Yes.

*Jacobs:* You're on a salary here, so by the time you go on the set, you're getting paid.

*Berge:* Yeah. As a producer, coproducer, you make a deal for the show, and that's what you get.

*Jacobs:* And this is something that's negotiated and could change from picture to picture.

*Berge:* That's exactly right.

*Jacobs:* Project to project.

*Berge:* Yeah. You get one set fee for the show. If you're on as producer and it takes you three months, it's fine. If it takes you two years . . .

*Jacobs:* It's the same amount of money.

*Berge:* Yup. So then it starts all over again. At least, you hope it does!

# Appendix C

# Sample Proposals and Scripts

**Jackson·Walsh**
**& Associates, Inc.**

THE GREAT AMERICAN DREAM MACHINES

Proposal for an advertising account contract
presented to:

Mr. Clyde Fessler
AMF/Harley-Davidson
Harley-Davidson Motor Co., Inc.
Milwaukee, Wisconsin

Account Executive: Victor Feathers

3923 W. 6th. Street Suite 216
Los Angeles California 90020
213 · 387-3231

<u>A WORD ABOUT US</u>

Creative.

That's the word. But, there is a LOT of philosophy behind the word; behind us.

We're an agency which believes in America. In American products. The American Dream is a reality for us, as well as for the clients we represent. We want AMF/Harley-Davidson on our team. In this proposal we will show you why.

We selected Harley-Davidson for one <u>major</u> reason. You are America's motorcycle company. We have watched the Japanese machines, using American marketing and advertising practices, slowly erode your business. That business, according to your annual report to the stockholders was down 17% last year alone, primarily because your advertising was outstripped by Honda, Kawasaki and Yamaha.

We know that Harley-Davidson makes wonderful machines. Your powerful V-Twin engine, your workmanship, the legendary durability of the Harley-Davidson and the mile-after-mile comfort of your superbikes are all objects of pride for your company. AND...your products are made in America. So, why are your sales down?

Turn on a television set tonight and find out.

..."We <u>know</u>  why you ride"- Kawasaki

...a policeman giving the thumbs up sign on a Honda.

Turn on a radio and listen to...

..."Kawasaki lets the good times roll"...

And we'll BET you can hum that tune JUST from reading that line of copy. We will have America humming the Harley-Davidson song. We can sell Harley-Davidson's. And THAT is all we need to say about us.

2.

## <u>ON THE POSITIVE SIDE</u>
Sales!

That's what ANY agency promises to deliver. So do we. The
difference is that our fresh approach does it better, as the enclosed sample campaign indicates. On page 4 we have some other
ideas which go outside traditional channels to sell the product.

Here we'd like to deal with some traditional specifics.
You spent nearly 60% of your advertising budget last year on print.
We recommend reversing the media mix with a heavy emphasis on broadcast media. Your current approach to large display ads in the motorcycle trade magazines misses a large segment of potential buyers.
An exciting radio and television mix will correct this deficiency.
Kawasaki spent 52% of its budget on television, for example, with
a resulting 210 million dollars in sales. Their magazine figures
were only 25% of budget, with newspapers getting 2%, radio 3% and
point-of-purchase only 9%. We would recommend for Harley-Davidson
a heavier concentration on radio which reaches over 98% of the
American population every day at very low cost per thousand figures.
Radio also offers very good specific demographic targets.

Our campaign is designed to reach the HEART first, then the
head. This also reverses your current campaign objective. Harley-
Davidson engineering IS superb. We doubt that the AVERAGE potential
buyer <u>cares</u>. What he wants is fantasy gratification.

Our initial campaign is a strong EMOTIONAL appeal.
<u>HARLEY-DAVIDSON- THE GREAT AMERICAN DREAM MACHINES!</u>  Encapsulated in
that slogan is a wealth of fantasy-building:

     ...patriotism...the mythos of obtainable wealth a la Horace Greeley...

     ...prestige...a sense of belonging...power...national pride.

3.

We also move toward the nostalgia value of Harley-Davidson motorcycles with our banner lead:

Remember the feeling you used to get? Harley-Davidson gives it back!

There is strong appeal in evoking the sense memory of things like...

...your first pair of summer tennis shoes

...your first bicycle

...your first love affair

and so on. By linking these feelings to Harley-Davidson Motorcycles we have overcome a lot of the negative attitudes which many people still have toward motorcycles. To reach the guy in the suburbs who could become a Harley-Davidson buyer, we have many things to do away with in his mind:

...Fear of the machine, probably instilled by his parents with comments like, "They oughtta outlaw those things".

...Fear of the image of Hell's Angels; especially critical to Harley-Davidson Motorcycles.

...Fear of policemen; unfortunately still strongly identified with Harley-Davidson.

...Fear of being DIFFERENT! Astonishingly, recent research indicates that most Americans, in spite of what they profess, do NOT want to be different from their neighbors. We suspect this is the main reason one encounters so many "nice people" on HONDAs!

Paradoxically, these same fears can become the strongest POSITIVE factors in the decision to buy a motorcycle; especially if the fears are manipulated into fantasies.

On the next page we explore some concrete programs to describe this rather complex notion of human motivation.

4.

We are not <u>just</u> after the buyer who is ALREADY committed to motorcycling. We want the Honda rider to switch to Harley, but, more importantly, we want the first time buyer to "Go Harley" from the start. Here are specific programs to overcome the fears we talked about on the previous page.

1. <u>THE HARLEY-DAVIDSON GOOD GUY CLINIC</u>

Part of the fear of the machine is not understanding it. Our dealers will hold evening clinics in motorcycling. Here, the current or the prospective bike owner will take lessons in handling a motorcycle, riding in dirt, on the road and general safety and control aspects important to the rider. For the expert rider we offer classes in racing and stunt techniques under the close supervision of a professional rider. In short, the clinic is for everyone from rank novice to road racer.

The second part of the clinic instructs riders in owner maintenance. This is in many ways the scariest part of the game for the suburban novice. He doesn't want to look like a fool when he takes his girlfriend for a ride and the damn machine quits running. Some basic instruction will eliminate his fear forever and make a HERO of our Harley-Davidson dealer!

The clinic is open to anyone in the community, whether or not they own a motorcycle, whether or not they own a HARLEY. And THAT is WHY it's the "Good Guy" clinic. What we SELL is that Harley-Davidson is interested in safer and more trouble free <u>motorcycling</u>, period. AND...we're the only ones to be so public spirited. Bring us your Honda...your tired Kawasaki and we'll show you how to take care of it...while we sell you a Harley!

People who pass the course get a nifty patch for their jackets and a decal for their bike which reads:
CERTIFIED HARLEY-DAVIDSON RIDER/MAINTENANCE SPECIALIST.

2. <u>THE HARLEY-DAVIDSON AMERICAN DREAM TOUR</u>

If you buy your Harley-Davidson during the month of July, we'll FLY you to Milwaukee to pick it up and join our American Heritage Tour. Our caravan, with a maintenance and comfort vehicle in the lead, will take you and your passenger through the Land of Lincoln to the historic battlefield at Tippecanoe. Our trail is over quiet country roads...etc.

The idea here is very simple. The guy buys a bike to be "free", but is scared to venture off on his own. So, we give him the dream trip on his bike in perfect safety and in the company of other riders who are EXACTLY like him. This idea made Wally Byam the King of Caravans with his Airstream trailers. It satisfies the same urge to merge with the great outdoors which fills every campsite in America with motorhomes and campers. Our tour follows a simple route through the Midwest with organized campsites at the end of each day's short ride. For an additional fee, we arrange shipment home of the bike at the end of the tour and the customer gets a jacket patch and decal which reads:
OFFICIAL HARLEY-DAVIDSON GREAT AMERICAN DREAM TOUR.

5.

Our Dream  Tour also takes care of another objection raised when a married man wants to buy a bike. Mom wonders how she's going to fit in. On our couples tour, she'll have the time of her life, and we can end up selling her a bike as well!

## THE HARLEY-DAVIDSON SAFETY SCHOOL

A giant Harley-Davidson Number 1 van pulls up to the school yard. Out of it rolls a fleet of Harley-Davidson motorcycles with instructor/trick riders. We stage a one or two day demonstration for driver education classes, putting the high school kids in the saddle under close supervision. We have the local policeman there with his Harley Police Special, too.

Inside the van we have audio-visual presentations. Exciting films show our motorcycles in action: racing footage, Evel Knieval, motocross riding, trials competition, and plain old fashioned sport riding through the beautiful scenery of Door County.

The idea we're selling here is safety and interest in the true sport of motorcycling. Part of our Great American Dream is that the young rider will learn respect for the machines and will ride safely to live and enjoy the dream. This is another area where we can capture public attention as the "concerned motorcycle company". To continue an ongoing program of safety, we include our local Harley-Davidson dealer in the school's driver education program.

These are a few of the unique ideas which we propose as part of our service as your advertising agency. We know that in America, Harley-Davidson should be, can be and WILL be, Number One.

Since we are in Hollywood, in constant touch with the celebrities, the studios and the television production firms, and since much of our expertise lies in these areas, we can also promote Harley-Davidson motorcycles in a variety of ways aside from the conventional time-buy.

We invite you and whomever of your staff you feel would be appropriate, to come to Hollywood at our expense for two or three days. We want to prove that we can deliver and to show you how.

<u>SAMPLE SPEC SPOT COPY</u>

**Harley-Davidson Motorcycle Television Spot - 60**

Writer: Bob Jacobs     Account Exec: Victor Feathers

| VIDEO | AUDIO |
|---|---|
| **1. LS ROAD**<br>A billowing American flag SUPERED over. The road is a twisting rural one lined with trees in Autumn flame. A rider, neatly dressed in designer leathers comes toward us on a SPORTSTER. A pretty lady is riding with him, enjoying the ride.<br><br>dissolve to | (MUSIC UP- "Harley Song")<br><u>LYRIC</u><br>FREEDOM RIDES THE AMERICAN ROAD, ALONG WITH YOU AND ME... |
| **2. CU ANOTHER RIDER**<br>A good looking young exec type. PULL BACK to reveal another sylvan scene on the California Coast. He and a young, beautiful woman are on a SUPERGLIDE near Big Sur. Ocean sparkles B.G.<br><br>dissolve to | HARLEY PUTS YOU <u>IN</u> THE SCENE FROM SEA TO SHINING SEA!... |
| **3. MS ANOTHER RIDER**<br>He is on a full-dress ELECTRAGLIDE rolling down a rural road with red barns and silos: American "heartland". We FOLLOW. | ON BYWAYS OF THIS SPRAWLING LAND,<br>PAST RIVER, LAKE AND STREAM...<br>HARLEY-DAVIDSON TURNS YOU ON TO FEEL THE AMERICAN DREAM!<br>(Instrumental continues under) |
| **4. MONTAGE**<br>Quick cuts of a Motocross, a young woman on an SX250, a boy on an SX175 fording a river, and a couple, typifying young urbans, setting up camp in the woods, 2 SS250's in FOREGROUND. | <u>NARRATOR</u><br><br>HARLEY-DAVIDSON IS AMERICA'S MOTORCYCLE COMPANY. PART OF THE AMERICAN DREAM SINCE 1903. GETTING BETTER. PERFECTING OUR MACHINES FOR AMERICAN ROADS, AMERICAN RIDERS, AMERICAN DREAMERS. RIDE THE HARLEY-DAVIDSON DREAM MACHINE. YOU WON'T WANT TO WAKE UP! |
| **5. CU HAPPY RIDER**<br>We pull back quickly in an aerial shot and see 100 riders, all on various model Harley's in a procession down a rural highway. These are SUPERED over the Harley Number 1 logo.<br><br><br><br><br><br>Fade to black. | (Song continues)<br><br>COME JOIN THE HARLEY-DAVIDSON CLUB AND FEEL THE AMERICAN DREAM!<br><br><u>NARRATOR</u><br><br>HARLEY-DAVIDSON MOTORCYCLES-THE GREAT AMERICAN DREAM MACHINES.<br><br>(FX- MOTOR SYNTHESIZED FADING) |

# Jackson·Walsh
## & Associates, Inc.

COPY FOR HARLEY-DAVIDSON MOTORCYCLE PRINT AD     0002-77

(Banner-) OUR NUMBER 1 IS THERE FOR A REASON!

Actually it's there for several reasons.

We win races. LOTS of them.

We set and KEEP land speed records.

We set and KEEP jumping records with EVEL KNIEVAL.

(Ask HIM why we're number 1!)

But those aren't the IMPORTANT reasons.

YOU are.

You're an American rider. We're America's motorcycle company.

Harley-Davidsons have been built to be Number 1 with you since 1903.

Our V-Twin engine is the strongest one in town. Take it from L.A. to
New York sometime and see for yourself.

We EAT mountains, deserts, the great plains. Then we give you carefree
city street riding for dessert.

Our Number 1 is YOURS. Because  you're part of the American Dream.

HARLEY-DAVIDSON MOTORCYCLES- The Great American Dream Machines.

# Jackson·Walsh
## & Associates, Inc.

COPY FOR HARLEY-DAVIDSON MOTORCYCLE PRINT AD      0001-77

(Banner-) REMEMBER THAT FEELING YOU <u>USED</u> TO GET?...

...in your first new pair of tennis shoes for your tenth summer?

...on your very first Christmas bicycle?

...in your FIRST car?

...on your FIRST date?

HARLEY-DAVIDSON REMEMBERS THAT FEELING, TOO...

AND GIVES IT BACK TO YOU!

Harley-Davidson is AMERICA'S motorcycle company. We've been

part of the American dream since 1903. Getting better.

<u>Perfecting</u>  our machines.

Making them stronger. More durable. More FUN!

Our bikes are made for <u>American</u> riders. For <u>American</u> roads.

For American <u>dreamers</u>.

Our Number 1 is there for a reason. We've EARNED it, year after year,

in the toughest competition in the world—<u>American</u> racing!

You can find the "nicest people" anywhere. You can find YOURSELF on

a HARLEY-DAVIDSON.

HARLEY-DAVIDSON MOTORCYCLES—THE GREAT AMERICAN DREAM MACHINES.

3674 Knapp Street Road
Oshkosh, Wisconsin
54901

the Film Farm


THE MECHANISMS OF JOY

Proposal for a Recruiting Film for

Product Engineering Group
Mercury Marine

Presented to:

Director of Product Engineering

by

Bob   Jacobs, Ph.D


Where Ideas Grow

1

## SECTION ONE

## INTRODUCTION

In our past couple of meetings, musings and meanderings around the world of Product Engineering at Mercury Marine, we have explored a problem which you have identified; a problem which lends itself to a unique and dynamic solution in the form of a quality film presentation. First, let's define and detail the problem. Then we will propose the format for the solution and the reasons why The Film Farm should be the choice to execute that solution.

You need to recruit high-caliber design engineers to fill both present and projected vacancies in Product Engineering in the Fox Valley. The target candidate for these positions is a man or woman between the ages of 25 and 40, usually with a degree and/or extensive experience in mechanical engineering. The primary candidate would be someone already working in the field at places such as 3M, Texas Instruments, Ford, GM, Chrysler, Boeing Aircraft and  so on. The secondary candidate would be an undergraduate or graduate student at a major university. The salary range and fringe benefit package in this specialty field offered by Mercury Marine is competitive with other major corporations.

In spite of this apparent equity in the field, conventional methods of recruiting candidates for your positions have encountered obstacles, severely limiting your choice of the best people available. In our discussions, we have conjectured at several of the possible reasons why gifted young  engineers may

2

be reluctant to apply for work at Mercury Marine. These include all of the following, not necessarily in prioritized order:

[1] The perception by many people in other states that Oshkosh and Fond du Lac, Wisconsin are cultural backwaters is a significant consideration. The very fact that people in the industry who work in New York and Los Angeles say, "You must be from Oshkosh", when they mean, "You're a real hick" is indicative of the mentality in question.

[2] Another impression of our part of the country is difficult to refute. Winter is long, bitter, costly in terms of home heating, and frightening to many folks who are used to "the sun belt" or the beaches of Southern California.

[3] The recent highly publicized fact that Wisconsin is consistently one of the highest taxed states in the country, especially in the areas of personal income and property taxes, is a major deterrent to many American white-collar workers, especially to those in the salary bracket under consideration.

[4] There is a conception among the technical elite that boat motors are prosaic and that there is little if any challenge or excitement left in the field. Under the intense publicity blaze of recent space technology, many engineers feel that aerospace is the cutting "edge of the envelope", the place where the "action", and therefore **they** ought to be.

[5] Wisconsin itself, when it is thought of at all, is regarded by many otherwise intelligent people as an unexciting land of dairy farms, corn fields, beer-swilling, pot-bellied foundry workers and, even at this late period of political

3

history, the arch-conservative, closed-minded culture which has only produced Senator Joseph McCarthy and polka dancing.

Those of us who live here certainly recognize finely-ground kernels of whole grain truth in the foundations for such ideas about our state and the industry. The facts are that for nearly six months each year our trees are leafless, that from December through March the wind blows and the snow flows, that heating costs **can** eat up a large chunk of the family budget for the unwise and unwary, that one aspect of our society has a hard-drinking, hard-laughing, "blue-collar", four-wheel drive, Wednesday night bowling mentality, and that personal taxation is, indeed, a heavy burden for Wisconsinites to bear. And, if this were the **entire** story — and 10-horsepower trolling motors for bass fishermen were the only challenge for a Mercury Marine engineer to contemplate—we would all throw up our hands at **ever** luring a rational man or woman to such a terrible fate, pack up our bags and move **anywhere** else on the planet!

But, we know better.

We live here.

We work here.

We know that any whole picture is not represented by a few pixels therefrom!

And obviously, there is **something** which keeps us here. In fact, there are **many** things which keep us here and which, when presented properly to our prospective candidates, will encourage them to want to join us.

In the next few pages we will explore some concepts for

4

presenting the whole picture and the perfect format for doing it.

## THE MEDIUM IS THE MESSAGE

We have agreed that the format for this highly directional appeal should be a departure from the norm: a dramatic, motion-packed, emotionally stimulating "movie". There are two methods for recording whatever story we end up choosing. One is video. The other is motion picture film.

Before coming to our recommendations for the recording medium (film or video), we'd like to recap the justification for choosing this radical departure from more standard recruiting techniques.

First, it is impractical to expect that we can overcome the already identified mindset of our candidate in a conventional print ad, or job announcement in trade/tech periodicals. There is, as Mercury Marine and other major corporations already know, proven effectiveness in reaching target audiences with well designed film or video programs. We are a nation, like it or not, which is conditioned to view programs on film or video screens. We are "sold" on concepts, products and ideas by manipulation of our emotional and sometimes even our rational selves by the verisimilitude of the moving images of light. Using proven techniques, some of them time-tested in the cauldron of television advertising, we implant messages in our medium, designed to convince our candidate that his or her preconceptions about our geographic area and our company's products are not only incomplete, but in error. Since we know our target audience, choosing and carefully scripting the most appropriate final form

5

for our program to reach that candidate is the next step in our process.

### Film or Video as the Medium

There are two disparate "looks" to the media of film and video. Television programs and commercials with the intent of selling the concept of "quality" are shot on motion picture film. The look of film is difficult to describe. "Slick", "three-dimensional", "glossy", "professional" are adjectives which have been used in the attempt. Familiar examples are simple to give. Television shows like "Cagney and Lacey", "Hill Street Blues", "M*A*S*H" and all other dramatic series are recorded on film. So are **all** major, national TV spots.

The "video look" is easier to describe. "Live", "one-dimensional" and "bright" are suitable adjectives. Simply compare the "look" of the 6 o'clock news or a Pierquets' TV spot with a Miller, Budweiser, or Ford commercial along with any of the shows named above and you have the idea.

We have the capability to shoot in either medium. Here are the advantages we see for recommending film:

[1] Lighting for film can be more dramatically compelling than the flatter ratios needed for video.

[2] Film imparts a subtle feeling of high quality in the viewer.

[3] A film can be shown to large audiences in theater or auditorium settings.

[4] Film can be transferred to video with infinitely better results than video can be transferred to film.

6

The negative side of the equation is that it is difficult to intercut scenes shot on film with scenes shot on video (not technically, but esthetically). If the final project is going to incorporate a great deal of existing Mercury Marine footage already recorded as video, then our advice would be stay with that medium. The cost factor would be only slightly higher shooting the original on film.

## SECTION TWO

## THE CONCEPT

Crafting a script to tell our story is the heart, soul and backbone of the project. We have two primary considerations:

[1] The ideal target candidate.

[2] Getting the project to that candidate.

Our person is presumed to be intelligent, informed, curious, upwardly mobile, probably an urbanite and also, to face facts, just as probably a man. If the person is a woman in the field, she will no doubt have the same characteristics, however. Because of the type of input we are going to want from this person as a member of the Mercury Marine Team, we are also presuming an inherent sense of adventure and one who enjoys testing his or her limits in a variety of ways. Our major appeal is going to be to someone who feels either bored, boxed-in or frustrated by the limitations of their present position.

While our perfect candidate is represented by a rather narrow spectrum of the entire population, we want to maximize the exposure to most of the potential prospects. Therefore, we propose a standard television length format. There are four from

7

which to choose. A commercial TV one-hour is 48 minutes. A PBS hour is 54 minutes. A commercial half-hour is 26 minutes and a PBS half-hour show is 28.9 minutes. It is possible for us to "cut" a program in both the commercial and PBS lengths no matter whether we opt for the hour or half-hour format. The shorter version is more suited for educational classroom, trade/technical conventions and service club showings.

### THE PSYCHOLOGY OF THE SCRIPT

Now that we know our intended viewer and the right format to use, the next step is to construct a script. And here's what our script has to do: **MOTIVATE** the viewer to want to work for Mercury Marine in Wisconsin. Our goal is to initiate a flood of resumes onto your desk!

Since we anticipate making a film which will be of general enough interest to run as a television program, we are **not** considering a "sales pitch" per se. Even if we were to make this a direct appeal to Mr. and Ms. Engineer, we would not want to appear to be pleading with them. There are two antique axioms which apply to the psychology of our script: "Nothing succeeds like success" and "Everybody loves a winner".

Our script is going to be a positive statement, therefore, about Mercury Marine Product Engineering and about the numerous bounties of the State of Wisconsin.

Our title, **The Mechanisms of Joy**, at once sets the thematic statement of our piece and intrigues the viewer to discover what these wonderful mechanisms might be. With the highly visual dynamics at our disposal, we know there will be no

8

difficulty in demonstrating several things about working for Mercury Marine. The sheer fun in our products is demonstrable. We can <u>see</u> them at play in a stunning variety of situations from quiet fishing to world class racing to the <u>adult</u> fantasyland at Disney World; a place which has proven that none of us, and most especially the kind of candidate we're after, never **really** "grows-up"!

Our working conditions nurture the perpetual inquisitive "kid" in every one of us. And as for "pushing the edge of the envelope", the present and the future of our marine technology is as fraught with science fiction devices as anything to do with outer space. Our explorations are with "inner space"; the waterways and oceans of Planet Earth and discovering the best and most efficient ways to move in and through them. We see this facet in our gem as central to the theme. We do not build the juggernauts of destruction, nor the prosaic mechanisms of ordinary transportation or commerce. We **build** "the mechanisms of joy"!

Finally, our product engineers are not always limited to a small part in a vast complex of other parts as engineers frequently are at other corporations. At Mercury Marine, our engineers are limited only by the boundaries of individual imagination.

With this understanding of the psycho/philosophical approach, we are now ready to explore a few considerations for the final shape of the script.

9

## THE ELEMENTS OF THE SCRIPT

We suggest basing a dramatic story around the life of a single Product Engineer at Mercury Marine. We envision having a professional actor play the part. There are several very competent, correct-looking performers available to us in the Fox Valley. We want to build our story around this single central character as he approaches and successfully goes through a critical moment in his career.

We suggest this device based on the principle that viewers can identify with a single person or family with similar lifestyles and insights to their own better than they can absorb large, generalized concepts. We are using one engineer to symbolize and represent the "gestalt" of <u>Mercury Marine Product Engineering</u>.

As a gross example of this dramatic technique, it is impossible for individuals to become terribly involved with or moved by the concept of "slavery". The highly acclaimed and successful television miniseries on that historical event, *Roots*, however, focused on the trials and tribulations of one family's history, giving us all the human insight we needed to comprehend their ultimate triumph. The viewer's involvement with our engineer will impart to that viewer the positive message which we have agreed is central to our presentation: Mercury Marine is a great place to work, and the Fox Valley of Wisconsin is a great place in which to live.

In working out the plot and the dramatic structure of our script, through a period of time in the life of our central

10

character, we move through four basic stages.

[1] Exposition. This first portion of the script introduces us to the central character, the location, and other characters with whom he will interact and sets the stage for the action with which we will become involved.

[2] Point of attack. This is the place in the story where the action begins. It is usually brought on when the central character sets out to achieve a goal.

[3] Rising action. The story picks up pace as the character encounters two dramatic devices called "complication" and "crisis". The complication is some set of circumstances which stand in the way of the character's goal. The crisis is reached when the character has to overcome that complication to achieve the goal.

[4] Resolution and denouement. The resolution of the crisis leads to the third dramatic script device of the "climax" where the character triumphs. Denouement is simply letting the audience see the happy results of the victory in the life of the central character and a place for summing up the message if necessary.

All of these elements follow the plot. Plot means literally "action" and can normally be defined very succinctly: "Boy meets girl, boy loses girl, boy gets girl". Here, for example, is the plot of *Hamlet*: "A young prince has trouble making up his mind whether or not to avenge the death of his father".

The plot is also called "the spine" of the piece. Everything which fleshes out that spine into a full-blown creation with depth and scope hangs on the skeleton of the

11

screenplay.

Attached, part by part, to the spine of our script will be all of the clarifications of the misconceptions about Wisconsin and working on boat motors which we discussed earlier. Those ill conceived notions about Mercury Marine Product Engineers are the easiest to overcome. The freedom of our engineers, the in-depth involvement with each project which an engineer enjoys, the state-of-the-art facilities and support equipment with which he works, and the highly visual, dynamic end-products actually in use are visualizations of the very essence of "the Mechanisms of joy". We can make the computer graphics, the test stations, the metallurgy and so on appear just as exciting visually as anything from the aerospace industry and more. We will demonstrate that our engineer is, indeed, "pushing the envelope" of "high-tech". We also want to show **where** he gets to do so.

We do not intend to make "excuses" for Wisconsin, for we know that none need to be made. The "kernels of truth" which we discussed earlier only need to be shown after they have been planted in rich soil and have grown to mature plants for harvesting in the minds of our viewers. Let's consider those we have agreed upon.

[1] It is true that life in Wisconsin does not follow the pace of urban centers like Los Angeles or New York. But we are far from being a "cultural backwater". The arts and sciences flourish here in cities like Milwaukee and Madison. Both are short hops by either automobile or airplane from our sylvan residence in the Fox Valley. The Valley, itself, is not a "hick

12

town", but rather a slowly expanding urban corridor with fine music, art, theater, institutions of higher education, museums and world class attractions like the E.A.A. Aviation Center and the annual Convention and Fly-in.

Urbanites will be shown a place where middle income people can and do enjoy the goodness of country living, if they choose, on farmettes where no one even thinks of locking doors or worrying about major robbery, where children can learn about nature by growing up in it. In our small towns we still find cheerful neighbors who care about us and about their community and where, again, we do not have to barricade ourselves behind quadruple dead-bolted doors of terrifically overpriced apartments, or fear for ourselves, our wives or our children walking our pleasant, beautifully maintained, tree covered streets night or day. Our values are intact in the midst of the terrors of our urban cousins. We are communities of porch sitters and dog-walkers where the nightly news is filled with feature stories in the main, since there is so little crime to report. Set that notion in the mind of a guy in Houston or Atlanta, show him the red barns and silos of Grandma Moses, the joggers and bicyclists of our autumnally incarnadined countryside and we have set the hook of envy right off the bat!

[2] Yes, Winter is long and harsh. It can also thrill the soul of the poet with its enormous beauty; the crystalline glitter of fresh-fallen snow, the cheerful glow of a house at Christmas looking like a picture postcard, the opportunities for new and adventurous sports like ice-boating, cross-country and

13

downhill skiing minutes away from where we live, snowmobiling, ice fishing and brisk hikes. There is a grandeur to winter as part of the visible passing of the seasons of our planet which many find  endearing and spiritual as we compare and contrast the coming of spring and summer. Life in our climate presents new challenges to people who enjoy challenge. And we have already concluded that it is that very personality whom we are trying to reach.

For our engineer, Winter also has a flip side with trips to the Florida facility. We won't deny winter, but we will show  it for what it is; simply another sparkling facet of existence in harmony with the spinning of the Earth.

[3] Wisconsinites pay high taxes. Wisconsinites  also enjoy incredible services in comparision with most other states as a result. For example, Wisconsin secondary students typically score near the highest in the  nation  on  annual college entry examinations. We have a proud history of education here with a top-ranked university system which is enormously accessible to every resident. In the fields of elder care, special education, and other social services, Wisconsin ranks second to none. And while we pay for these services, we also enjoy an overall cost of living which ranks toward the bottom of the national scale for housing, clothing, food, entertainment and so forth. We may pay more in property tax on a percentage basis than our friends in Texas, for example, but we can afford the house we choose to buy!

[4]    Our  state  does  indeed  have  a  blue-collar element. But that element is a source of pride, not scorn. Our

14

workers are imbued with the "work ethic" as no others in the country. We have craftsmen, not "assemblers". And many of our citizens enjoy the hearty laughter of the local tavern, the bowling alley or the fishing tournament. We are a diverse conglomeration of ethnic types, taking pride in the heritage left us by the rock-hard pioneers who settled here. We also have a socially elevated class in Wisconsin which enjoys symphony music, art museums and live theater without the preciosity displayed by many urban snobs. It is our cultural intermixing, that freedom of association and our characteristic casualness of dress and manner which lends any Wisconsinite a sense of belonging, of having roots and of loving this land of rolling fields, forests, streams, lakes and rivers.

And, in the experience of our central character, we will blend all of these elements of the script and of the story together to produce a revelry of sights and sounds which will leave all but the most blasé yearning to become a part of it all.

### AT YOUR SERVICE

Any film begins with the written word. We are ready to begin scripting *The Mechanisms of Joy*. The elements are all waiting to be assembled. We propose the following schedule to implement the project.

[A] Research and scriptwriting: October 14 through November 14.

[B] Production: November 18 through May 1, to enable us to show the transition of seasons.

[C] Postproduction: May 1 through June 1.

15

## BUDGET

It is impossible to present a detailed production budget since the amounts will depend upon the exigencies of the script from which the actual budget must be drawn. We can, however, provide the actual cost of research and scriptwriting and a "ballpark" figure between which the production budget will fall for either shooting on original film or original video. (The top figure represents an estimated minimum, the bottom an estimated maximum).

[A] Research and Scriptwriting..............$ 1,200.00

[B] Production for Film.....................$ 5,000.00
                                             20,000.00

[C] Production for Video....................$ 4,000.00
                                             20,000.00

[D] Postproduction for Film.................$ 3,000.00
                                              7,000.00

[E] Postproduction for Video................$ 2,500.00
                                              7,000.00*

Mercury Marine shall own all rights to the script upon completion and approval. At that time we will present a detailed, accurate production budget estimate for your consideration. We invite you to solicit comparison bids on the production at that time.

## TERMS

[A] Research and Scriptwriting: $600.00 on contract signing, $600.00 balance on script approval by the client.

[B] Production and Postproduction: One half on contract

---

* These are not the actual budget figures for this project. The client retains a proprietary right of confidentiality over the real cost. These are typical figures for such a production, and are included here only as a rule of thumb.

16

signing, one half balance due on delivery of final print.

## CONCLUSION

We believe that you have a challenging and worthwhile project, the goals for which are achievable by us at the highest quality and the lowest cost. Our bid for this project will be on a cost recovery basis, paying only for the actual materials and services needed. We want to prove to you that Mercury Marine does not need to go outside the Fox Valley to provide itself with the best film and video production services available. We regard this as our chance to do so. A copy of some of our previous credits is attached.

We are excited at the prospect of working on this entertaining and stimulating project and look forward to a long and happy association with you.

# Caterpillar, Inc.

## Thermal Spray: The High-Tech Solution

***Instructional Video Script by Dr. Bob Jacobs***
fade in

(MUSIC UP—lively tempo)

MONTAGE

We see a fast-paced intercut sequence of CAT products in the field, with an emphasis on over-the-road trucks, cut in time to the music to show the power and durability of the machines. Hot desert, humid forest, etc. SUPER TITLE OVER:

  CORINTH THERMAL SPRAY COATINGS

dissolve

EST. AMT-MOSSVILLE

  ANNOUNCER V.O. (music fades under)

  IT'S A TOUGH WORLD OUT THERE WHERE CAT HAS TO COMPETE, DAY AFTER DAY. WE'RE KNOWN FOR QUALITY—DEPENDABILITY— LONG LIFE. IT'S BEEN OUR ADVANTAGE FROM THE START. AND AS THE GLOBAL COMPETITION HEATS UP, WE NEED TO KEEP THAT ADVANTAGE.

dissolve

EST. THERMAL SPRAY LAB—DAY

A team of engineers working on a plasma spray SEQUENCE.

  ANNOUNCER V.O.

  ENGINEERS AT OUR MOSSVILLE TECH CENTER WORK AROUND THE CLOCK, LOOKING FOR NEW ANSWERS TO OLD PROBLEMS— FIGHTING THE EFFECTS OF CORROSION, METAL STRESS, AND HEAT . . . THOSE GREMLINS THAT EAT AWAY AT OUR BEST WORK AND LEAD TO EQUIPMENT FAILURE.

CLOSE ON ENGINEERS AT MONITOR

Two ENGINEERS are looking at a coating cross section at microscope monitor. Out of that monitor we ZOOM (fx) to

EST. THERMAL SPRAY ROOM—DAY

Technician is preparing to light the torch.

ANOTHER SHOT

As the flame is lit and the robot arm begins spraying.

  ANNOUNCER V.O.

  THE BEST WAY THEY'VE FOUND TO EXTEND LIFE, RETARD WEAR, . . .

dissolve

ANGLE ON

EST. HIGHWAY TRUCK IN RUGGED ENVIRONMENT

As it rolls by us.

  ANNOUNCER V.O.

  . . . AND GIVE OUR CUSTOMERS THE BEST REASON TO GO ON CHOOSING CAT PRODUCTS IS ALL IN YOUR HANDS.

effect

The TRUCK is replaced by

EST. SHOT—THERMAL SPRAY LINE— CORINTH

An OPERATOR is doing a HAND-HELD spray job on a connecting rod component. We cut to a couple of different angles to form a sequence of this as the ANNOUNCER enters the frame, talking directly to us.

  ANNOUNCER

  THERMAL SPRAY IS THE BEST WAY YET TO COAT A VARIETY OF PARTS FOR LONGER LIFE AND DURABILITY. AND THOUGH IT'S BEEN AROUND FOR A HUNDRED YEARS OR SO, IT'S ONLY DURING THE PAST FEW THAT THIS HIGH-TECH

PROCESS HAS COME INTO ITS OWN. MODERN THERMAL SPRAY IS FASTER, CHEAPER, MORE EFFICIENT AND ENVIRONMENTALLY SAFER THAN WELDED BONDING. THAT'S THE FORMULA FOR A VERY BRIGHT FUTURE FOR ALL OF US. AND RIGHT HERE IN CORINTH, MISSISSIPPI, IS WHERE IT COMES TOGETHER, WITH YOU AT THE HEART OF IT.

The ANNOUNCER walks out as we cut to

A DIFFERENT ANGLE ON THE OPERATOR (SEQUENCE)

We focus on the part and on the OPERATOR'S face, making a visual connection between his/her concentration and the beauty of the flaming process. This LOOKS very dramatic and important. The MUSIC swells to underscore that theme.

ANNOUNCER V.O.

SOME FOLKS THINK IT'S JUST A JOB. BUT THIS IS JUST A JOB THE WAY HEART SURGERY IS JUST A JOB. THIS IS WHERE HIGH-TECH AND HIGHLY SKILLED WORKER JOIN UP!

CLOSE ON THE PART BEING COATED

ANNOUNCER V.O.

YOU SEE, WE'RE DIFFERENT FROM EVERY OTHER COATING PROCESS. THERMAL SPRAY LIQUEFIES THE COATING MATERIAL AND BONDS IT PERMANENTLY TO THE SUBSTRATE. WE CAN APPLY AN ALMOST UNLIMITED RANGE OF COATING MATERIALS TO MEET A WIDE RANGE OF DEMANDS. . . .

ANGLE ON DISPLAY OF APPLICATIONS AS ANNOUNCER WALKS THROUGH

ANNOUNCER V.O.

. . . THESE INCLUDE WEAR COATINGS, THERMAL INSULATION, CORROSION-RESISTANT, ABRASIVE, ELECTRICALLY CONDUCTIVE AND RESISTIVE COATINGS, AND A VARIETY OF POLYMERS. WE USE METALS, CERAMICS, CARBIDES, AND PLASTICS. SO IF YOU'RE IN THERMAL SPRAY, YOU'RE SMART, SCIENTIFICALLY TRAINED, AND HIGHLY SKILLED. AND AROUND HERE, YOU'RE WALKING TALL!

dissolve

EST. THERMAL SPRAY BAY—SETTING UP

We follow an operator preparing to fire up the machine.

ANNOUNCER V.O.

IT WORKS LIKE THIS. OXYGEN AND FUEL ARE MIXED TOGETHER TO FORM A VERY HIGH TEMPERATURE JET COMING OUT OF THIS GUN. POWDERED PARTICLES OF THE COATING MATERIAL ARE FED FROM THIS HOPPER DOWN THE LINE WHERE THEY GET INJECTED INTO THE FLAME. THEY MELT INSTANTLY AND ARE SHOT ONTO THE SURFACE BY THE EXPANDING GAS FLOW, WHERE THE NOW LIQUID MATERIAL SPREADS AND SOLIDIFIES INTO A THIN COAT ON THE SURFACE. IT SOUNDS . . . WELL . . . SIMPLE!

ANGLE ON PART

As the flaming gun begins to spray material.

dissolve

ANOTHER ANGLE ON A SPRAY BAY

As the ANNOUNCER walks in with a spray gun in his hand.

ANNOUNCER

AND . . . IT IS SIMPLE IN THEORY. PREPARE THE PART, LOAD UP THE HOPPER, INSTALL THE PROPER NOZZLE, ADJUST THE GASES, FIRE IT UP, AND LET 'ER RIP. WITH PROPER PREPARATION AND ATTENTION TO DETAIL, IT LOOKS EASY. BUT YOU AND I BOTH KNOW THE TRICK TO MAKING THINGS LOOK EASY. WE HAVE TO MASTER

THEM FIRST. SO LET'S GO THROUGH THE BASIC STARTUP WITH A CORINTH PROFESSIONAL.

ANGLE ON PROFESSIONAL

He/She will SHOW us through the following elements, with COMMENTS from the ANNOUNCER. EACH SEGMENT will be a complete sequence with close-up details as needed.

ANNOUNCER V.O.

(1. Startup procedure)

REMEMBER THAT THE MOST CRITICAL PART OF THE THERMAL SPRAY PROCESS IS TO BOND THE COATING TO THE PART. THERMAL SPRAYING DIFFERS FROM WELDING, YOU SEE, IN THAT WELDING MELTS THE COATING AND THE BASE MATERIAL TOGETHER TO FORM A METALLURGICAL BOND. IN THERMAL SPRAY, THE MOLTEN PARTICLES COOL UPON IMPACT WITH THE SUBSTRATE, FORMING A MECHANICAL BOND.

ANGLE ON PROFESSIONAL WORKER

PROFESSIONAL (SOT)

THE BOND STRENGTH OF OUR METCO 452 IS AROUND 7 THOUSAND PSI. BUT YOU HAVE TO BE CAREFUL. THE BOND STRENGTH WILL BE A LOT LOWER IF YOU DON'T PREPARE THE PART PROPERLY. PREPARATION BEGINS WITH GRIT BLASTING.

ANGLE ON GRIT BLAST MACHINE

PROFESSIONAL V.O.

THE FIRST STEP IS TO DEGREASE THE PART COMPLETELY. OTHERWISE, OIL CONTAMINATES THE GRIT. DEPENDING ON THE PART, YOU MAY HAVE TO MASK OFF AREAS—LIKE THIS—THAT YOU DON'T WANT COATED, SO THEY AREN'T BLASTED. UNWANTED OVERSPRAY WILL CLEAN RIGHT OFF THE NON-GRIT-BLASTED AREAS.

ANGLE ON GRIT BLASTER

As PROFESSIONAL fires it up. We see the process.

ANNOUNCER V.O.

ALWAYS USE 90 PSI TO GRIT BLAST STEEL SUBSTRATES LIKE THIS ONE. IF THE SUBSTRATE IS ALUMINUM, WE TURN IT DOWN TO 60 PSI. OTHERWISE, YOU'LL IMBED GRIT INTO THE SOFT METAL.

ANGLE ON BLAST NOZZLE AND SUBSTRATE

ANNOUNCER V.O.

HOLD THE BLAST NOZZLE PERPENDICULAR TO THE SURFACE, AND MOVE IT BACK AND FORTH TO COVER THE SURFACE. TECHNICALLY SPEAKING, WE'RE MAKING THE TEXTURE 200 TO 300 MICROINCHES ROUGH.

ANGLE ON PROFESSIONAL

As he/she finishes grit blasting, lays down the gun, and walks to a table while talking to us. We CUT IN CU to each PIECE as it is discussed.

PROFESSIONAL (SOT)

WE'RE LOOKING FOR THE PIECE THAT'S JUST RIGHT. (Picks up piece) THIS ONE WAS BLASTED TOO SHORT A TIME. SEE, THE SURFACE ISN'T ROUGH ENOUGH FOR THE COATING TO TAKE HOLD. WE'VE ALSO LEFT TOO MUCH CONTAMINATION BEHIND—LIKE THIS SCALE—OR OTHER SURFACE IMPERFECTIONS.

ANOTHER ANGLE

As PROFESSIONAL picks up another piece.

PROFESSIONAL (SOT)

TOO LONG AND THE BLASTING WILL KNOCK DOWN THE PROFILE AND ACTUALLY REDUCE THE SURFACE ROUGHNESS.

CLOSE ON FINAL PIECE

As it is picked up.

PROFESSIONAL (SOT)

BUT DONE JUST RIGHT, THE PIECE SPARKLES LIKE THIS, INSTEAD OF BEING DULL. THERE'S NO LEFTOVER DUST OR GRIT PARTICLES. AND NOW WE WANT TO HANDLE THE PART WITH CLEAN COTTON GLOVES SO WE DON'T GET ANY OIL ON IT, EVEN FROM OUR HANDS.

ANOTHER ANGLE

As PROFESSIONAL sets down the clean part and picks up a rusted one.

PROFESSIONAL (SOT)

FINALLY, YOU WANT TO GRIT BLAST JUST BEFORE YOU SPRAY. ONCE STEEL IS BLASTED, IT OXI-DIZES VERY QUICKLY, SO IT'LL RUST IF IT'S LEFT OVERNIGHT.

ANGLE ON GOOD, SPARKLING PART AGAIN

PROFESSIONAL V.O.

ALWAYS REMEMBER—THERMAL SPRAY COATINGS ARE MECHANI-CALLY BONDED, SO PROPER GRIT BLASTING IS REALLY IMPORTANT.

ANGLE ON WORKER

Who demonstrates hammering on a component coating with grit blast, then on a component without grit blast.

CU COMPONENT

Showing the result.

dissolve to

EST. THERMAL SPRAY BOOTH

We see an OPERATOR preparing to spray a part. The ANNOUNCER enters the picture carrying the Metco 6P instruction manual.

SUPER GRAPHIC
THERMAL SPRAY PROCESS

Equipment Operation

ANNOUNCER

THIS IS THE BIBLE AS FAR AS STANDARD OPERATING AND SAFETY PROCEDURES ARE CON-CERNED. ALWAYS FOLLOW THE BOOK WHEN USING THIS HIGH-TECH AND POTENTIALLY DAN-GEROUS EQUIPMENT. OK? WE NEED YOU TO STAY WHOLE AND HEALTHY!

CLOSE ON OPERATOR

As she adjusts the oxygen and fuel flow-meters.

ANNOUNCER V.O.

CHECK THE BOOK FOR THE PARAMETERS GIVEN FOR WHAT-EVER MATERIAL YOU'RE SPRAY-ING, AND SET THE FLOWMETER READINGS ACCORDINGLY.

CLOSE ON METERS

ANNOUNCER V.O.

BE SURE THAT THESE GAUGES ARE SET RIGHT AND THAT YOU HAVE ENOUGH GAS IN THE TANK TO COMPLETE YOUR JOB.

CLOSE ON GUN VALVE

ANNOUNCER V.O.

OPEN THE GUN VALVE TO THE FULL OPEN POSITION TO CHECK READINGS. LINE THE BALL UP DIRECTLY IN FRONT OF YOU, AND TAKE YOUR READINGS FROM THE DEAD CENTER. THIS IS CRITICAL.

ANGLE ON THE GUN

As she lights it.

ANNOUNCER V.O.

BEFORE LIGHTING UP, BE SURE THAT THE VENTILATION IS ON AND WORKING RIGHT IF YOU'RE IN AN ENCLOSED BOOTH. TURN THE VALVE TO THE STARTUP MARK, AND IGNITE IT. ONCE THE GUN LIGHTS, QUICKLY TURN THE VALVE TO THE FULL OPEN POSI-TION.

ANGLE ON POWDER FEEDER

As the OPERATOR does what the ANNOUNCER is describing.

ANNOUNCER V.O.

TURN ON THE POWDER FEEDER, AND SET THE CORRECT FLOWMETER READING AND HOPPER PRESSURES. BEFORE YOU START, IT'S A GOOD IDEA TO BLOW OUT THE BLACK POWDER FEED HOSE WITH FILTERED COMPRESSED AIR. SOME RESIDUE MAY HAVE BEEN LEFT IN THE HOSE FROM THE LAST OPERATION, AND YOU DON'T WANT ANY CONTAMINANTS IN YOUR JOB.

ANGLE ON THE SPRAYER

As the OPERATOR checks the powder flow.

ANNOUNCER V.O.

WHEN THE POWDER STARTS FLOWING AND YOU'RE SURE THE RATES HAVE STABILIZED, YOU'RE GOOD TO GO. JUST FOLLOW THE GUIDELINES FOR STAND-OFF DISTANCE AND GUN SPEED, AND ENJOY THE SHOW!

MONTAGE

We see a fast-paced sequence of the entire process cut in time to some zippy, uplifting music. This piece features the OPERATOR on-site, making her or him the STAR!

dissolve out

ANGLE ON ANNOUNCER

As he walks into a demonstration area. On a TABLE we have PARTS to illustrate what he talks about. He picks each up as he describes it, and we cut in CUs.

SUPER GRAPHIC
Process Variables Affecting Quality

ANNOUNCER

WHEN EVERYTHING GOES RIGHT, IT'S A REAL FEEL-GOOD! BUT JUST TO KEEP YOUR FEET ON THE GROUND, HERE ARE A COUPLE OF THINGS THAT CAN GO WRONG—

AND SOME GOOD ADVICE ON HOW TO PREVENT THEM.

ANGLE ON BURNT STEEL PART

ANNOUNCER V.O.

STAND-OFF DISTANCE—THAT IS, THE DISTANCE FROM THE GUN TO THE SUBSTRATE—IS REALLY CRITICAL. TOO CLOSE AND THE POWDER WON'T HAVE TIME TO MELT IN THE FLAME. YOU'LL BURN THE SUBSTRATE.

ANGLE ON ANOTHER PIECE

This one shows the result of too large a stand-off distance.

ANNOUNCER V.O.

THE SPRAY ANGLE IS IMPORTANT, TOO. A 90-DEGREE ANGLE IS THE BEST. TOO SHORT AN ANGLE AND THE COATING SHADOWS ITSELF LIKE THIS.

GRAPHIC

We show a schematic of shadow effects.

dissolve

ANGLE ON ROTATING PIECE BEING COATED PROPERLY

ANNOUNCER V.O.

REMEMBER THAT THE LAYDOWN RATE IS IMPORTANT, TOO. THINK OF THERMAL SPRAYING AS PAINTING. SEVERAL THIN LAYERS ARE ALWAYS BETTER THAN ONE THICK ONE. YOU CONTROL THE LAYDOWN RATE BY THE SPEED OF THE GUN AS WELL AS BY THE SPEED OF THE ROTATING PART. THE METCO 452 LAYDOWN RATE IS 0.004 INCHES PER PASS.

dissolve

ANGLE ON PART

It demonstrates a coating put down with too high a laydown rate.

ANNOUNCER (SOT)

OBVIOUSLY, SOMEONE GOOFED ON THIS PART. THAT'S WHAT YOU GET FROM LAYING IT ON TOO THICK AROUND HERE!

ANGLE ON INSPECTION AREA— CORINTH As the OPERATOR checks several pieces that have been sprayed. We see each piece in CU.

ANNOUNCER V.O.

SO, TAKE TIME TO PULL YOUR OWN INSPECTION WHEN THE SPRAYING'S DONE. YOU'RE THE BEST QUALITY-CONTROL PERSON WE'VE GOT, AFTER ALL. LOOK FOR ANOMALIES IN THE COATING, LIKE . . .

CU VALVE WITH CRACKED COATING

ANNOUNCER V.O.

. . . CRACKS INDICATING THE LAY- DOWN RATE IS TOO HIGH OR THE SUBSTRATE OVERHEATED.

CU DISBONDED PART

ANNOUNCER V.O.

DISBONDING LIKE THIS . . . PROB- ABLY DUE TO POOR GRIT-BLAST- ING TECHNIQUE.

CLOSER ON PART

ANNOUNCER V.O.

LOWER COATING THICKNESS THAN EXPECTED LIKE THIS IS GENERALLY CAUSED BY POWDER FEEDER CLOGGING OR INCOR- RECT GUN GAS FLOW SETTINGS.

CLOSE ON ANOTHER PART WITH BUMPS

ANNOUNCER V.O.

AND LUMPS LIKE THIS, WHICH YOU MIGHT GET IN AUNT TILDY'S GRAVY, ARE DEFINITE SIGNS OF POWDER CLUMPING. MAKE SURE THEY DON'T GET PAST YOUR EAGLE EYE BECAUSE THEY COULD RUIN AN OTHERWISE PER- FECT DAY IN THE FIELD!

dissolve

EST. MACHINE IN FIELD

A TECHNICIAN is repairing it.

dissolve

EST. INT. AMT THERMAL SPRAY SHOP

As the ANNOUNCER enters. We FOLLOW him to see each piece he talks about here.

SUPER GRAPHIC
Maintenance

ANNOUNCER (SOT)

THERE'S NO SECRET THAT A SKILLED WORKER IS ONLY AS GOOD AS HIS OR HER TOOLS. KEEPING YOUR GEAR IN PROPER ORDER IS FUNDAMENTAL TO HIGH QUALITY. HERE ARE A COU- PLE OF AREAS THAT NEED CLOSE ATTENTION, SINCE THEY'RE VUL- NERABLE TO DAMAGE.

CLOSE ON SIPHON PLUG BEING ASSEM- BLED

ANNOUNCER V.O.

AFTER THE CHALLENGER SPACE- CRAFT ACCIDENT, WE ALL LEARNED THE IMPORTANCE OF O- RINGS. WATCH FOR THE THREE OF THEM HERE ON THE SIPHON PLUG. THEY CAN BE DAMAGED BY THE SLEEVE WHEN ASSEMBLING THE GUN. BE SURE THE O-RINGS ARE WELL LUBRICATED WITH DRY GRAPHITE LUBE.

CLOSE ON THE VALVE CORE

ANNOUNCER V.O.

WHEN THE VALVE IS HARD TO TURN OR THE GUN IS HARD TO LIGHT, GREASE THE O-RINGS HERE ON THE VALVE CORE LIKE THIS. NOW, THIS IS THE ONLY PART OF THE GUN THAT GETS VALVE LUBE. IF YOU USE IT ON THE FRONT OF THE GUN, THE GREASE WILL GET TOO HOT, MELT, AND PLUG UP THE POWDER

PASSAGES. REMEMBER . . . KEEP YOUR POWDER DRY!

ANGLE ON BRAIDED HOSE

ANNOUNCER V.O.

BE VERY CAREFUL WITH THE BRAIDED HOSE ON THE POWDER HOPPER WHEN YOU FLUSH THE FEED HOSE WITH AIR. THE INSIDE IS LINED WITH LATEX TUBING. IT DETERIORATES EASILY AND CAN'T TAKE PRESSURE.

ANGLE ON POWDER HOPPER AND JARS

The OPERATOR is shaking the jar, getting ready to add it to the hopper.

ANNOUNCER V.O.

THE BIG THING TO REMEMBER HERE IS THAT ANY KIND OF FINE POWDER WILL TEND TO CLUMP UP ON HUMID DAYS. GIVE THE JAR A GOOD SHAKE BEFORE ADDING THE MIXTURE TO THE HOPPER. AND MAKE SURE YOU DON'T LEAVE POWDER JARS OPEN. JUST AS IMPORTANT, EMPTY OUT THE POWDER FEEDERS EVERY NIGHT BEFORE GOING HOME.

PUSH IN CU ON POWDER

dissolve

CU FLAME PATTERN

As the ANNOUNCER speaks, the FLAME PATTERN changes as follows:

too rich

too lean

powder pulsing

SUPER GRAPHIC
Troubleshooting

ANNOUNCER V.O.

A GOOD OPERATOR KNOWS HOW TO TROUBLESHOOT, AS WELL AS HOW TO USE THE EQUIPMENT ACCORDING TO THE METCO MANUAL. FAMILIARIZE YOURSELF

WITH THE RIGHT FLAME PATTERN, COMPARED TO ONE THAT'S TOO RICH . . . TOO LEAN . . . OR IS PULSING POWDER. REMEMBER, YOU ARE THE FIRST LINE OF DEFENSE AGAINST SUBSTANDARD SPRAY COATINGS.

dissolve

THERMAL SPRAY AREA—CORINTH

We see WORKERS preparing to start up the spray process. The ANNOUNCER walks in FOREGROUND. As he names PARTS, we SUPER them in a BOX over his shoulder.

ANNOUNCER

THERE YOU HAVE THE STORY. THERMAL SPRAY IS TODAY'S ANSWER TO TOMORROW'S PROBLEMS. WHETHER IT'S MORE HEAT RESISTANT VALVES, MORE DURABLE CYLINDER HEADS, LONGER LASTING WATER PUMP SHAFTS, OR ANY OF HUNDREDS OF NEW COMPONENTS, THE FUTURE OF CATERPILLAR MACHINES IS IN YOUR SKILLED HANDS. TREAT IT WITH CARE.

ANNOUNCER walks off screen as we PUSH IN on the SPRAYER. MUSIC swells up and under as we

dissolve in

CATERPILLAR LOGO

and

fade out

---

I have read and approved the above script. Producer is herewith authorized to shoot the video in accordance with this script with no further substantial changes, aside from any which may arise as exigencies of location or technical impractibility.

For Caterpillar:

---

# Selected Bibliography

## Advertising and Marketing

Baker-Woods, Gail. *Advertising and Marketing to the New Majority: A Case Study Approach*. Belmont, CA: Wadsworth, 1995.

Belew, Richard. *How to Win Profits and Influence Bankers*. New York: Van Nostrand Reinhold, 1973.

*Building Strong Relations with Your Bank*. SBA publication no. 107. Fort Worth, TX: Small Business Administration, 1994.

Hampe, Barry. *Making Videos for Money: Planning and Producing Information Videos, Commercials, and Infomercials*. New York: Henry Holt, 1998.

Jewler, A. Jerome, and Bonnie L. Drewiany. *Creative Strategy in Advertising*, 6th ed., Belmont, CA: Wadsworth, 1998.

——.*Guerilla Marketing: Secrets for Making Big Profits from Your Small Business*. Boston: Houghton Mifflin, 1998.

——.*Online Marketing Handbook: How to Promote, Advertise, and Sell Your Products and Services on the Internet*. New York: John Wiley, 1998.

——.*The Barrows Popularity Factor: An Easy to Use Mathematical Formula That Will Let You Quantify the Relationship between Your Advertising and Sales Actually*. Burlingame, CA: R.M. Barrows, 1996.

More, Roy L. *Advertising and Public Relations Law*. Mahweh, NJ: Lawrence Erlbaum, 1997.

Siegel, David. *Creating Killer Websites: The Art of Third-Generation Site Design*, 2nd ed. Indianapolis: Hayden, 1997.

## Credit Policies

Blake, William Henry. *Retail Credit and Collections*. SBA publication no. 31. Fort Worth, TX: Small Business Administration.

*Collection and Enforcement of Judgments 1998*. Winston-Salem, NC: Wake Forest CLE, 1998.

## General Business and Management

Alexander, Carol. *Risk Management and Analysis: Measuring and Modeling Financial Risk*. New York: John Wiley and Sons, 1998.

Breslin, William J. *Negotiation Theory and Practice*, 2nd ed. Cambridge, MA: Harvard Law School, 1993.

Godin, Seth, ed. *Information Please Business Almanac and Desk Reference*. Boston: Houghton Mifflin, annual.

Monash University. *Implications of System Thinking for Research and Practice in Management.* Victoria, BC: Monash University, Faculty of Business and Economics, 1998.

Redmond, James, and Robert Trager. *Balancing on the Wire: The Art of Managing Media Organizations.* Boulder, CO: Coursewise Publishing, 1998.

Urquart, James R. *The IRS, Independent Contractors, and You.* Santa Ana, CA: Fidelity Publishing, 1998.

# Government Forms and Reports

*Your Business Tax Kit.* Washington, DC: Internal Revenue Service, annual.

# Management

Bracey, Hyler, and Jack Rosenblum. *Managing from the Heart.* New York: Dell, 1993.

Cleland, David I. *Strategic Management of Teams.* New York: John Wiley and Sons, 1996.

Chemers, Martin M. *An Integrative Theory of Leadership.* Mahweh, NJ: Lawrence Erlbaum, 1997.

——. *Sales Management: Theory and Practice,* 2nd ed. New York: Macmillan, 1998.

——. *Managerial Communication: Bridging Theory and Practice.* Upper Saddle River, NJ: Prentice Hall, 1999.

Drucker, Peter. *The Practice of Management,* rev. ed. New York: Harper and Row, 1980.

Nelson, Bob, and Peter Economy. *Managing for Dummies.* Indianapolis, IN: IDG Books Worldwide, 1996.

# Personnel

Caroselli, Marlen. *Great Session Openers, Closers, and Energizers: Quick Activities for Warming Up Your Audience and Ending on a High Note.* New York: McGraw-Hill, 1998.

Kennedy, Peter. *Macroeconomic Essentials for Media Interpretation.* Cambridge, MA: MIT Press, 1997.

Rabe, William F. *Matching the Applicant to the Job.* SBA management aid no. 185. Fort Worth, TX: Small Business Administration.

Raphelson, Rudolph. *Finding and Hiring the Right Employee.* SBA management aid no. 106. Fort Worth, TX: Small Business Administration.

*Seven-Step Guide to the Design and Development of an Equal Opportunity Plan.* Washington, DC: U.S. Department of Justice, Office of Justice Programs, Office for Civil Rights, 1998.

# Video Writing and Producing

Browne, Steven E. *Video Editing: A Postproduction Primer.* Boston: Focal Press, 1997.

Cartwright, Steve R. *Pre-production Planning for Video, Film, and Multimedia.* Boston: Focal Press, 1996.

Koster, Robert. *The On Production Budget Book.* Boston: Focal Press, 1997.

Lutzker, Arnold P. *Copyrights and Trademarks for Media Professionals.* Boston: Focal Press, 1997.

Lyer, Des, and Graham Swainson. *Basics of Video Production.* Boston: Focal Press, 1995.

Miller, Philip. *Media Law for Producers,* 3rd ed. Boston: Focal Press, 1998.

Van Nostran, William J. *The Media Writer's Guide.* Boston: Focal Press, 1999.

Watts, Harris. *Directing on Camera: A Checklist of Video and Film Technique.* Boston: Focal Press, 1997.

# About the Author

Dr. Bob Jacobs is a professor and Coordinator of Radio/Television Production in the Department of Communication at Bradley University in Peoria, Illinois. He also owns and operates an independent production company and is a prolific freelance writer and producer. He has published articles and book chapters for a wide variety of periodicals and magazines. He recently completed his first novel, *Season of the Beast*. He has been a writer, producer, and director in film and television since graduating with a degree in cinema from the University of Southern California (USC). He is the author of dozens of commercial and industrial scripts on a variety of topics. He is profiled in *Who's Who in Entertainment, Who's Who in America,* and *Who's Who in Education.*

Bob Jacobs began his career as an actor under contract to Warner Brothers and then Twentieth Century Fox. His main credit as an actor was in the film version of *South Pacific.* After the premiere of the movie, Bob decided that his future lay behind the camera and went to USC to learn how to make movies. His film and TV credits include Walt Disney Productions and Burt Sugarman Productions. His network credits include *Walt Disney Presents, The Dionne Warwick Chevy Special: Souled Out,* and *The Bell Festival,* a musical series with Zubin Mehta and the L.A. Philharmonic. He cocreated a TV musical series called *The Midnight Special,* which ran for more than 10 years. He produced three feature-length movies, *The Fry Cook* and *Exit Dying,* both of which he also directed, and *Dreams Come True.* A featurette called *The Cremation of Sam McGee,* narrated by the late William Conrad, is in distribution worldwide with Encyclopaedia Britannica Films.

Bob has been a writer, producer, and director of corporate and industrial films and videos as well as dozens of regional and national television commercials. Clients have included NASA, Columbus Shock Absorbers, the Moog Corporation, the Ariens Company, Jewelers Mutual Insurance Company, the National Beef Council, the Greater Cleveland Growth Association, and Caterpillar, Inc. In Wisconsin, he produced a daily opinion drop-in radio show; in Maine, he was a video and television feature producer; and in Ohio, he produced and directed a national feature series called *Postcards from Cleveland,* an award-winning weekly magazine-format television program for the Fox affiliate station, and a weekly basketball program for the Sports Channel cable network.

He produces a national award-winning weekly feature series called *Postcards from Home* for the NBC affiliate station in Peoria. He wrote, produced, and directed a musical program featuring composer Peter Shickele. The program received Emmy nominations for "Outstanding Director—Edited" and "Outstanding Entertainment Program—Edited." Other honors include an international award in Badajoz, Spain, for his production of *Peoria 911*. He is a member of the National Academy of Television Arts and Sciences (NATAS), the Broadcast Education Association, the American Federation of Television and Radio Artists (AFTRA), and is a charter member of the University of Southern California Cinema/TV Alumni Association.

Bob holds a B.A. in cinema from the University of Southern California and a Ph.D. in dramatic art from the University of California—Santa Barbara. He has lectured on independent production at the University of Texas, the University of Minnesota, Purdue University, the University of Maine, Cleveland State University, California State University—Long Beach, California State University—Humboldt, Milwaukee Area Technical College, and the University of Wisconsin—Milwaukee. He has also acted as a consultant to a number of corporations and independent production companies throughout the country. He and his wife, Martina "Max" Jacobs, a television news producer, live on a farm 35 miles from the nearest city.